Modernity, Medicine and Health

Social change has gathered momentum through the fourth quarter of the twentieth century and has had a considerable impact on health and medicine. *Modernity, Medicine and Health* brings together a variety of influential sociologists who present their theories on the nature and depth of change, and on the modernity/postmodernity debates, applying them to issues of health and healing. Among the issues covered are the parameters of the future of medical sociology itself, the potential and limitations of the postmodern perspective, the interface with public health, analyses of class and gender, new notions of citizenship, complementary medicine, and life and death in postmodern times.

Modernity, Medicine and Health will be invaluable reading for those studying medical sociology and of interest to all those engaged in social theory.

Graham Scambler is Reader in Sociology and Director of the Unit of Medical Sociology at University College London. **Paul Higgs** is Lecturer in Medical Sociology also at University College London.

D0023954

Modernity, Medicine and Health

Medical sociology towards 2000

Edited by Graham Scambler
and Paul Higgs

London and New York

First published 1998
by Routledge
11 New Fetter Lane, London EC4P 4EE

Simultaneously published in the USA and Canada
by Routledge
29 West 35th Street, New York, NY 10001

Typeset in Galliard by RefineCatch Limited, Bungay, Suffolk
Printed and bound in Great Britain by
Creative Print and Design (Wales), Ebbw Vale

British Library Cataloguing in Publication Data
A catalogue record for this book is available from the British Library

Library of Congress Cataloguing in Publication Data
Modernity, medicine, and health: medical sociology towards 2000 /
edited by Graham Scambler and Paul Higgs.
     p.   cm.
Includes bibliographical references and index.
   1. Social medicine.   2. Postmodernism.   I. Scambler, Graham.
II. Higgs, Paul.
RA418.M66   1998
306.4'61 – dc21   97–34889

ISBN 0–415–14938–X (hbk)
ISBN 0–415–14939–8 (pbk)

Contents

List of contributors

Zygmunt Bauman is Emeritus Professor of Sociology, University of Leeds and University of Warsaw. Among his recent books are *Life in Fragments* (1995) and *Postmodernity and its Discontents* (1997).

Gillian Bendelow is Lecturer in Applied Social Studies at the University of Warwick. Her current research interests are in the area of gender, pain and emotions, and children and health. She is currently writing a book, *Gender and Pain*, based on her doctoral research in this area, and is convenor of the BSA study group on emotions.

Michael Bury is Professor of Sociology and Head of the Department of Social Policy and Social Science at Royal Holloway, University of London. He teaches on the MSc in Medical Sociology at Royal Holloway and is joint editor of *Sociology of Health and Illness*. Professor Bury's research interests in medical sociology are in the fields of chronic illness and disability, ageing and health and cultural aspects of health and medicine. His new book *Health and Illness in a Changing Society* was published by Routledge in 1997.

Mike Featherstone is Research Professor of Sociology and Communications at Nottingham Trent University. He is founding editor of *Theory, Culture and Society* and the *TCS* book series, and co-editor of *Body and Society*. His numerous publications include *Consumer Culture and Postmodernism*, *Undoing Culture: Globalisation, Postmodernism and Identity*, and co-edited volumes on *The Body: Social Process and Cultural Theory*, *Cyberspace/Cyberbodies/Cyberpunk: Cultures of Technological Embodiment*, and *Images of Ageing*.

Nicholas Fox is Senior Lecturer in Sociology, School of Health and Related Research, University of Sheffield. He is the author of *The Social Meaning of Surgery* (Open University Press, 1992) and *Postmodernism,*

Sociology and Health (Open University Press, 1993), as well as numerous articles on postmodern social theory.

Mike Hepworth is Reader in Sociology at the University of Aberdeen. His research interests include images of ageing, the social construction of decline in later life, and literary gerontology. He has published widely in the sociology of crime, deviance and ageing, he is a founding member of the editorial board of *Theory, Culture and Society* and an editor of *Body and Society*.

Paul Higgs has been Lecturer in Medical Sociology at University College London since 1994. Previously he was Lecturer in Social Gerontology at St George's Hospital Medical School, London. His publications include *The NHS and Ideological Conflict* (1993) and he is currently completing a book (with Chris Gilleard) *Cultures of Ageing: Self, Citizen and the Body*, which expands on some of his interests in the social theory of old age.

Richard Levinson is Candler Professor of Public Health and Associate Dean of the Rollins School of Public Health at Emory University, Atlanta, Georgia, USA. He is also a Professor in Emory's Department of Sociology, and Honorary Senior Lecturer in the Department of Psychiatry and Behavioural Sciences at University College London Medical School. Previously he taught at Indiana University and served as Chief of the Behavioral Epidemiology and Evaluation Branch at the US Centers for Disease Control and Prevention. He is currently involved in research on access to health services among persons with chronic health conditions in the US.

Mike Saks is Professor and Dean of Faculty of Health and Community Studies at De Montfort University. He has presented many national and international conference papers and published widely on the health professions and alternative medicine. His most recent books are *Alternative Medicine in Britain* (Oxford University Press, 1992), *Health Professions and the State in Europe* (co-edited with Professor Terry Johnson and Professor Gerry Larkin, Routledge, 1995) and *Professions and the Public Interest: Medical Power, Altruism and Alternative Medicine* (Routledge, 1995).

Annette Scambler has taught sociology and women's studies for the Open University for fifteen years. She has honorary lectureships at University College London and at Imperial College. She is also Visiting Professor at Emory University, Atlanta, USA. She has researched women's health issues and her publications include (co-author) *Menstrual Disorders* (1993) and (co-editor) *Rethinking Prostitution: Purchasing Sex in the 1990s* (1997).

Graham Scambler is Reader in Sociology and Director of the Unit of Medical Sociology at University College London. He is also Visiting Professor at Emory University, Atlanta, USA. He has conducted and published a number of studies in the sociology of health and illness and has a long-standing interest in social theory and philosophy. Recent books include (editor, 4th edition) *Sociology as Applied to Medicine* (1997) and (co-editor) *Rethinking Prostitution: Purchasing Sex in the 1990s* (1997).

Simon Williams is a Lecturer/Warwick Research Fellow in the Department of Sociology at the University of Warwick. His current research interests centre on the relationship between social theory and the sociology of health and illness, with particular reference to issues of emotions and embodiment. Recent publications include a co-edited volume (with Gillian Bendelow) *The Emotional in Social Life: Critical Theory and Perspectives* (Routledge), another co-edited volume (with M. Calman) *Modern Medicine: Lay Perspectives and Experiences* (UCL Press) and a forthcoming book (with Gillian Bendelow) *Embodying Sociology: Critical Perspectives on the Dualist Legacy*.

Introduction

Graham Scambler and Paul Higgs

Few inside or outside of sociology would dispute the enhanced pace and profundity of social change in the final quarter of the twentieth century. Examples range from macro-level changes, like the implosion of the Soviet power bloc at the end of the 1980s, to micro-level changes, like the rapid consumerist diversification and export of Western styles of identity and self. There is considerable and often heated dissension, however, on how such dramatic, and prima facie fundamental or far-reaching, changes are to be characterized, understood and, more tendentiously, accounted for or explained. This has led to protracted debates within mainstream sociology around issues of periodization and to reconceptualizations of 'sociological knowledge' which challenge the conventional thrust of the discipline. As this volume indicates, medical sociology has been significantly and increasingly affected both by social change, in its multifarious macro- and micro-forms, and by the mainstream debates this has generated.

In this brief introduction we draw on a broad, complex and sometimes tangled literature in an attempt to clarify some of the key debates about change and, more specifically, to address some basic issues of terminology. We start, because of the frequency, intensity and ambivalence of their usage, by considering the two dichotomies, 'modernity/postmodernity' and 'modernism/postmodernism'. We turn then to modern versus postmodern perspectives on the enterprise of sociology itself. Finally, after highlighting some key issues confronting sociologists debating not just dynamic social change but the future of their own discipline, we reflect on the ramifications for medical sociologists in particular and the rationale for the present volume.

MODERNITY/POSTMODERNITY

The modernity/postmodernity dichotomy suggests periodization and implies a transition from modernity to a new epoch or social formation. Modernity is generally used to refer to the distinctive social formation characteristic of 'modern' societies, namely, those emerging initially in Europe in the fifteenth century. These are contrasted with their pre-modern predecessors, modernity being contrasted in particular with 'antiquity'. The idea of 'the modern', however, was only fully crystallized much later, during the European Enlightenment in the eighteenth century. The 'project' of the Enlightenment, and thereafter of modernity, commended a secular concept of universal reason which bore the promise of ineluctable progress to the good society as well as to the comprehension and control of nature. Modernity as a social formation has, since the late nineteenth century, come to be identified with the 'progressive economic and administrative rationalization and differentiation of the social world' (Featherstone 1988: 197–8). More specifically – and many would say paradigmatically – it is associated with: the nation-state, together with an international system of states; a dynamic and expansionist capitalist economic system based on private property; industrialism typified by Fordism; the growth of large-scale administrative and bureaucratic systems of social organization and regulation; the dominance of secular, rationalist, materialist and individualist cultural values; and the formal separation of the *private* from the *public* (Hall *et al.* 1992).

References to postmodernity signal the approach or arrival of a new social formation, distinct from and succeeding modernity. Predictably, it is more difficult to define or characterize postmodernity than modernity (and, paradoxically perhaps, there are those who would protest that only a disciple of modernity would [need to] attempt such a task). But many writers associate postmodernity with the demise of the – Western, and essentially Eurocentric – project of modernity, condemning its terminally flawed foundationalist defence of universal reason, its rationalist metanarratives, and its failure to deliver – either at all, or at least constructively – on its promises. Concerning postmodernity as a social formation, many emphasize: the declining importance of the nation-state and nationalism in the face of, on the one hand, a growth in supra-national bodies and a globalization of markets and communication systems, and, on the other hand, a concurrent process of 're-tribalization' or displacement of national by local political and cultural loyalties; a shift from mass to segmented production, primarily oriented to consumerism; new and predominantly post-industrial or post-Fordist 'flexible' patterns of work; the increasing role of mass media and information technologies; shifts in the social production and circulation of knowledge; the superseding of 'old' class-based politics by the activities of 'new' social movements around the politics of lifestyle and identity; and a fragmentation, diversification and relativization of culture commonly regarded as liberating.

MODERNISM/POSTMODERNISM

It would be convenient if the putative epochs of modernity and post-modernity could be said to be characterized by distinctive cultural constellations or modes of thought and values, modernism and post-modernism respectively, but although many have adopted this approach – for example, equating the project of modernity with 'modernism' – others would maintain that doing so significantly misrepresents much current theoretical discourse. When we refer to the cultural configuration allied to modernity, we write of 'modernism', rather than modernism.

In so far as there is continuity in usage of the terms 'modernism' and 'postmodernism', it is in relation to art. Modernism (at least) is associated primarily with art, and especially with aesthetic movements consciously opposed to classicism. Emergent in Europe in the 1880s these movements peaked around the time of the First World War. Prominent among them were those of the avant-garde, like Dadaism and Surrealism. The avant-garde attacked the 'institution of art', its targets being both the apparatus of distribution on which works of art depend and the status of art epitomized by the concept of autonomy. Antiauratic, its objective was the reintegration of art into the praxis of life.

The term 'postmodernism' became popular among artists, writers and critics in New York in the 1960s, its use spreading rapidly and somewhat indiscriminately around Europe and to and fro across the Atlantic from the 1970s onwards. Linked to the arts, it was associated, in the words of Featherstone (1991: 7–8) with:

> the effacement of the boundary between art and everyday life; the collapse of the hierarchical distinction between high and mass/ popular culture; a stylistic promiscuity favouring eclecticism and the mixing of codes; parody, pastiche, irony, playfulness and the celebration of the surface 'depthlessness' of culture; the decline of the originality/genius of the artistic producer; and the assumption that art can only be repetition.

A certain consistency with aesthetic modernism is detectable here, encouraging some to refer to 'second-wave modernism'; but post-modernism has proved altogether more radical and pervasive than modernism.

It is more radical, for example, in that while modernism made *representing* reality problematic, postmodernism makes *reality* problematic: postmodernism collapses the distinction between signifier and referent (Lash 1990). It is more pervasive in that while modernism's impact was largely confined to art, postmodernism's is felt throughout contemporary culture: it has been interpreted, moreover, as heralding the 'end of' the rationalism inherent in Enlightenment-inspired disciplines like sociology.

MODERN/POSTMODERN SOCIOLOGY

Sociology has its origins in modernity. While few, if any, would now maintain that it can be adequately grounded in the foundationalist philosophies pioneered during and after the Enlightenment, there has been much discussion about whether the discipline might yet be grounded in a post-foundationalist defence of universal reason, and hence be allied to a 'reconstructed' project of modernity; whether it can be grounded and practised rationally in the absence of a commitment to universal reason; or whether sociology, if it is to survive at all, now needs to be 'groundless' and postmodern(ized). It remains unclear just what form a postmodern sociology might take. Presumably, responding to Lyotard's (1984) injunction, it would be cast loose from the Enlightenment-style metanarratives that have either informed or bedevilled (depending on one's stance) most orthodox sociological work to date. Nor would it be able to adjudicate between competing claims to knowledge of the social world 'from a position of presumed, or usurped, privilege' (Gurnah and Scott 1992: 144). In fact, a postmodern sociology would amount, drawing on Lyotard's Wittgensteinian terminology, to *one* more or less discrete network of language games *among numerous and disparate others*. Lyotard applauds the fragmentation and dissensus this implies; postmodern thought, for him, 'refines our sensitivity to differences and reinforces our ability to tolerate the incommensurable'.

For some critics, Lyotard is here (merely) displacing one set of meta-narratives with another (Sarup 1993). His very advocacy of fragmentation and dissensus, which he prescribes as conducive to localized creativity, testifies to his commitment at the level of grand narrative. And to many the relativism implicit in Lyotard's – and others' – definitions of the postmodern is subject to familar forms of interrogation. Putnam

(1981), for example, refers to the centuries-old 'truism' that a relativistic position cannot be stated without inconsistency, any such statement itself being non-relativistic (ironically, in light of Lyotard's debts to Wittgenstein, Putnam cites the latter's well-known case against the methodological solipsist in this connection). Whether or not most forms of postmodernism, including a putative postmodern sociology, are internally inconsistent (and Rorty [1989] for one would seek to 'evade' such a loaded 'modernist' charge), it is evident (at least) that the case for a sociology of postmodernism is difficult to resist (Lash 1990). Gellner (1992: 24) is characteristically scathing about postmodernism as a 'living and contemporary specimen of relativism', but readily acknowledges the need for its analysis as a cultural phenomenon.

SOME REFLECTIONS ON ONGOING DEBATES

We started by asserting, uncontroversially enough, that momentous social changes have occurred over the course of the last generation. The crucial question which almost as many pronounce as premature as attempt to answer is: do these changes, considered in combination, bear testimony to a new social formation? An affirmative response would appear to justify references to postmodernity. There are many, however, who admit to momentous change, and even concur with accounts of change commonly proffered by postmodernists, who prefer to write of 'high' or 'late' modernity. These theorists see recent change as internal to the development of a global and relexive modernity, and some specifically refer to 'reflexive modernization' (Beck 1992; Beck *et al.* 1994). As Owen (1997: 15) notes:

> the proponents of postmodernization locate the emergence of post-modernism in its sociocultural and sociopolitical forms as part and parcel of the process of emergence of postmodernity and, in this respect, external to modernity; whereas the theorists of reflexive modernization situate postmodernism in these senses as internal to late modernity.

It is pertinent to ask what would count as a 'new social formation', to insist on the specification of criteria. To date there has been an understandable reluctance to be specific. Few, it seems, would yet be willing to proclaim the end of capitalism, although many have suggested a new phase of – for example, 'disorganized' – capitalism (Offe 1985; Lash and Urry 1987); and many more have been willing to announce the advent of a post-industrial era. Some, of course, urge a rejection of such a 'modernist' deployment of periodization. It might be argued, however, that, if heightened attention is currently being directed towards the study of *discontinuity*, especially, but by no means exclusively, on the part of advocates of postmodernity, this may well be at the price of a neglect of *continuity*. Consider, for example, the concept of social class. It has become almost commonplace to maintain that class is less salient in post-industrial than it was in industrial capitalism, to refer to class de-alignment, even to pronounce the 'death' of class (Pakulski and Waters 1996). And yet the weight of both empiricist and more subtle investigation can be read as suggesting, quite to the contrary, that class is very much alive and kicking (see Lee and Turner 1996). As we have already implied, debates about modernity/postmodernity hinge on the nature of this – ironically, perhaps still under-theorized – interface between continuity and discontinuity.

If a sociology of the postmodern is essential, it is important to note too that there are lessons for sociology in the development of postmodern thought. It is possible to hold strongly, for example, that postmodern articulations are often internally inconsistent and therefore flawed and/or that they represent, and even celebrate, a neo-conservative impotence in the face of the status quo ante, whilst nevertheless acknowledging that some postmodernists have proved innovative and provocative commentators on a changing social world. Certainly the writings of such diverse and original theorists as Foucault, Lyotard, Baudrillard, Deleuze and Guattari and others have – some would say, fortuitously – required sociologists to come to renewed terms with their discipline and its practices, as well as its conventional modes and focuses of investigation. At the very least, postmodernists may be important catalysts. Sociologists cannot, and should not, remain unaffected by their work.

Many issues of ontology and of reason and epistemology remain unresolved, and, arguably, certain of these have more substantive ramifications for the day-to-day practice of sociology than was the case a generation ago. It might reasonably be argued that postmodernists, like many of those who are committed to the project of modernity, tend not to confront issues of ontology. Worse, they commit what Bhaskar (1978: 16) calls the 'epistemic fallacy'. This refers to the tendency to transpose statements about being into statements about our knowledge of being, thus (fallaciously) reducing ontology to epistemology. If orthodox or 'modernist' sociologists tend to be tacit ontological realists, and postmodernists tend either to be tacit ontological idealists or, ascribing the realist/idealist distinction to the lost discourses of modernity, ignore (or evade) it, few theorists of either persuasion seem to have openly and convincingly addressed general issues of ontology. Although more of both persuasions have adopted stances on general issues of reason and epistemology, there has evolved of late a general propensity to dogmatism around universalistic and, increasingly often, relativistic approaches in relation to understanding the social world. There is scope for more detailed and imaginative work: for example, drawing on the contributions of 'modernists' and postmodernists, it might be maintained – possibly through recourse to concepts such as those of necessary and contingent intersubjective conventions – that there are universal and local aspects to the use of reason and to knowledge. The irresolution or under-theorization of the ontological, rational and epistemological dimensions of alternative 'frames' for interpreting the social world has, whether we be in high/late modernity or in postmodernity, a more immediate impact than hitherto on the sociological enterprise.

SOCIAL CHANGE AND MEDICAL SOCIOLOGY

So far the schematic and illustrative comments we have made on the nature of recent change, and on appropriate ways of defining and accounting for it, have not been explored in relation to medical sociology. They are of course as relevant to the study of health, illness and healing as to any other domain. Bury (1997) has recently emphasized the challenges of social change, in all its forms, for contemporary medical sociology. Of course how one specifies and responds to these challenges depends on how 'modernist/postmodernist' one's perspective is. Few 'modernists' would dispute the importance of examining and monitoring the implications for people's health of, for example: material and cultural facets of globalization; the shifting distribution of poverty and deprivation; inter- and intra-national changes in stratification and power; changing work patterns; crises of Western welfare statism; the 'reform' of health professions and health care systems; new types of ecological and other environmental risk and risk behaviours; processes of individualization and de-traditionalization; and the emergence of lifestyle and identity politics. Many postmodernists have signalled or emphasized the importance of these same factors, although their concepts of 'examining' (let alone 'monitoring') typically differ. Their contributions range widely, for example from the consideration of macro-issues like the social construction or fabrication of health risks and needs, frequently leading via the work of Foucault to concepts like Armstrong's (1995) 'surveillance medicine'; to a rethinking of the putatively neglected body in 'modernist' thought (Turner 1992) (associated with a questioning of expert medical discourses on 'abnormality', 'disability' and so on); to the micro-analysis of forms of healer/client encounters (see Nettleton 1995).

In this volume contributors representing a diversity of theoretical viewpoints reflect on the challenges facing medical sociology and its engagements with the health domain at a time of rapid change, be it in high or late modernity or in postmodernity, on the eve of the millennium. It is revealing just how different the social and theoretical terrains have become since one of us was involved in a similar venture just a decade ago (Scambler 1987). A volume of this length and kind can never hope to be comprehensive, but those contributing cover a broad range of themes and topics, often from different, and sometimes incompatible, viewpoints. Our hope is that there will be something here for most reflexive colleagues with a concern for the interface between theory and research at a time of indisputable, and perhaps unusually unpredictable, change for society and for medical sociology.

Mike Bury stresses the key role health and medicine have played in the dynamics of recent change, and, through an examination of the pivotal processes of 'objectification', 'rationalization' and 'subjectification', appraises the advantages and disadvantages of embracing the notion of postmodernity. While recognizing that postmodernity 'points to important elements of change in late modern cultures', he insists that medical sociology need not and should not abandon much of its substantive and methodological legacy. Nicholas Fox sees more promise in the postmodern. Building on his earlier work, and developing his concept of 'arche-health', he draws especially on the writings of Deleuze and Guattari, and on Cixous's distinction between the 'Gift' and the 'Proper', to spell out its potential. Graham Scambler uses the writings of Habermas to argue in favour of a continuing commitment to a 'reconstructed' project of modernity. The implications of such a commitment for sociology in general, and for medical sociology in particular, are then explored in relation to the potential for a further rationalization and decolonization of the lifeworld.

Richard Levinson explores the changing relationship between medical sociology and public health medicine. He demonstrates how a sociology 'of' and at the 'interface' with public health can illuminate why both colleagues 'in' public health and public health practitioners in the USA systematically overlook the social inequities that threaten the population's well-being. Paul Higgs and Graham Scambler touch on some of the same underlying issues in their discussion of the continuing salience of class for understanding enduring health inequalities. A critique of extant ways of conceptualizing and operationalizing class is accompanied by a plea for greater theoretical engagement and some pointers for future research. Annette Scambler offers a critical consideration of the influence of postmodern thought on feminism in general and links between gender and health and healing in particular. She acknowledges some specific gains from postmodern discourse but finds the thrust of much postmodernist thinking inimical and subversive to the feminist project.

Simon Williams and Gillian Bendelow offer an account of the 'postmodernist/post-structuralist position on pain and the body (without organs)'. They see both merits and limitations in this perspective. They then articulate their own views on pain and the body, which they present as combining a foundationalist or realist ontology with a social constructionist or relativist epistemology. Mike Featherstone and Mike Hepworth focus on debates about the limits of the social in the ageing process. They show that it is no longer possible to generalize about the ageing process on the basis of biological assumptions about the 'ages of life', contending that models of ageing into old age must be increasingly postmodern, 'by which we mean they must anticipate even advanced forms of bio-cultural destabilization'.

Paul Higgs opens his chapter by reflecting on changing discourses of risk and citizenship in relation to health and welfare. He uses the Foucauldian notions of 'governmentality' and 'technologies of the self', and the emergence of new and distinctive approaches to ageing, to throw light on recent marked policy shifts towards the provision of health care and welfare statism. Mike Saks explores the extent of the potential for postmodern thought to help understand the changing relationship between orthodox allopathic medicine and complementary medicine. He qualifies his commendation of postmodern insight with some general concerns about the concept of postmodernism itself and some specific concerns about pragmatic issues of policy and practice. Finally, Zygmunt Bauman contributes a discussion of the nature and depth of changing orientations towards death in pre-modern, modern and postmodern times. His discussion simultaneously addresses changing conceptualizations of health and the human body, closing with a wide-ranging and – for medical sociologists especially, suggestive – account of the postmodern body as a 'receiver of *sensations*' and 'instrument of *pleasure*'.

REFERENCES

Armstrong, D. (1995) 'The rise of surveillance medicine', *Sociology of Health and Illness* 17: 393–40.

Beck, U. (1992) *Risk Society: Towards a New Modernity*, London: Sage.

Beck, U., Giddens, A. and Lash, S. (1994) *Reflexive Modernization: Politics, Tradition and Aesthetics in the Modern Social Order*, Cambridge: Polity Press.

Bhaskar, R. (1978) *A Realist Theory of Science*, Hassocks: Harvester Press.

Bury, M. (1997) *Health and Illness in a Changing Society*, London: Routledge.

Featherstone, M. (1988) 'In pursuit of the postmodern: an introduction', in M. Featherstone (ed.) *Postmodernism*, special issue of *Theory, Culture & Society* 5(2–3).

—— (1991) *Consumer Culture and Postmodernism*, London: Sage.

Gellner, E. (1992) *Postmodernism, Reason and Religion*, London: Routledge.

Gurnah, A. and Scott, A. (1992) *The Uncertain Science*, London: Routledge.

Hall, S., Held, D. and McLennan, G. (1992) 'Introduction', in S. Hall, D. Held, and G. McLennan (eds) *Modernity and its Futures*, Cambridge: Polity Press.

Lash, S. (1990) *Sociology of Postmodernism*, London: Routledge.

Lash, S. and Urry, J. (1987) *The End of Organized Capitalism*, Cambridge: Polity Press.

Lee, D. and Turner, B. (1996) *Conflicts about Class: Debating Inequality in Late Industrialism*, London: Longman.

Lyotard. J.-F. (1984) *The Postmodern Condition*, Manchester: Manchester University Press.

Offe, C. (1985) *Disorganized Capitalism: Contemporary Transformations of Work and Politics*, Cambridge: Polity Press.

Owen, D. (1997) 'Introduction', in D. Owen (ed.) *Sociology after Postmodernism*, London: Sage.

Nettleton, S. (1995) *The Sociology of Health and Illness*, Cambridge: Polity Press.

Pakulski, J. and Waters, M. (1996) *Death of Class*, London: Sage.

Putnam, H. (1981) *Reason, Truth and History*, Cambridge: Cambridge University Press.

Rorty, R. (1989) *Contingency, Irony and Solidarity*, Cambridge: Cambridge University Press.

Sarup, M. (1993) *Post-structuralism and Postmodernism*, Hemel Hempstead: Harvester Wheatsheaf.

Scambler, G. (ed.) (1987) *Sociological Theory and Medical Sociology*, London: Routledge.

Turner, B. (1992) *Regulating Bodies: Essays in Medical Sociology*, London: Routledge.

Chapter 1

Postmodernity and health

Michael Bury

To begin writing about postmodernity and health is no easy task, if only because the terms are so difficult to define. 'Postmodernity' like 'postmodernism' or even 'postmodern society' can mean almost anything the author likes. Likewise, the term 'health' conveys a number of positive and negative values, depending on the context and purpose of use. For some, especially those already sympathetic to the idea that we live in postmodern times, this definitional problem is moot; for 'signification' is now only loosely connected with that being signified. 'It all depends' becomes the cliché of our period. Indeed, clichés become the meeting point between modernity and postmodernity, as context and function supersede shared meanings (Zijderfeld 1979). 'Postmodernity' and 'postmodernism' end up being applied to all and sundry phenomena.

In this chapter an attempt is made to outline a critical approach to postmodernity and health that begins with these problems of terminology but goes on to evaluate current debates in medical sociology. This involves a discussion of sociological views of disease, illness and medicine, as well as health, and the ways in which the latter term – health – has come to have particular cultural salience. Although 'postmodernity' and 'postmodernism' have not been used widely in medical sociology, there are key areas of 'post-structuralist' thinking, especially that influenced by Foucault, which are central to the debates in question. On occasion medical sociologists have explicitly invoked 'postmodernism' as a frame of reference (e.g. Fox 1993). This chapter does not seek to impose strict definitions of 'postmodernity' or 'postmodernism' on this range of writing, but will indicate, as it develops, what intellectual currents are being drawn upon.

The chapter proceeds along the following lines. Having commented a little further on the general problem of terms and related conceptual issues, I then outline a series of arguments concerning the nature of postmodernity. Borrowing from Lyon's (1994) and Featherstone's (1992) expositions, these sections are organized by discussing the processes of 'objectification', 'rationalization' and 'subjectification'. These processes, as will be made clear, are held to be at the centre of the transformations that have characterized modern society, and which appear to point towards, if not usher in, postmodernity. In each case the general processes involved are outlined and their relevance to health illustrated. The final section of the chapter attempts to weigh up the value of arguments about postmodernity for future developments in medical sociology.

POSTMODERNISM, POSTMODERNITY AND THEIR VICISSITUDES

One of the main difficulties in approaching the 'terminological inexactitude' of the current topic is to know what level of analysis is being referred to. Lyon asks the question whether postmodernity is 'an idea, a cultural experience, a social condition or perhaps a combination of all three' (1994: 4). He goes on to examine 'the postmodern' and 'postmodernity' by linking the former to cultural processes and the latter to social ones, though he sees it as impossible entirely to separate the two (Lyon 1994: 6). Both suggest a radical rethinking of the processes that have characterized modern society. The general idea is that the 'project' of modernity, especially its belief in progress, social improvement and a 'providential view' of the future, is no longer tenable; there is, in short, a 'forsaking of providentialism' (Lyon 1994: 7). Nevertheless, by distinguishing between the two terms and contrasting them with earlier features of modern society and 'modernism', different issues can be revealed.

As indicated, the term 'postmodernism' is probably best applied to cultural transformation, and often used with respect to architecture, art, film and literary criticism. Where modern society elevated 'high art' based on (apparently 'objective') aesthetic criteria (e.g. truth, beauty) held to be self-evidently of value to all cultivated or civilized individuals, postmodernism lauds 'low' art as equally valuable. Soap operas vie with musical operas for cultural analysis. Each is seen to contain narrative forms which cannot be ordered in terms of hierarchy. Soap operas or comedy shows with their catch phrases, for example, provide elements of repetition, ritual and story-telling for mass audiences that are seen as equally meaningful as, say, the tragedies of musical operas, aimed at the cultural elite (B. Martin 1981: 65). Subjectivity, in terms of taste and distinction, takes over from the dictates and authority of cultural experts defending the value of high art. To repeat a much quoted example of high/low inversion, the poetry of Keats is no better or worse than that of Bob Dylan.

Lyon makes the point that postmodernism not only inverts the 'high/low' cultural distinction, but also draws attention to the increasing importance of images and icons in cultural life. He states that there is an 'exchange of the printed book for the TV screen, the migration from word to image, from discourse to figure' (Lyon 1994: 7). Such processes increasingly 'simulate' experience. In Baudrillard's terms 'simulacra' substitute for experience. At an everyday level cookery and gardening books, as well as those on sex and health, provide us with representations of experiences, many of which we will never have. At a wider level, historical processes feed back into simulated forms. Thus for Baudrillard the Gulf War became a video show and history itself has become little more than a series of simulacra, forever recycled. Grand narratives do not simply come to an end, as envisaged, by, amongst others, Lyotard (1984) but are replayed endlessly. Baudrillard states:

> We are so used to playing back every film – the fictional ones and the films of our lives – so contaminated by the technology of retrospection, that we are quite capable, in our present dizzy spin, of running history over again like a film played backwards.
>
> (Baudrillard 1994: 11)

Postmodernism as a term and an idea points to the way events and products vie with each other in the cultural sphere and can hardly be separated. Thus we watch 'news' of death and destruction in Bosnia or Rwanda, or films about nature, or medical dramas, while waiting to see if our lottery number has come up, with odds of perhaps 14 million to one. The technology of the films and the lottery play through our subjective minds with equal force. Or so it appears in a culture of postmodernism.

'Postmodernity' on the other hand, refers to some of the underlying social and technological processes that underpin or interact with postmodern cultures. Globalization, the endless expansion of modern capitalist economic forms, now seems to be unstoppable. Not only has the 'grand narrative' of communism, and perhaps even of socialism, collapsed with the Berlin wall (for an analysis of the implications of this for postmodernity, see Bauman 1992), but capitalist commodity production is now found in every part of the globe. Even though it might be the case that some of the features of this process are to be distinguished by their 'disorganized' character (Lash and Urry 1987) the consequent 'globalization' of capitalist/technological productions pushes far beyond the boundaries of the former 'metropolitan' centres and international character of modern capitalism (but see Hirst 1996).

Giddens has argued that globalization significantly reorganizes time and space, especially as the result of computer technology. Most importantly for local communities and for individuals, globalization means that, 'no one can "opt out" of the transformations brought about by modernity: this is so, for example, in respect of the global risks of nuclear war or of ecological catastrophe' (Giddens 1991: 22). The technological processes now at work touch everyone, whether directly or indirectly. No one can escape the logic of the new technologies, and most people wish to participate in the benefits which many of them bring.

This last point brings to the fore the associated process of consumerism, which can be seen to characterize the shift from modernity to postmodernity – at the economic level a shift from an emphasis on productive capacity and output to one on consumer goods, competition and customer service. This relates to the centrality of cultural products, of 'simulacra' discussed above. Consumer choice acts as another means of reinforcing an ever stronger element of subjectivity in social and economic life. Today, lay people are obliged to have views about a whole range of products and lifestyles, including those pertaining to health. These views are then expected to be translated into 'informed choices' concerning (health-producing) lifestyles, for example with respect to the consumption of tobacco and alcohol (Burrows and Nettleton 1995). Consumer choice may also include alternative healing practices (acupuncture, reflexology, even shamanism) alongside or instead of allopathic medical practice, itself increasingly employing a consumerist dimension. Indeed, the systems that earlier catered for *needs* in such areas as health and welfare now emphasize *preference* and customer satisfaction. Such 'signals' substitute for price mechanisms in 'post-Fordist' welfare states – if patients cannot actually be made to buy the services they receive, they can at least express views about them. 'Flexible production' and 'segmented consumption patterns' in the economic sphere now relate to forms of welfare that are themselves increasingly characterized by cost-cutting and 'internal market' structures (Burrows and Loader 1994). In contrast to the logic of modern societies such as Britain, where health and welfare were often seen as 'external' to capitalist dynamics, postmodern societies tie them in ever more closely.

Finally, these initial comments need to touch on the problem of meaning which bridges postmodernism and postmodernity. To return to Lyon once more, the problem of the meaning of social life and the strain towards 'authenticity' in experience and behaviour in modern societies has long been a feature of sociological writings. The example given by Lyon is that of the work of Simmel. According to Lyon 'Simmel straddles the worlds of sociology and cultural analysis' (1994: 10) and in depicting the logic of modern cultures foresaw the 'widening gap between the objective culture, seen in technology for instance, and the increasingly alienated individual, frustrated in the quest for genuine individuality' (1994: 10). Postmodernity throws this problem into sharp relief, as reflexiveness and individual choice have to be exercised against a cultural and social backcloth of ever greater complexity. The loss of grand systems of thought, the inversion of high and low culture appear to set people adrift from the ability to make sound ethical and personal choices. Despite robust attempts by writers such as Charles Taylor (1991) to defend 'authenticity' in contemporary life it is held that post-modernity simultaneously opens up massive dynamics in social life and constrains experience within them. Postmodernity, from this viewpoint, turns out to be a problmatic 'state of mind' (Bauman 1992: vii)

The role of health and medicine in these processes is far from peripheral. Health, illness and medicine have reflected and contributed to the fashioning of modern culture and society (Lawrence 1995). Indeed, they have taken on increasing salience over the last decades. The processes that run through the cultural and social forms of modern life, and which appear now to be straining towards postmodernity – the processes of objectification, rationalization and subjectification – can therefore be fruitfully examined with respect to health-related matters.

OBJECTIFICATION

The process of objectification refers to the progressive tendency in modern life to separate activities and forms of knowledge that were once linked to local or private settings into more publicly available ones. In Featherstone's words: 'forms of knowledge originally embedded within everyday life become progressively separated and subjected to specialist development' (Featherstone 1992: 162). Expertise in many fields develops rapidly under modern social conditions, ranging from the religious, economic, political and cultural fields, to those of science, including medical science.

From a Marxist perspective the obvious features of modern capitalistic political economy illustrate the general lines of development dramatically. As Lyon puts it: 'The emerging industrial society was characterized by a steadily increasing division of labour, in which tasks became progressively more specialized' (1994: 23). The 'public sphere', to use a phrase explored in an examination of modernity's internal momentum by Habermas (1991), becomes more than the site for trading goods, but it is based on a rapid development of private property. For Marx, of course, the production of commodities signals the power of objectification in which the products of labour are progressively separated from the labourer and stand in relation to everyday life in an increasingly objective and 'mysterious' fashion.

These processes carry through a range of institutional settings. Again, as Lyon puts it: 'Tasks once performed by the family or the church were taken over by schools, youth cultures and the mass media, on the one hand, or by local hospitals and welfare departments, on the other' (1994: 23). He goes on to point out that in the twentieth century, sociologists such as Parsons examined in detail the way in which such objectification led to a progressive 'differentiation' of tasks and the superseding of tradition by merit. Here, a free market of skills and abilities would overcome the tendency of modern life to suffer from acute forms of disintegration as well as differentiation.

Developments in medicine and health can help to provide a sharper focus on such general processes. As Lawrence (1995) points out, the objectification of disease and illness rested on two interrelated processes. First, the development of science at the end of the eighteenth and then progressively in the nineteenth centuries, separated disease from the experience of the sufferer and relocated it in a system of thought about the human body based on the findings of pathological anatomy. This application of science was part of a general attack on the authority of elite physicians (and on the aristocracy in general) and allied medical thought with progressive bourgeois approaches to new technologies. As already mentioned, the development of the hospital was important in this process of objectification, especially in the latter half of the nineteenth century. 'Bedside medicine' gave way to 'hospital medicine' as people were turned into patients and as comparisons were made between different 'cases' rather than an exhaustive documentation of the unique features of each individual (Jewson 1976).

Second, Lawrence describes the development of what he calls a 'bounded profession'. What he means by this is that by the turn of the twentieth century the medical profession as we now recognize it came into being. This involved the acceptance of an 'objective' view of disease, based on the idea of specific causes linked to discrete and specific dis eases, especially infectious diseases and germ theory. The medical profession therefore marginalized both the practitioners who did not accept this view of disease and illness, and the 'heterodox' ideas that they might hold. 'Marginal medicine' became exactly that, marginal to the dominant theories and approaches of an increasingly assertive and 'bounded' group of highly organized experts. The separation of disease from the individual was therefore encoded in the idea of the 'doctor–patient relationship'. To fall ill meant to call in the doctor, increasingly meaning someone working within the confines of a regulated professional organization and someone working with a scientific view of disease.

Different sociological perspectives have been brought to bear on this objectification process in medicine. For those following Foucault, the clinical 'gaze' brings the newly arrived patient under the control of the powerful expert. The heterogeneity of illness as a lived experience is constrained by the perceptions and scientific codes of the medical profession. Here the medical profession is seen as being central to modernity's differentiated and ever more sophisticated social control apparatuses. Moreover, the intolerance of the heterogeneity of illness by modern medicine, and of its place in everyday experience, means that illness is 'sequestrated' from everyday life and transferred into an object of medical discourse. The recognition, labelling and legitimation of illness is transferred from the 'lifeworld' of the person to become part of the 'monopoly' of the profession of medicine (Freidson 1970). Only the doctor can know the truth about illness through the language of disease, and the patient becomes a passive agent: for Foucault, a 'docile body' caught in the web of medical knowledge and medical power.

To repeat the point, just as economic life, education, punishment and welfare are increasingly separated from the 'undifferentiated' world of everyday life, and relocated in the factory, school, prison and welfare department, so illness and the body are, literally as well as metaphorically, transferred to the clinic and hospital. Thus medicine reflected and helped to constitute the major institutional and intellectual or 'discursive' fault lines of modern life. During the period since Freidson first published *Profession of Medicine* in 1970 (and perhaps later, with influential writers such as Illich and Foucault) numerous critiques of the objectifying processes of modern medicine have been produced, inside and outside of sociological circles. In this body of work more and more areas of life are seen to fall under medicine's 'objectifying' gaze. Many examples could be cited.

The area of reproductive health is an obvious case in point. Feminist critics such as Oakley have spelled out what they take to be the consequences of the 'medicalization' of childbirth. In a series of studies (e.g. Oakley 1980, 1984) Oakley argued that modern medicine increasingly 'sequestrates' childbirth from the everyday world of women, and of lay practices and practitioners. The consequence of this, according to Oakley is that the doctor–patient relationship takes over, in which, 'the patient's attitude to pregnancy is ignored by the examining doctor, who instead focuses his and the patient's attention narrowly on its medical management' (Oakley 1980: 30). Although the sixty-six women in this particular study showed little sign of resisting the medicalizing process, or of demanding alternative approaches, Oakley felt able to sustain her critique based on the discontent expressed by at least some in her study, about the way childbirth was managed (Oakley 1980: 216). Subsequently, other feminist writers such as Emily Martin (1987) have polemicized against the 'destructive travesty of parenthood' produced by medical monopoly of women's bodies and the reproductive process (E. Martin 1987: 67).

Throughout the critical literature on medicine's growing 'monopoly' over illness and health (from disability to mental illness, and from lifestyle to an ever-widening set of 'risk behaviours') several themes emerge which point to the supposed contradiction in modern medicine's approach. Implicit in these critiques is a view of modernity as a whole, especially its general tendency towards objectification and separation of 'embedded' experience from everyday life.

As has been shown, the processes at the heart of the 'project' of modernity, though ostensibly progressive, are argued to be deeply contradictory. Of all the writers on medicine mentioned above, perhaps Lawrence is alone in recognizing the 'elective affinity' between medical science and political *reform* in early modernity. However, in the main, and in Lawrence's own argument concerning the late nineteenth and early twentieth centuries, the lay person is seen as being made 'invisible' and obliged to be passive in the face of expert advice. In an eloquent essay on his own illness, in which the positive value of medicine's intervention in managing disease is recognized, Arthur Frank (1991) describes how, particularly in hospital, he experienced being treated as though his life (his feelings about his altered body, his fears and concerns, as well as his own views about the illness and treatment) were unconnected with the object of the doctors' attention. This sense of separation, of 'differentiation' and loss of meaning is held to be central to modernity's thrust.

Although it is recognized that 'de-medicalization' can sometimes occur (Conrad 1992), sociological and other critiques of modern medicine have constantly stressed the issue of professional power and the involvement of medicine in modernity's social control mechanisms. These arguments have implied, if not always explicitly spelled out, an important 'meta-theme' that needs now to be explored further. This is that, despite the rise in professional power and the dominance of scientific thought, the clash with everyday experience does not entirely disappear. If it did, it is difficult to see how any critique, let alone change, would be forthcoming. If medical or expert monopoly was completely dominant a 1984 situation would exist, with perhaps only an individual Winston Smith seeing through the processes at work. By turning to the rationalizing of experience which accompanies obectification processes we can see how the logic of modernity turns in on itself and begins to create the conditions for a new phase: that of postmodernity.

RATIONALIZATION

In Lyon's treatment of the shift from modernity to postmodernity, rationalization is an important process, involving 'the gradual adoption of a calculating attitude towards more and more aspects of life' (1994: 24). Underlying rationality and science and the development of the capitalist economy lies a calculating attitude that has assisted in marginalizing judgements and decision-making that were once based on traditional modes of thought. In Weberian thought, 'The acme of efficient, productive organization . . . was the bureaucracy' (1994: 24). Every sphere of modern life was touched by rationalizing processes, and the bureaucratic institutions that carried them forward.

It is this latter point which marks a shift in thinking about modernity/ postmodernity. For, where objectifying processes and the rise of professional expertise had separated key areas of experience from everyday life, the rationalizing process re-enters the everyday world and infuses it with a new and powerful dynamic. In Featherstone's discussion, this phase in modern life means that expert knowledge 'is fed back in order to rationalize, colonize and homogenize everyday life' (Featherstone 1992: 162). The tendency of modernity to separate knowledge from 'the lifeworld' turns into powerful mechanisms that advocate the 'transformation, domestication, civilization, repair and healing of what are the shortcomings of everyday life' (1992: 163). The contradictory nature of this process is not hard to detect. The need for 'repair and healing' (one thinks, for example, of the widespread advocacy of counselling in the present time) arises directly from the tendency of modern life to undermine local knowledge and lay structures that might sustain mental health and self-identity.

In any event, everyday life becomes infused with the effects of rationalizing processes. The role of medicine and the experience of health and illness are once again central. The extension of the 'medical monopoly' and 'medicalization of everyday life', already discussed, take us to the heart of the problem. It is not just that modern medicine spawns powerful experts who stand separate from and above the individual, important though this is. It is also that once the institutional development of modern medicine is established in the shape of the clinic, hospital and laboratory, its practices and perceptions begin to infuse everyday life in myriad ways.

According to David Armstrong (1983, 1995), since the 1950s medicine has moved out from its 'citadel' in the hospital and clinic (in which it objectified the patient's body and experience of illness) to survey normal populations. Epidemiology and the social survey combined, not simply to map the pattern of disease, but to investigate normal populations for the early signs of abnormality. Thus all aspects of bodily and mental experience, as well as behaviour, could fall under the purview of medicine's calculating gaze. It might be added that similar processes were at work in the development of medical specialities such as geriatrics, where the study of 'normal ageing' and the processes of senescence was advocated, alongside the documentation of disease *in* old age (Katz 1996).

Scientific methods and powerful statistical techniques could therefore go beyond the examination of medical cases to the study of an endless array of 'normal' processes. The measurement and calculation of mental states, in which substantial minorities of apparently healthy urban populations could be seen to be suffering from psychiatric symptoms, were increasingly supplemented by the measurement of virtually all other aspects of daily experience. Concepts such as 'well-being', 'life satisfaction' and 'quality of life' entered the social and medical lexicon from the 1960s onwards, producing a bewildering array of questionnaires, interview schedules and scales that were 'validated' on normal populations. Acronyms and short-hand terms such as 'ADLs', 'QALYs', the 'NHP' or the 'SF36' became increasingly popular among clinicians and social researchers alike (Carr-Hill 1995). (For a summary of many of these measures see Bowling 1991, 1995, and for a discussion of the place of 'quality of life' in health care, see Bury 1994.)

The point being made here is not simply that calculation and rationalization extended the surveillance potential of modern (medical) expertise. Such surveillance is certainly important to modern societies, as the techniques developed by science and professional expertise re-enter the everyday realm. And equally important is the argument that this helps to extend the social control mechanisms over an apparently docile population. There is little doubt that such surveillance has become characteristic of our age. By 'coding information' in expert formats the origins and purposes of the surveillance, including its social control function may be obscured (Giddens 1991: 149–50).

But, perhaps more importantly, everyday life itself undergoes a power transformation through rationalizing processes, in which 'docility' in the face of monopolistic professional expertise shifts to an emphasis on active consumerism and lifestyle. Health rather than illness become the watchword under such conditions, as more and more areas of life become subject to rational calculation and choice. The language of health risks exemplifies this 'reflexive' process, as lay people absorb expert knowledge and reorganize their lives accordingly, being expected to know how to 'choose' a healthy lifestyle (for a more detailed discussion of health and risk, see Gabe 1995). A new phase of 'homogenization' occurs in which 'surveillance plus reflexivity means a "smoothing of the rough edges" such that behaviour which is not integrated into a system . . . becomes alien and discrete' (Giddens 1991: 150).

A healthy lifestyle and 'body maintenance' are obviously important in today's culture. Strictures concerning smoking, alcohol consumption, drug use (licit and illegal), food and diet, exercise, the proper use of the mind, the ability to deal with stress or traumatic events such as death, together with many other aspects of everyday life, become subject to the public discourses produced by an ever growing array of professionals and semi-professionals. Indeed, the boundary between the lay everyday world and the world of the expert becomes eroded, as the tendency of 'lay experts' (for example, the victims of crimes committed by the mentally ill) significantly to influence public debate and policy testifies.

Under these circumstances, rational calculation, especially of risk to health, becomes an almost obsessive preoccupation, or so it seems to those who detect a major shift in the logic of modernity throughout such developments. The change in emphasis, from the examination and specification of disease in terms of pathology, to the widespread calculation of risks to health among 'normal' populations, signifies a broadening of medicine's remit beyond its original 'objectifying' tendency to a new 'postmodern' set of processes. These transform modernity's reliance on expertise and the 'docile' body into a more fragmented and less authoritative scientific voice on the one hand, and a more active and sometimes resistant stance of the lay person on the other. The more the lay person is enjoined to be active in calculating and acting on risk, the more a complicated form of subjectivity comes to the fore. This crucial aspect of modernity/postmodernity is the third process that needs to be examined further here.

SUBJECTIFICATION

The link between rationalization and subjectification lies in the notion of 'reflexivity'. The idea that modernity has created an intense sense of personal identity and selfhood has been widely discussed (Taylor 1989, 1991; Giddens 1991). One of the motifs of such work concerns the aforementioned question of authenticity. If, as Goffman maintained, the self is a product of the 'performance' we present in everyday life, or if, as Foucault later argued, it is a construct produced by different forms of 'discourse', how can an authentic sense of self or identity be achieved? In performance or discursive acts we may endlessly reflect on ourselves and the world around us, for example, by considering the health risks of our behaviour or the impact of the environment, but any self-knowledge so obtained will be like any other – partial and always open to contestation by other constructs, other definitions. A 'contestable culture' results in which no form of authoritative knowledge holds sway (Giddens 1991; Beck 1992).

The fear of the resulting meaninglessness in life, or, perhaps more accurately, the anxiety produced by a surfeit of meanings, may be the defining characteristic of our age (Taylor 1989: 18). Reflexivity holds out the promise of a surer grasp of the world around us and our place within it, yet its operation undermines its desired effects. We now feel obliged to hold opinions on the way specific stressors, or even foods, influence health, as well as on the environment or genetics. Indeed, a reflexive approach to future health risks, through assimilating information produced by screening techniques, including 'predictive genetic screening', may dominate a great deal of everyday life in the future (Davison 1996) despite the uncertainty that such information might also produce. Indeed the anxiety about 'probable futures', created by discourses on risk, may be greater than the ability of people to act on the (often statistical) information provided.

Even more important, perhaps, is the idea that we are now supposed to be in touch with our innermost feelings, ready to talk about the truth of our collective and individual pasts, as well as about our feelings in the here and now. Self-identity needs to be 'constructed', balancing the demands of a consumer society, the assimilation of technical information and an awareness of spiritual needs. A consumerist–pluralist view of health (and health care) feeds into and reflects the processes at work. Health and even longevity can be enhanced, by choices of behaviour and health-promoting 'products', whether orthodox or heterodox. The construction of the self as a form of 'bricolage', rather than the product of membership of social collectivities, seems increasingly salient in this connection (Davison 1996).[1]

Here, perhaps, we glimpse the defining characteristic of postmodernity, in the age of the subjective. For Foucault, the development of modern society involved not simply a shift from sovereign power to disciplinary power (that is from the power of the king or state to the surveillance of the school, factory, prison and hospital, or social survey), but also the emergence of 'pastoral power', a caring view of the person's subjective state. In Arney and Bergen's (1984) colourful phrase the 'last great beast' is 'tamed' as subjectivity comes under the scrutiny of an ever growing array of 'caring professions'. If subjectivity and the lay everyday world were excluded and marginalized under the processes of objectification and rationalization they are now brought centre stage as 'those in the helping professions and mass media occupations . . . supply a variety of means of orientation and practical knowledge for everyday life' (Featherstone 1992: 163)

Even more important from the Foucauldian view is that subjectification ushers in a new form of power and domination. The clearest expression of this is in Foucault's later work on sexuality. The ability of lay people, today, to reflect more openly and speak more freely about sex is often portrayed as a reaction to earlier 'repressive' regimes, that is, a move in the direction of authenticity. Yet sexuality has been brought under the scrutiny of an array of scientists and professionals, from nineteenth-century sexologists and psychiatrists to today's counsellors and television 'experts'. Relays between 'technologies of the self' in which people are now obliged to speak the truth about themselves, and earlier forms of discipline and surveillance produce 'complex structures of domination' (Dreyfus and Rabinow 1982: 175). Far from openness and reflexivity loosening the bonds of repressive power they now combine to produce 'regimes of truth' that are ever more pervasive. Far from being passive, the subject must now speak.

Such processes may be observable in health and medicine more generally, aside from the example of 'bio-power' and sexuality. One of the most obvious examples in the British context can be found in debates about medical general practice. In the immediate period following the setting up of the National Health Service doctors in general practice frequently complained of low morale. As doctors trained to deal with disease, their everyday work appeared mundane. By the early 1980s many still complained of patients bringing them 'trivial complaints' and of low status, an issue that still reverberates, from time to time, in the late 1990s (Cartwright and Anderson 1981).

However, as Armstrong (1979) has pointed out, it would be a mistake to see this picture as entirely one of passive patients and disease-oriented ('objectifying') medicine. For, throughout the 1950s and 1960s a different form of discourse on disease, illness and medicine could also be found in British medical general practice. Through the work of the psychoanalyst Michael Balint and others, doctors were encouraged to adopt what Armstrong calls 'biographical medicine' in their approach to patients. This entailed two interlinked processes which touch on the issue of subjectivity. The first of these is that doctors were enjoined to see their patients as more than just the carriers or harbingers of disease. Balint suggested that doctors should attend to the emotional and psychological worlds that the patient might inhabit, and which, indeed, might be the reason for consultation in the first place. Many of the 'trivial' conditions presented by patients might be a 'somatic' cover for more deep-seated needs, which, it was argued, the general practitioner was in a good position to recognize. Listening to patients was as important as pronouncing on what was wrong with them.

Second, doctors were also encouraged to examine their own subjectivity. Rather than seeing themselves as superior and distant from their patients, they too, if reflective, would be able to identify their own needs and feelings more clearly. This would not only help in exploring sources of dissatisfaction and frustration, but also in gaining a greater insight into the healing process. By recognizing that illness and the doctor–patient relationship involved a series of 'offers and responses' between the parties, rather than the uncovering of an objective reality by the doctor acting as a scientific expert, a more complete view of illness could be produced. In so doing the doctor would also be able to recognize his or her 'apostolic function' and to see that interactions in the clinic often involved the 'doctor as drug', as much as the tablets being prescribed from the pharmacy (for a recent discussion of the 'Balint legacy', see E. Balint *et al.* 1996).

In this scenario health and medicine could be put on a new footing by reintroducing the 'heterogeneity' of everyday life and the emotions into a relationship that had become spoiled by unrealistic expectations of objectivity and science on the part of both doctor and patient. However, for commentators such as Armstrong, this process involves the production of an even more pervasive set of 'discourses' on subjectivity (Armstrong 1986: 30). In an attempt to overcome the charge that medicine was too narrowly based on a 'reductionist' pathological anatomy, a new kind of zeal is created to develop 'radical alternatives' by elite members of the professional group in question, in this case GPs. From a Foucauldian viewpoint, the adoption of the patient's view and of 'holistic' perspectives, in ever more elaborate professional discourses, far from 'liberating' the patient threatens to widen 'medical hegemony' based on an ideology emphasizing an 'individual ethic' (Armstrong 1986: 33).

This shift from an 'objectivist' and 'rationalist' mode of thought to one based on subjectivity can be found in several areas of modern medicine outside of general practice. Another important example is that of nursing. May (1992) has drawn attention to the way in which nurse education and, it is presumed, nursing practice, has changed markedly in recent years. In the main, modern nursing has been based on the objectification of the body, in the sense that everyday work has focused on its maintenance, care, repair and hygiene. Informal or 'heterogeneous' elements, including the suffering of the patient, subjective distress and the emotions, were left out of the picture. Like the doctor, the nurse was either expected to ignore them as irrelevant to the clinical task in hand (May 1992: 591) or deal with them on an 'informal' basis.

Now, May argues, a second wave of nurse education, and of related discursive practices in the profession more generally, is under way. Patient-centred nursing now helps to create forms of 'pastoral power' in which the nurse, rather than asking the patient to report neutrally on their bodily discomforts, wants to know how the 'whole person' feels. Patients are thus led through a form of 'secondary socialization' in which 'emotional work' can become central to the nursing process. Far from being marginalized or a source of 'external' stress for the nurse, the emotional and everyday 'lifeworld' of the patient becomes all-important. May states that: 'Pastoral power, then, finds its expression in a therapeutic gaze directed at the production of truth about the subject' (1992: 597). The power of the professional in this latest phase is expressed not in domination and control 'from above' – in the sense of the result of hierarchy – but in the immediate interactional and discursive contact between individuals. Power under conditions of postmodernity is not 'seized' or 'exercised' but is 'productive' and 'constitutive' of social relationships. In this latest phase signs of resistance to professional power are recycled by the practitioner as a concern for the patient's emotional and subjective well-being.

For some who follow this argument, the reintroduction of heterogeneity – emotions, subjectivity – into social life is to be celebrated, as those aspects that were hidden from public view (or were only the object of rational scientific enquiry) can now appear from 'behind the scenes'. The expressive revolution of the 1960s, to use Martin's telling phrase (B. Martin 1981) created conditions in which voices, once silent, could now be heard. Today the effects of child abuse, the 'hidden' experience of women, the impact of racism or the experience of emotional distress, pain and despair in illness or death can all now appear in the light of day. Postmodernity reinforces the tendency to 'transform the cultural sphere' which has taken place over the last thirty years (Featherstone 1992: 159). In this way heterogeneity offers up the politics of possibility. Postmodernity means difference and contingency and the disorganized nature of postmodern life means that objectification and rationalization processes lose their ability to effect social control in all spheres.

For others the process of 'subjectification' is seen as a totalizing move, from which the individual cannot escape. Authenticity is at best an illusion, as all thoughts and feelings about self and identity are pervasively influenced by discourse of one form or another. Any attempt at resistance can be seen as avoidance or 'denial' and new forms of discourse can always encompass deviant cases. A more pessimistic tone is struck by those who see any attempt to avoid discursive and pastoral power being met with yet another attempt to understand, care and control. When Tony Bulimore, the round-the-world yachtsman was offered counselling following four days in a capsized boat in the South Atlantic in January 1996, he was reported as saying that he would rather go to the pub and have a beer. It was widely suggested in the press that such an individual might not see the need for a caring professional hand now, but in the future he most certainly would. We are all, today or tomorrow, likely to be in need of treatment or counselling.

POSTMODERNITY, HEALTH AND ILLNESS

These opposing strains in analysis – the emphasis on fragmentation, difference and possibility, and the emphasis on increasing organization and surveillance in daily life – act as two sides to the coin of postmodernity. The more optimistic strain celebrates the apparent end of modernity, or at least the glimpse of its final transformation. In the field of health and illness 'health' itself becomes deconstructed into a series of possibilities, termed in one recent text 'arche-health' – health in the making, so to speak (Fox 1993: 40–1). In this formulation 'objectivist', 'rationalist' or even 'subjectivist' views of health as 'the absence of illness' or 'total physical and mental well-being' are eschewed in favour of a postmodern view which sees 'health' only as a possibility, located in 'flows of desire' and as 'the *play of pure difference*' (Fox 1993: 41, italics in original). No form of 'essentialist arche-health' is offered, only the heady prospect of 'possibilities of a *politics* of arche-health through the deconstruction of [modernist] discourses on health and illness' (1993: 41, italics in the original).

But in such an approach the more pessimistic note of postmodernity is sounded at the same time. Postmodernity seems to mean a never-ending relay between knowledge and power; every development in understanding is either an illusion, the false belief that the emperor really is wearing clothes (Bury 1986), or another move to survey and control. To suggest anything more definite or progressive is to slip back into modernity's old ways, namely to appeal to objective/rational, even subjective, views of health, and the role of medicine, with all their 'essentialist' or 'foundationalist' overtones. And this is to be avoided at all costs. Indeed, as all forms of 'modernist' discourse produce an illusion of an 'essential' reality, postmodernist analysis finds itself pointing only to possibilities. As Lupton puts it, in the context of feminist approaches to women's health:

> Poststructuralist feminist scholars now claim that women's experiences of the body cannot be separated from the discourses and practices which constitute them, that there is no 'authentic' body waiting to be released from the bounds of medicine.
>
> (Lupton 1994: 160)

The move from modernity to postmodernity cannot easily be seen in terms which suggest progress, improvement or greater authenticity. Under such circumstances, critique can offer no more than critique itself and, in the fields of health and medicine, the existing values of public health and medical sociology themselves become the focus of deconstruction. Insofar as there is a project to be pursued, it can only be advanced by undermining and contesting 'accepted understandings about public health and health promotional practices' (Lupton 1995: 14). To do more would be to repeat, in never-ending moves, the mistakes of modernist thought – the desire to know, organize and control. This would include a view of sociology as a 'privileged discourse' (Bauman 1992: xxv) untenable in a postmodern society. As elsewhere in postmodernist writings, the legacy of modernity is taken to be, on balance, negative and a failure – at the least, it is taken to have run its course.

In a wider context, Baudrillard (1994) has argued that the tendency to repetition is the key to a pessimistic non-conclusion for modern society. It is not that modern history has come to an end, but that under conditions of postmodernity the events of the twentieth century become effaced as endless 'balance sheets' are drawn up. The 'realities' of the twentieth century – the violence and the failures (including those of science and medicine) are lost in the 'hurry to cover up the worst before the bankrupt proceedings start (everyone is secretly afraid of the terrifying balance sheet we are going to present in the year 2000)' (Baudrillard 1994: 12). Ironically or not, however, postmodernist writings appear to add to the process identified by Baudrillard. By emphasizing the central role of discourse, other aspects of the actual legacy of modernity are left unevaluated. The attempts to tackle disease and illness and to pursue health as a valued goal, for example, take second place to the examination of *texts*, through which such efforts have variously been expressed, and through which 'realist' accounts have been socially constructed.

How, then, can the arguments about postmodernity themselves be assessed, given the existence of 'moves within moves' that seem to enclose any evaluative attempt? Perhaps the answer lies in accepting Baudrillard's (strongly moral yet ironic) invitation to regard 'events' as having a reality which 'exceeds meaning and interpretation' (Baudrillard 1994: 12), if we take this to mean experience rooted in people's lives, rather than that seen in academic or professional debate, or in media representations. As stated, paradoxically postmodernity often appears to leave us with nothing more than the examination of discursive practices and texts. To this we might counterpose the lived realities, for example of health, disease and illness, as they have unfolded throughout the modern period. To rescue these from effacement in postmodernist writings (or in postmodern society) may not provide us with an un-problematic 'authentic' body, or a true account of the past, but it might allow for at least a minimal guide across what is becoming an all too hazardous terrain.

The problem is, of course, that any attempt to evoke the 'realities' of 'lived experience' exposes the analysis to the charge of avoidance. Surely, the answer will come, any evidence about such matters is bound to be no more or less than a product of objectifying, rationalizing or subjectifying discourses. There can be no access to 'reality' except through discourse, and because of this discourse is all we can apprehend. To argue otherwise is to 'privilege lived experience', or assert an 'essentialist' view of health, both of which are fatally flawed. But if assumptions are to be 'undermined and contested', those of postmodernity and health can also come into the frame. Through this tactic it may be possible to glimpse some of the social dynamics related to health, underlying the arguments. By 'deconstructing the deconstructions' the *reconstruction* of lived experience might emerge. Perhaps even a sociology of health and illness might come back into view. Three aspects of the argument will be examined briefly in this concluding move: questions concerning agency, knowledge and power.

Agency

One of the main difficulties with arguments about postmodernity is the sense that human agency has disappeared. The processes at work, for example the development of a strong cultural emphasis on subjectivity, appear to have occurred without conscious intention or deliberate human action. Echoing Marxist and structuralist thought before it, postmodernist writing often displays a 'functionalism' which suggests that social action is 'constitutive' of hidden structures of power. Thus Foucault argues that a sense of freedom from sexual 'repression' might seem to be liberating today, but such a development is only to be understood as a 'regime of power-knowledge-pleasure that sustains the discourse on human sexuality in our part of the world' (Foucault 1981: 11). In other words, a subjective sense of freedom, improvement or positive change (e.g. speaking about that which was once forbidden) cannot be accorded value as an active human achievement in its own right. The only approach to be adopted is to see such processes as a function of new and merely *different* forms of discourse.

Yet there are other approaches which challenge such assumptions. For example, though modern medicine first objectifies disease in bio-medical science, and is then supplemented by health promotion, with its emphasis on subjective assessments and informed choices about risk and lifestyle, voices can be heard which do not passively reproduce or extend these discourses. There is a range of available reports which suggest a more critical and active appraisal in everyday life. A lack of consideration of these reports in postmodernist writings leads to an overstatement of the relays between power and knowledge, and a neglect of agency and resistance.

To take just one example, Davison's work (Davison *et al.* 1991, 1992) on 'lay epidemiology' and heart disease in South Wales shows how official 'discourses' on health and lifestyle are *actively* assimilated and judged in everyday settings. Davison suggests that lay people compare what they hear with what they know of illness from their personal and collective experience in specific communities. Official discourses do not hold sway *sui generis* as a 'regime of power/knowledge'. In the case of heart disease, lay people have a definite sense of who is likely to be a 'candidate' for a heart attack and compare what experts say against a stock of knowledge gained from several sources, and from 'sedimented experience' produced within particular cultures.

Even more to the point, the rapid expansion of discursive practices in matters such as health opens up questions which lay ideas actively address. Again, in the case of heart disease, lay people are quick to see that notions of statistical risk, which are at the centre of health promotion activity, are open to serious doubt. Lay experience suggests that exposure to risk does not always lead to illness and that the avoidance of risk does not always result in maintaining health. Lay people are just as likely to question as to accept the logic and evidence in discourses on health. Active responses shape the impact of expertise in everyday settings.

Interpretive research which has reported on lay ideas in this way suggests that 'medical dominance' in the period of 'objectifying' science, or 'subjectivity' under more recent postmodern conditions, are less pervasive than they appear (Williams and Calman 1996). As May has also suggested, again in the context of discourses on modern nursing, 'it should not be assumed that the practices through which subjectification is undertaken render the patient powerless. In fact the opposite may be true' (May 1992: 599). By engaging lay people at the subjective level an *active* response is as likely as a passive one. If the lay person or patient is asked if he or she would like to speak 'the truth' about themselves the answer may well be 'No' (1992: 600).

Knowledge

As indicated, the emphasis on difference and possibility in postmodernist writings, especially those on health, takes much of its intellectual legitimacy from the work of Foucault. In *The Birth of the Clinic* the essentials of his view of knowledge are made clear. Knowledge of the body and of disease are the products of a specific configuration of the patient and doctor, partly through the 'reorganization of the hospital' (Foucault 1976: 196). Foucault states:

This structure, in which space, language and death are articulated – what is known, in fact, as the anatomo-clinical method – constitutes the historical condition of a medicine that is given and accepted as positive.

(1976: 196)

In other words, the way modern medical scientists and doctors have displayed the realities of disease, and the ways in which lay people have come to accept them, are the product of specific historical conditions. It follows, according to Foucault, that the modern medical construction of the 'order of the solid, visible body', is 'only one way – and in all likelihood neither the first, not the most fundamental way in which one spatialises disease. There have been and will be other distributions of disease' (Foucault 1976: 3). Modern medicine's 'positive knowledge' about disease is merely the product of the power which the medical profession has to determine what is, and what is not, 'true' about disease.

Suggestive though such an argument is, two points of 'deconstruction' reveal major difficulties with it. The first is concerned with the view that knowledge is entirely bound by cultures and histories. To argue that modern (medical) science is only one way of looking at the world, or the reality of disease, runs the risk of seriously underestimating the transformations that have been brought about by these perceptions and related actions (illustrative of the organizational and technical thrust of modernity as a whole). The ability of modern medicine effectively to prevent, treat and cure major diseases, especially since 1945, places it in an entirely different league to 'other perceptions' (past, present or in the foreseeable postmodern future), however mixed the record of modern medical practice is. Numerous examples could be cited. The eradication of smallpox, the ability of modern surgery successfully to replace damaged hip joints and the reduction of severity of symptoms in diabetes, renal failure, heart disease and many other conditions show that, contrary to Foucault, modern medical science *is* the most fundamental and far-reaching form of knowledge ever to have been produced with respect to the human body. Medicine's limitations, serious errors and flaws, leading to deleterious side effects, harm and iatrogenic illness, testify equally dramatically to the same point.

To argue that such knowledge is *merely one* interest-laden way of looking at the world, seems entirely to misunderstand the nature and continuing effects of modern knowledge production. With the rapid development in recent years of fields such as surgery, drug therapies, immunology, imaging techniques and genetics, there also seems little sign of this being dramatically set aside by alternative approaches. More likely is a pluralistic setting in which modern medical science will continue to occupy a powerful position, though displaced from having sole authority over all matters to do with health. Health promotion, alternative medicine and 'discursive practices' such as counselling will continue to grow, but modern medicine will still remain a major source of knowledge and action.

The second point that needs to be made about the Foucauldian and postmodernist approaches to knowledge concerns method. Much postmodernist writing sees knowledge, both lay and professional, as the result of methods that derive from particular cultures. Anthropological writings appear to reinforce the view that Western 'positivistic' (objective/rational) methods are just that – Western – involving such matters as a split between mind and body not found elsewhere, and, by implication, not applicable elsewhere.

However, the relativism implied by this approach – that all cultures are equally valid, and Western values and knowledge cannot therefore be 'privileged' – also misses the crucial point that Western scientific methods, rightly or wrongly, have largely displaced alternative approaches. As Gellner puts it: 'The world we live in is defined, above all, by the existence of a unique, unstable and powerful system of knowledge of nature, and its corrosive, unharmonious relationship to other clusters of ideas' (Gellner 1992: 60).

The scientific method becomes 'autonomous' in the sense that it becomes 'disembedded' from local cultures, and becomes applicable to problems in *any* culture. There are, of course, limits and problems with this argument, but today many important forms of disease (especially those causing physical illness) can be tackled in similar ways anywhere in the world, taking into account local circumstances and perceptions. At least, the *possibility* of doing so arises from the detachment of scientific methods from the specific interests of the cultural groups in which they were first formed, and to which they are now applied. Doctors in Caracas, Cairo or Cologne can read a chest X-ray or the results of blood tests in the same way, and routinely do, faxing the results to their international colleagues. Again, postmodernist ideas of knowledge and method which relativize (medical) science as being no more or less important than any other form of knowledge fail to address the importance of 'publicly available methods' of investigation and their massive effects, which modern science has brought to the fore. Indeed, it is something of an irony that postmodernity fails to see that the force of its case is fashioned by exactly the same methods (persuasive argument, logic, coherence, even empirical evidence) that it seeks to relativize.

Power

The third and last area that needs to be addressed in postmodernist arguments concerns the question of power. As I hope has been made clear in the foregoing, the development of 'objectification', 'rationalization' and 'subjectification' suggests transformations in the way power is 'realized' and experienced. Most important is the suggestion that power has become 'lighter' in form, shifting from 'sovereign' to 'disciplinary', and then to 'pastoral' forms of surveillance. Welfare, including medicine and health care, is central to these processes, exercising power by 'ordering bodies' and by generating pervasive forms of discourse that shape subjective perceptions and experience. In postmodernist perspectives, therefore, language takes on an all-important role in understanding power. The role of expert discourse is paramount, as those who have the power to pronounce and speak are able to shape public perceptions and private sensibilities.

Yet here, too, there are serious objections to be made. To return to Gellner's critique of postmodernism for a moment. While Gellner accepts that language and 'discursive practices' play an important role in social control in society he raises the following counter-critique:

> Indisputably, it is the case that concepts do constrain. Concepts, the available range of ideas, all that is suggested by a given language, and all that is expressible in it are part of the machinery of social control in any society. What is *not* obvious is just how important a part conceptual constraint plays, when compared to political and economic pressure. . . . If we live in a world of meanings, and meanings exhaust the world, where is there any room for coercion, through the whip, gun or hunger? The cosy world of the scholar is allowed to stand for the harsh world outside.
>
> (Gellner 1992: 63)

In the field of medical sociology, empirical research has continually provided evidence of the way social and material circumstances influence the pattern of health and illness, apart from the undoubted influence of medical concepts and knowledge. The popular notion that 'knowledge is power' is often taken to mean the reverse: that under postmodern conditions power is little more than knowledge and 'truth claims'. However, the idea that we live in a period of 'post-scarcity values' (Featherstone and Hepworth 1991: 375) where such discursive processes hold sway, flies in the face of the continuing effects of economic deprivation in contemporary societies – as reflected in the continuing debates about income differentials and social status and their impact on health, even where absolute poverty is less evident (e.g. Blane *et al.* 1996, Wilkinson 1996). Unless such sources of power are recognized postmodern ideas threaten to become little more than a gloss on the continuing trend of widening social inequalities.

Although those following Foucault have spoken of 'resistance', and though some of the strategies employed in resistance to surveillance have been documented in the health field (e.g. Bloor and McIntosh 1990) the postmodernist view of power remains unsatisfactory. As Taylor has pointed out, the sources and character of power in such arguments remain obscure, and this reflects difficulties with the notion of agency in postmodern writings discussed above. Under conditions of postmodernity no one (individual, group or class) seems responsible for anything, as power can be neither seized nor overthrown, as it is inseparable from 'regimes of truth'. As Taylor has pointed out, in this formulation 'power no longer appears, it is hidden, but the lives of all the subjects are now under scrutiny' (Taylor 1986: 74) and 'we cannot raise the banner of truth against our own regime' (1986: 94). Truth (or freedom or justice) cannot act as a check on power (for example, the potential power of doctors over patients) because each such claim can only be seen as an expression of social interests and social position. But, as Taylor concludes, what is the point of this exposition if it is not to point to a truth which will help to free us from the illusions we create for ourselves (1986: 99) as well as the effects of social determination? Foucauldian and postmodernist writings finally leave us with a view of power and resistance which suggests that there might be social progress, but which cannot grasp it firmly.

CONCLUDING REMARKS

In this chapter arguments concerning the transformation of modernity into postmodernity have been examined, particularly as they relate to illness, health and medicine. In this context the main processes held to be at work in this transformation, 'objectification', 'rationalization' and 'subjectification' appear to underpin a shift from medical scientific concerns with disease to more subjective concerns with health. In parallel, the power of medicine in the modern era is now seen to be giving way to more pluralistic structures, in which voices once unheard now emerge as new sources of influence. For example, the health of women or the disabled, once regarded as the 'object' of rationalizing medical power, are now being reconstructed by voices 'from below', in the shape of the women's and disability movements. A recognition of the importance of ethnic differences in health experience also comes to the fore (Kelleher and Hillier 1996). Health promotion, consumerism and alternative medicine, together with a diminution of the power of the medical profession, are held to add a powerful impetus to the processes at work. In this way, 'heterogeneity' re-enters everyday life and displaces forms of professional and expert discourse from their dominant position. Difference rather than 'abnormality', and pluralism rather than unrivalled professional power, now define postmodernity as it unfolds on a global scale.

While these ideas point to important elements of change in contemporary societies, and the need to incorporate them in medical sociology (Bury 1997), the chapter has raised serious doubts concerning the arrival of postmodern society. It has been argued that by exposing postmodernist ideas to a series of critical questions, the realities of modern experience reappear relatively intact. In the context of health and medicine this means that while health and health promotion are undoubtedly important cultural motifs today (linked to the rise of 'lifestyle' modalities), the medical treatment of disease and illness has by no means been effaced. Medical science and medical practice remain central to the lives of lay people in contemporary society, as do many other features of modernity, and have gained new impulses from powerful developments in scientific knowledge and therapeutics, whether for good or ill. These influences continue to exist alongside widespread and possibly growing doubt and scepticism among lay people in different cultural segments. To this extent the notion of postmodernity points to important elements of change in late modern cultures, but it finally fails to encompass the range of organizational and experiential elements that go to make up contemporary experience. A critical and engaged sociology of medicine needs to recognize the changes under way, but this does not mean the wholesale abandonment of its substantive and methodological legacy.

NOTE

1 At the time of writing, the death of Diana, Princess of Wales, has brought forth a plethora of comments about self-identity and contemporary experience. For example, the political scientist John Gray has argued that Britain is now:

a country [which] has accepted the challenge of modern times, which is the opportunity to invent one's life for oneself. . . . In mourning the Princess of Wales, the country honours the memory of someone whom circumstances forced to author her own life and went on to claim that freedom for others.

(*Guardian* 3 September 1997)

REFERENCES

Armstrong, D. (1979) 'The emancipation of biographical medicine', *Social Science & Medicine* 13A: 1–3.
—— (1983) *Political Anatomy of the Body: Medical Knowledge in Britain in the Twentieth Century*, Cambridge: Cambridge University press.
—— (1986) 'The problem of the whole-person in holistic medicine', *Holistic Medicine* 1: 27–36.
—— (1995) 'The rise of surveillance medicine', *Sociology of Health and Illness* 17(3): 393–440.
Arney, W.R. and Bergen, B. (1984) *Medicine and the Management of the Living: Taming the Last Beast*, London: University of Chicago Press.
Balint, E., Courtenay, M., Elder, A., Hull, S. and Julian, P. (1993) *The Doctor, the Patient and the Group: Balint Revisited*, London: Routledge.
Baudrillard, J. (1994) *The Illusion of the End*, Cambridge: Polity Press.
Bauman, Z. (1992) *Intimations of Postmodernity*, London: Routledge.
Beck, U. (1992) *Risk Society: Towards a New Modernity*, London: Sage.
Blane, D., Brunner, E. and Wilkinson, R. (eds) (1996) *Health and Social Organization: Towards a Health Policy for the 21st Century*, London: Routledge.
Bloor, M. and McIntosh, J. (1990) 'Surveillance and concealment: a comparison of client resistance in therapeutic communities and health visiting', in S. Cunningham-Burley and N. McKegney (eds) *Readings in Medical Sociology*, London: Tavistock/Routledge.
Bowling, A. (1991) *Measuring Health: A Review of Quality of Life Measurement Scales*, Buckingham: Open University Press
—— (1995) *Measuring Disease*, Buckingham: Open University Press.
Burrows, R. and Loader, B. (eds) (1994) *Towards a Post-Fordist Welfare State*, London: Routledge.
Burrows, R. and Nettleton, S. (1995) 'Going against the grain: smoking and "heavy" drinking amongst the British middle classes', *Sociology of Health and Illness* 17(5): 668–80.
Bury, M. (1986) 'Social constructionism and the development of medical sociology', *Sociology of Health and Illness* 8(2): 137–69.
—— (1994) 'Quality of life: why now? A sociological view', in L. Nordenfelt (ed.) *Concepts and Measurement of Quality of Life in Health Care*, Dordrecht: Kluwer.
—— (1997) *Health and Illness in a Changing Society*, London: Routledge.
Carr-Hill, R. (1995) 'Welcome to the brave new world of evidence-based medicine', *Social Science & Medicine* 41(11): 1467–8.
Cartwright, A. and Anderson, R. (1981) *General Practice Revisited: A Second Study of Patients and their Doctors*, London: Tavistock.
Conrad, P. (1992) 'Medicalisation and social control', *Annual Review of Sociology* 18: 209–32.

Davison, C. (1996) 'Predictive genetics: the cultural implications of supplying probable futures', in T. Marteau and M. Richards (eds) *The Troubled Helix: Social and Psychological Implications of the New Genetics*, Cambridge: Cambridge University Press.

Davison, C., Davey Smith, G. and Frankel, S. (1991) 'Lay epidemiology and the prevention paradox: the implications of coronary candidacy for health promotion', *Sociology of Health and Illness* 13(1): 1–19.

Davison, C., Frankel, S. and Davey Smith, G. (1992) 'The limits of popular lifestyle: re-assessing "fatalism" in the popular culture of illness prevention', *Social Science & Medicine* 34(6): 675–85.

Dreyfus, H.L. and Rabinow, P. (1982) *Michel Foucault: Beyond Structuralism and Hermeneutics*, Brighton: Harvester Press.

Featherstone, M. (1992) 'The heroic and everyday life', *Theory, Culture & Society* 9: 159–82.

Featherstone, M. and Hepworth, M. (1991) 'The mask of ageing and the postmodern life course', in M. Featherstone, M. Hepworth and B.S. Turner (eds) *The Body: Social Processes and Cultural Theory*, London: Sage.

Foucault, M. (1976) *The Birth of the Clinic: An Archaeology of Medical Perception*, London: Tavistock.

—— (1981) *The History of Sexuality*, Vol. 1, Harmondsworth: Penguin Books.

Fox, N. (1993) *Postmodernism, Sociology and Health*, Buckingham: Open University press.

Frank, A. (1991) *At the Will of the Body: Reflections on Illness*, Boston: Houghton Mifflin.

Friedson, E. (1970) *Profession of Medicine: A Study of the Sociology of Applied Knowledge*, Chicago: University of Chicago Press.

Gabe, J. (1995) 'Health, medicine and risk: the need for a sociological approach' in J. Gabe (ed.) *Medicine, Health and Risk: Sociological Approaches*, Oxford: Blackwell.

Gellner, E. (1992) *Postmodernism, Reason and Religion*, London: Routledge.

Giddens, A. (1991) *Modernity and Self-Identity*, Cambridge: Polity Press.

Habermas, J. (1991) *The Structural Transformation of the Public Sphere*, Cambridge, MA: MIT Press.

Hirst, P. (1996) 'Globaloney', *Prospect* February: 29–33.

Jewson, N. (1976) 'The disappearance of the sick man from medical cosmology 1770–1870', *Sociology* 10: 225–44.

Katz, S. (1996) *Disciplining Old Age: The Formation of Gerontological Knowledge*, Charlottesville: University Press of Virginia.

Kelleher, D. and Hillier, S. (eds) (1996) *Researching Cultural Differences in Health*, London: Routledge.

Lash, S. and Urry, J. (1987) *The End of Organised Capitalism*, Cambridge: Polity Press.

Lawrence, C. (1995) *Medicine in the Making of Modern Britain 1700–1920*, London: Routledge.

Lupton, D. (1994) *Medicine as Culture*, London: Sage.

—— (1995) *The Imperative of Health: Public Health and the Regulated Body*, London: Sage.

Lyon, D. (1994) *Postmodernity*, Buckingham: Open University Press.

Lyotard, J.-F. (1984) *The Postmodern Condition: A Report on Knowledge*, Manchester: Manchester University Press.

Martin, B. (1981) *A Sociology of Contemporary Cultural Change*, Oxford: Blackwell.

Martin, E. (1987) *The Woman in the Body*, Milton Keynes: Open University Press.

May, C. (1992) 'Individual care? Power and subjectivity in therapeutic relationships', *Sociology* 26(4): 589–602.

Nettleton, S. (1995) *The Sociology of Health and Illness*, Cambridge: Polity Press.

Oakley, A. (1980) *Women Confined: Towards a Sociology of Childbirth*, Oxford: Martin Robertson.

—— (1984) *The Captured Womb: A History of the Medical Care of Pregnant Women*, Oxford: Blackwell.

Taylor, C. (1986) 'Foucault on freedom and truth', in D.C. Hoy (ed.) *Foucault: A Critical Reader*, Oxford: Blackwell.

—— (1989) *Sources of the Self: The Making of the Modern Identity*, Cambridge: Cambridge University Press.

—— (1991) *The Ethics of Authenticity*, Cambridge, MA: Harvard University Press.

Wilkinson, R.G. (1996) *Unhealthy Societies: The Afflictions of Inequality*, London: Routledge.

Williams, S. and Calman, M. (1996) *Modern Medicine: Lay Perspectves and Experiences*, London: UCL Press.

Zijderfeld, A. (1979) *On Clichés: The Supersedure of Meaning by Function in Modernity*, London: Routledge & Kegan Paul.

Chapter 2

The promise of postmodernism for the sociology of health and medicine

Nicholas Fox

Promises are gifts. And when promises come to fruition (which all promises do, or they are not promises but empty words) it is doubly sweet because – despite the waiting and the anticipation – we have known all along, we have trusted and been certain, that they would be fulfilled. The trip to the zoo, the first night of married passion, the Promised Land of the Israelites, feel so good when finally happening, because they were presaged in the promise. Moses would not have been so willing to wander for years in the desert (and die before he arrived) were the Promised Land to have been the Land that Could Be Yours One Day or the Land I Might Give You if You're Good. The Promised Land was already a gift, which could not be taken away: the Israelites could trust God not to renege, they were empowered, knowing that his love was unconditional, that however badly they behaved, one day the gift would be in their hands.

Promises thus stand in place of that which is promised: they are a sign of what is to be given. English banknotes carry a promise from the British government that, on demand, it will 'pay the bearer the sum of such-and-such'. In theory at least, we could exchange these promissory notes for 'real money', although the latter would in turn be a further signifier of the wealth of the nation which backs the currency. Like the Promised Land, banknote promises are special because of the trust, and the faith, which sustain them; they are built on relationship, and without relationship they are meaningless (as is witnessed when currencies collapse). This relationship of trust empowers; it allows us to travel in time, to look forward (in both senses) to a future fulfilment, and be confident of a continuity of relationship. As the root of the word 'promise' reminds us, they 'go before' what is to come, they are the guarantor of what has already been given, but is not yet here and now.

Promises are not coercive; their recipients can choose whether to take up the promised gift or not. We can leave our banknotes under the bed, to use when we wish. That is why promises are such special gifts – they are gifts given without expectation of reciprocity. They offer a future, but do not force it down our throat, demanding we be grateful. Promises free us, make new possibilities available, they are the victory of life over death, a becoming-other in place of stagnation. They are inscribed in letters of love.

THREE PROMISES

In this chapter I shall suggest some things which become possible as the postmodern approach to the sociology of health and medicine unfolds and develops. It is doubly appropriate to speak of the promise of postmodernism, for the ethics and politics of this position (at least as I shall explore them) are about 'becoming' rather than being, about diversification and multiplicity, about relationship and giving. Within this ethos, it is inappropriate to enter into rancorous debate between 'modernism and 'postmodernism' as applied in social theory; debates which substitute fear and misunderstanding for exploration, dialogue and engagement. The promise of postmodernism lies in its emphasis on openness, diversity and freedom.

The first promise of postmodernism is the promise to open up the discourses which fabricate our bodies and our health and illnesses. The discourses of medicine and its collaborators in the modernist human sciences seek to territorialize us as 'organisms' – Bodies-with-Organs (Deleuze and Guattari 1984), doomed to face the ministrations of these disciplines – to 'health', 'beauty' to a 'full and active life', to patience in the face of the failure of senses and memory, to accept, to *be*, never again to become other. Against these formulations, we are now rediscovering that our embodiment is provisional. We are cyber-bodies, already stretching the limits of our humanity, free to roam, to make ourselves other. So I shall speak not of a health fabricated by the Body-with-Organs, but of *arche-health*, a 'health' which is much more than 'health', which cannot be spoken because to speak it would inscribe it, and of *nomads*, subjectivities resisting and refusing discourse, not patients but impatients.

The disciplines of the self are so seductive: they permeate the way we act, what we eat, how we regulate our behaviour, how and to whom we make love (Foucault 1986). Even the care we offer each other is territorialized, as the rationality of the modernist market place encroaches even into the privatized spaces where emotion and love are hidden away.

Relationships are based on reciprocity: caring *about* someone becomes caring *for* someone (Gardner 1992). Care is transformed into a *vigil* (Fox 1995a) through the activities of theorists (including social theorists) which has the power to territorialize those who care and those who receive it, from cradle to grave.

The second promise of postmodernism is that – despite this disciplining work of the academy and of practitioners of health and care – it is possible to engage with those we encounter in those environments in ways which are not disciplinary, and which indeed challenge discipline. Such engagements are not about 'empowering', because what is involved is not *power* at all, but love and the *gift*. It is the antidote to academic or clinical hubris, a recognition that we cannot disengage from the world and our lives through the construction of a realm of the academic or the clinic – or that, if we do try to disengage, the tragic irony of this will face each of us when we are confronted by our mortality and our human-ness. This promise of postmodernism is a hard one. It reminds us of the context of all our energetic actions, that we are human and must die, and that those we love will die and be gone one day too.

Yet our human-ness is not tragic, it is a reason to celebrate. The ethics and politics of postmodernism are based in difference, in acknowledging diversity, that the world and its inhabitants do not fit into neat academic categories. So as we grieve for our finitude, we delight in our human diversity. We are no longer theorists separated from those we study, or practitioners distanced from our patients or clients (relationships of the kind that Cixous [1986] called the *Proper*), but participants, sharing and giving of ourselves.

The final promise of postmodernism is that we can start this right away, and that it is for all of us: social theorist, practitioner, parent, lover. It is that it is possible to engage with others in ways which will open up possibilities, not close down the way people think or behave. We can give of ourselves without seeking reciprocity (indeed, we give in this way all the time and never know it). That we can love and care, not wanting that the other be *like* something, but that the other is Other. That we can be nomadologists (Deleuze and Guattari 1986), creating new spaces to inhabit whatever we do, with whomever we engage.

THE DETECTIVE AND THE NOMAD

The post-Enlightenment or modern period celebrates rationality. Foucault (1970) identified this period with the development of the modern scientific disciplines of labour, life and language (economics, biology and philology) and the human 'sciences' which built on them (sociology, psychology and the study of literature and myth). Modernity and modernism are thought of as coinciding with philosophical commitments to truth, rationalism and rationalization; with progress: the belief that scientific analysis is the means by which the world will come to be known; and with humanism: the centring of the human subject as the wellspring of knowledge and good.

The ethos of modernism is typified in the consulting detective Sherlock Holmes, complete with fawning public in the shape of Watson, always ready to be astounded by the latest discovery. The figure of the postmodern is not Western at all, it is far from that Victorian rationalist with his comfortable consulting rooms and servant/surrogate mummy, Mrs Hudson. It is the nomad.

The nomad does not put down roots, or manipulate her environment to suit her needs and wishes. She does not seek control, she takes what is on offer, assimilates it, and moves on. She is at war with the forces which would territorialize her, the rationalism which values the stable, the static and the instrumentalism of matching actions to goals (Deleuze and Guattari 1986). Civilization, norms, taste, social distinctions mean nothing to her: she is at one with her environment, yet never part of it. She is a warrior without a strategy (Deleuze and Guattari 1986; Plant 1993).

The association of postmodernism, whether sceptical or affirmative (Rosenau 1992), with fragmentation, multivocality, radical doubt over metanarratives, epistemological relativism and anti-essentialism generate this nomad. The nomadism of postmodernism can be derived variously from the work of Foucault, Lyotard, Deleuze and Guattari, Cixous and others. For the sake of brevity, I shall simply draw on two elements of the work of Jacques Derrida. The first concerns Derrida's (1976, 1978) analysis of *différance*: the fundamental *undecidability* which resides in language and its continual *deferral* of meaning, the slippage of meaning which occurs as soon as one tries to pin a concept down. *Différance* is unavoidable once one enters into a language or other symbolic mode of representation, in which signifiers can refer not to referents (the 'underlying reality'), but only to other signifiers. While trying to represent the real, one finds that the meaning which one is trying to communicate slips from one's grasp. We are left not with the reality, but with an approximation which, however much we try to make it 'more real', is always already deferred and irrecoverable.

Derrida argued that the recognition of *différance* forces us to abandon any essentialism or foundationalism in our search for the real, to see instead the movements of difference which constitute the world. This subversion of essentialism leads to Derrida's critique of *logocentrism.* Logocentrism concerns the claim to be able to achieve the *logos,* an *unmediated* knowledge of the world: such claims have informed philosophy since Socrates (Derrida 1976), and are continually replicated in the variety of discourses which have sought to explain the world, be they philosophical, religious or scientific. A claim to this unmediated knowledge is an indicator of authenticity, of reality, of being able to 'speak the truth'. In scientific discourse, logocentrism inheres in the claim that scientific method makes reality accessible, without the intervention of any mediating process which might distort our perception. Natural science fought against a rival theological logocentrism, a struggle which continues in the debates between science and fundamentalist religions today. With the Enlightenment, humans became an object of study in the empirical sciences of economics, biology and linguistics, and in the human and social sciences (Foucault 1970; Hamilton 1992). To put it another way, since then, empirical and human sciences have been able to legitimate (though not incontestably) their particular claims to presence.

The critique of logocentrism opens up a new focus for a postmodern social theory; precisely an interest in *how claims to presence are constituted in discourse.* It rejects the possibility of a transparent mediation of knowledge of the world by the human observer. Applied to a social theory of 'health', the postmodern position asks some questions which focus upon the creation of knowledgeability about illness and health. How do discourses on health and illness, be they medical, lay or sociological, claim authenticity, how do they claim authority, and how is it that we are willing to accept their 'knowledge' of the character of health and illness?

Foucault's dramatic illustration of the contested character of the human body in the opening pages of *The Birth of the Clinic* (1976: ix–xii) describes the great changes between the eighteenth and nineteenth centuries in how those who explored the interior of the body saw. Something which at one point in history was made visible by power/knowledge in one way, would appear quite differently under a different regime of knowledge, even when the observers claimed a continuity of discipline (in this case, anatomy). New disciplines within medical science, physiology, embryology, immunology, have since vied to fabricate the body authentically, to speak the truth about it. More recently, psychology and sociology have had an impact, with some of their concepts incorporated in medical discourse, as a biopsychosocial model of medicine transforms the early bio-medical body (Armstrong 1987). Medical sociology and health psychology both oppose and collaborate with medical discourses on health and illness, while concepts such as the 'sick role' and 'stigma' have entered into lay discourse, so powerful are their claims to speak the truth of the body.

So there is no 'truth' out there concerning the way the body really is. We may have sense-data from that materiality, but to consciously perceive requires the activation of meaning, and this is possible only through language. Similarly, every datum from the internal world of sensation and pain is refracted through the lens of language as we process it into 'experience' of ourselves and our bodies. Such experiences come to have a life of their own, and logocentric claims as to their authenticity lead us to accept or refuse to accept their facticity. For Cupitt, the next step (the 'anti-realist' move) is to acknowledge that the world-in-language is the only world we inhabit, that it is not a mirror or duplicate, but the only world we have (1994: 47). It is the world within which we live out our lives, love, grieve, suffer and die, and it is enough.

In this way, postmodernism challenges the facticity of the human body as constituted in biology or in modern social theory. In place of the biological 'organism' or Body-with-Organs, we have a body which may be inscribed by such discourse, a philosophical surface which Deleuze and Guattari (to emphasize its non-biological status) call the Body-*without*-Organs (henceforth BwO). Foucault's various genealogies of power, knowledge and the disciplining of the body (1976, 1979, 1984, 1986) describe the inscription of this body by discourse, including those on health and illness. While this is not a physical inscription on the surface of a physical body, it is fair to speak of this inscription as material, in the sense that it may be 'read' on to a body, and to have material effects upon it. The BwO is a bodily, affective *subjectivity*, fabricated in 'the complex interplay of highly constructed social and symbolic forces . . . the body is a play of forces, a surface of intensities . . .' (Braidotti 1993: 44).

To give an example of this inscription of subjectivity: a reaction to a diagnosis of chronic illness may be a sense of great loss (Kleinman 1988). The diagnosis (which is a discourse couched in the language of biomedicine) inscribes the body, cutting across patternings of subjectivity which have previously constituted the person's sense-of-self. Now she responds with grief and sadness, fabricating cognitions, emotions and patterns of behaviour to inform and pad out this new subjectivity. Her sadness may be read (and mis-read) by others in demeanour and in interaction, reinforcing or refining the subject. The subject adopts new bodily strategies (self-care, risk reduction or perhaps abandonment), through which she in turn is reconstituted and re-read.

It is in such explorations that we find the first promise of postmodernism, to open up new possibilities for how we understand bodies, health and illness. Nomadology questions the valorization of 'health', offering the possibility for the radically different conception of human potential which I call 'arche-health' (Fox 1993). Outside medical discourses, health is rarely now defined simply as an absence of illness. The World Health Organization (WHO 1985) speaks of health as a state of 'complete physical, mental and social well-being', while Wright (1982) suggests an anthropological phenomenology of 'what it is to function as a human' with illness defined as circumstances of a failure to function which continues to be seen as human, and Canguilhem (1989) sees health and illness as positive and negative biological values. Illness is a 'notion of increasing dependency' for de Swaan (1990: 220), and Sedgewick identified illnesses as socially constructed definitions of natural circumstances which precipitate death or a failure to function according to certain values (1982: 30).

All these definitions (be they medical or sociological) have a politics associated with them, all try to persuade us to a particular perspective on the person who is healthy or ill, and are implicated in the inscription of the BwO. In other words, they are discursive, and are part of the modernist enterprise of *mastery*, in which a *responsibility to act* replaces any concern with the justice of the action (Bauman 1989).

The postmodern promise is the substitution of this responsibility to act with a *responsibility to otherness*. The need for such an ethics is highlighted in the work of Oliver Sacks (1991, 1995), who has documented the refusals and rejections of medicalizing definitions of health and illness among his patients. An artist who lost his colour sight refused a chance to restore it, having developed a way of seeing and creating in monochrome. The 'awakening' of people treated with L-Dopa for their Parkinsonism was, in some cases, a shattering experience. How many people are persuaded into 'cures' which cut across their subjectivity, inscribing a new medical identity – with no acknowledgement of their 'right' to otherness?

Arche-health is a becoming, a de-territorializing of the BwO, a resistance to discourse, a generosity towards otherness, a nomadic subjectivity. It is not intended to suggest a natural, essential or in any way prior kind of health, upon which the other healths are superimposed and it is not supposed to be a rival concept. Indeed the reason for using this rather strange term is its homage to Derrida's notion of *arche-writing*, which is not writing but that which supplied the possibility of writing, that is, the system of difference upon which language is based: *différance* – that which differs and is deferred. Similarly, arche-health:

1 is the *becoming of* the organism which made it possible for the first
   time to speak of health or illness;
2 is present, in the sense that a trace of it is carried, in every discourse on
   health, however and with whatever logos that discourse has constituted itself;
3 can never become the object of scientific investigation, without falling
   back into discourse on health/illness. It is not the outcome of deconstruction of these discourses, it *is* deconstruction: difference and
   becoming;
4 is multiple in its effects. As difference, it is meaningless to speak of its
   unity or its division.

Every BwO has an arche-health, which is its *becoming other*. Whereas
health and illness territorialize the BwO by their discourses, arche-health
is the refusal and resistance to this discourse. Your, or my, arche-health
may be more or less developed, depending on how territorialized our
subjectivities are by the discourses of medicine and the social sciences. It
is the path towards the BwO, one which is a life-long journey:

> You never reach the Body-without-Organs, you can't reach it, you are
> forever attaining it, it is a limit. . . . But you're already on it, scurrying
> like a vermin, groping like a blind person, or running like a lunatic:
> desert travels and nomad of the steppes. On it we sleep, live our
> waking lives, fight – fight and are fought – seek our place, experience
> untold happiness and fabulous defeats: on it we penetrate and are
> penetrated: on it we love. (Deleuze and Guattari 1988: 150)

The ethics and politics of arche-health is deconstructive, reminding us
to ask hard questions of the modernist disciplines which inscribe us into
subjectivity through their conceptions of, and preoccupations with,
'health' and 'illness'.

THE GIFT AND THE PROPER

Imagine on one hand the people in our lives who say: 'be this . . . do
this for me . . . I want you to be like this'. Their discourses reflect their
desire (which is a lack or a wish) for you to be like them, to take on an
identity which supports their own sense of self. Such talk *territorializes*
the BwO, patterning it with a subjectivity which creates it in the image of
that lack or wish.

On the other hand there is the person who says: 'here's some space for
you . . . go for it . . . get on with it . . . I trust and have confidence in you

. . . take my generosity of spirit'. This kind of engagement is a *gift* which enables, opens up new possibilities, allows the BwO to differentiate, to *de-territorialize* for a moment, to establish a nomad subjectivity, to resist.

Which kind of person are you? If you are an academic or a member of the practical professions concerned with health and care, it is likely that – like it or not – you are the first kind, although educators and professionals who are 'facilitative' in their practice may have broken with such disciplinary approaches. Modernism's *will to mastery* is Sherlock Holmes at work again, always categorizing, diagnosing, analysing, testing hypotheses, developing theory. Consequently it is very hard to de-territorialize our BwOs from the discourses which have grown up in medicine, nursing and the social sciences. We need all the help we can get.

I suggested earlier, following White (1991), that the ethics and politics of postmodernism replaces the commitment to mastery and action with a commitment to otherness and difference. In writing of a gift, this term is used advisedly, recalling my remarks concerning promises, and drawing on the writing of the feminist post-structuralist Cixous. She opposes Gift relationships to what she sees as the masculine realm of the Proper (property, possession, propriety), of possessive desire based in a wish and a lack, identity and dominance (Cixous 1986; Moi 1985). If we are concerned with an ethical engagement with other people – be they lovers, children, clients, students or colleagues, then the characteristics of such Gift relationships would seem particularly appropriate as the basis for our relationships. Gifts are concerned with, for instance, such values as:

generosity
trust
confidence
love
commitment
delight
allegiance
esteem
admiration
curiosity

Each of these values can easily elide into possessive relations: trust becomes dependency, esteem becomes reverence, generosity becomes patronage, curiosity becomes the gaze. And how few of these words are part of the discourse of professional care! How many suggest relations which could be seen as *unprofessional* and inappropriate to the highly theorized and formalized worlds of the academy and care settings of the modern world. Indeed, the exclusion of such relations and the constitution of such impersonal realms may supply the means whereby disciplines or professions can establish themselves, Thus, Dunlop (1986) has argued, the Western health care system provided the opportunity for a discourse on 'care', contributing to the inception of the distinctive profession of nursing.

The force and value of this distinction between the Gift and the Proper rests in the possibility that things could be different. It offers the potential for an ethics and politics of engagement based on a celebration of difference, not of identity (Haber 1994). The Proper is a possessive relationship, constantly requiring of its object that it behaves in certain ways, that it is defined (as 'patient', 'student', 'sociology'), and repeats the patterns of those who have been the objects of its discourse previously. Substituting Gift relationships changes everything: we engage with others now as others, not as those with whom we might wish to identify. Definition is replaced with metaphor and allusion, analysis and theory with poetics and expression, professional care by love and the celebration of difference.

But let me be clear about what a gift is, because it is possible to have Proper gifts! Gifts play a part in many societies (Mauss 1990), as a form of social bonding based in obligation and reciprocity (Hochschild 1983: 80–2). These are features of Proper relationships, and in the realm of the Proper a gift is thus threatening because it establishes an inequality, a difference, an imbalance in power. The act of giving becomes an act of aggression, an exposure of the Other (Moi 1985: 112). Gifts may also serve other purposes, as the commentary on the hypocritical giving of the Pharisees in the Christian New Testament reminds us: their 'gifts' were outward shows of godliness, intended to define their own superiority, and perhaps to store up credit for the afterlife. In contrast, the Gift is not given with any expectation of reciprocity; in the realm of the Gift, those who give do not expect gratefulness or even an acknowledgement of their effort. The true Gift is one which one does not even realize one is giving (Derrida 1992).

So we must be very cautious about these distinctions. Similarly, we must not underestimate the impact (and difficulty) of replacing the Proper in our disciplines of the academy and the caring professions. Substituting such relations with those based on Gifts is about replacing a modernist responsibility to act with a responsibility to otherness (White

1991). White suggests that this means adopting what he describes as a mood of 'grieving delight'. One grieves for human finitude, but delights and celebrates difference. Grief sensitizes us to injustice, while delight deepens our concern with celebrating difference in our humanity (1991: 129).

This takes us back to arche-health, which is about this dual engagement with the other. Whether an academic or a practitioner, we are to be guided by a responsibility to otherness which has as its objective the facilitation of becoming, of arche-health. Arche-health is possible only by the de-territorialization of the BwO, resisting its inscription of the relations of the Proper. The nursing theorist Rosemarie Parse developed a perspective on health as 'human becoming' (Parse 1987), and similarly Brykczynska speaks of a gift-like care as actualization, a sharing of a moment of joy, of being truly present alongside an other:

> True caring involves growth, mutual growth of carer and recipient of care; and it is this ability to grow, to change, to progress from pain to disintegration to purpose and equilibrium that gives the caring phenomena [sic] its impetus and rationale.
>
> (Brykczynska 1992: 237).

Yet even here it is necessary to ask what constitutes purpose and equilibrium, and by whom these are defined? There is no guarantee that acting in the world will lead to a facilitation of becoming, even within such a perspective. So, if we are to have a 'manifesto' of the Gift, it has to be a rather negative one, encouraging *inaction* rather than action! It might go something like this:

1 If you have to take sides, be on the side of the nomad thought: the wandering nomad broken free (for however short a time) from discourse. From such a position comes the reflection that acting is to be judged in terms of its consequences, not by any overarching discourse of good or truth.

2 If you must have values, celebrate difference and otherness. Structures and systems force us into sameness. Recognize the undecidability and openness of the world, its capacity always to become other.

3 If you must desire anything, desire in a spirit of generosity, not for mastery. Do not try to possess the object of your desire (the Other): make it possible that your relationship is a gift requiring no response or repetition. Accept the gifts which others may make available to you, and take pleasure in them for their own sake.

NOMADOLOGY FOR BEGINNERS

Because language is constitutive of subjectivity, that means that while it may be constraining (whenever we are persuaded to truth by 'discourse'), it can also be liberating. To return to Sherlock Holmes and the nomad. Holmes uses language, and the signs by which he makes sense of 'reality', as a physician diagnoses diseases from signs and symptoms, to deduce what occurred at a location. Every clue 'speaks' to him of what is absent, drawing upon a regime of truth based in assumptions about the world ('when you have eliminated the impossible, whatever remains, however improbable, must be the truth'). He is the modernist *par excellence*, persuading himself and us that his fabrications are synonymous with reality – even when reality is very strange.

The nomad (although there are no nomads, only nomadism and nomadic existence – it is a mood or an ethos, not a state of being) is like Holmes in one way, in that she is continually slipping into the detective's way of thinking, mistaking her constructions of reality for truth. She is attracted by discourses which offer certainty, she is at war with her own longing for a fixed point. Yet the medium of language which enslaves is also the medium of resistance to discourse. Achieving nomadism (and in realizing that it is never finally achieved), means contesting the patternings of subjectivity which discourses inscribe on the BwO, and the medium of this contestation is language (it must be, there is nothing else). I like this comment by the feminist post-structuralist Cixous, when she talks about the power of language:

> A feminine text cannot fail to be more than subversive. It is volcanic, as it is written it brings about an upheaval of the old property crust, carrier of masculine investments, there's no other way . . . it's in order to smash everything, to shatter the framework of institutions, to blow up the law, to break up the 'truth' with laughter.
>
> (Cixous 1990: 326)

Similarly, Deleuze and Guattari see writing as a way of 'de-territorializing', of breaking free from discourse, refusing to follow a single chain of meaning (1988: 7–9). Their own writing, in particular their book *A Thousand Plateaus* (Deleuze and Guattari 1988), is intended to de-territorialize its readers, to offer new possibilities and new subjectivities. It is also about living in the here and now, not in the pasts and futures dreamed up in discourse (Braidotti 1993: 44).

We can see just such a de-territorialization in the virtualization of 'reality' in the new cyber-culture. In May 1995, I took part in a plenary discussion at the Virtual Futures conference with the two performance artists Stellarc and Orlan, to talk about their work and the ethics associated with it. Stellarc has begun to explore the philosophical challenges of the cyborg (part-human, part-machine) in a series of performances, including the construction of an artificial third arm, and the control of this and other parts of his body by strangers via the Internet. Orlan's performance art entails changing her appearance through plastic surgery – some of which is conventional, while the creation of lumps on her temples challenges norms of human physiognomy and beauty. What they have in common is a questioning of the limits of the body, and of what it means to be human and to live in relationship with other 'humans'. They are interested, as are the cyberpunk writers, in developing the post-human, who is free from the constraints of the body. William Gibson writes of a future in which humans are downloaded into computers, and carry on a non-corporeal existence in cyberspace: we are challenged to reflect on our relations with such 'constructs', and on their humanity (Bukatman 1993). Within cyber-culture, there is also a new eclectic spirituality which challenges the limitations of realist philosophy and scientific secularism (Rushkoff 1994). The implications for the kind of postmodern nomadology which I have been exploring are – I hope – clear: technology, literature and art, and cyber-spirituality are variously testing the limits of embodied humanity, as constituted in the traditional discourses of the body.

But as I conclude these remarks, I want to turn back to the promise of postmodernism for those involved intimately with health and illness: 'patients' and their carers. Exploring care and the relationships between carers and those who receive care, I have been struck by the extent to which Proper relations impinge on an area which – intuitively – one might expect to reflect the Gift (Fox 1995a, 1995b). The ethics and politics of a commitment to difference and nomadism might thus involve a replacement of the Proper by the Gift in caring and healing relationships. If this is easy to say, then it seems that it is far harder in practice.

The ease with which a Gift relationship can become one of possession and repetition has been discussed by Bond (1991), who examined some of the consequences of rationalization and formalizing of informal caring – for family or friends – as a result of recent UK legislation encouraging moves away from institutional care, towards 'care in the community'. This legislation provides the possibility, amongst other policies, of rewarding informal carers financially, and providing training to ensure that good standards of care are achieved. Bond argues that this professionalization of informal care leads to a loss of the 'caring' element of the relationship through four processes: the implementation of expert knowledge, the legitimation of care through medical judgements of health and illness, the individualization of behaviour and its consequent depoliticization (1991: 11–12).

Within the framework developed above, this process could be interpreted as the loss of the positive investments which carers supply in caring and healing – of love, admiration, commitment, accord, involvement, generosity – substituting these with a relation of possession, in which the recipient of care is the property of the carer, upon whom the carer 'does' care. In place of the trust, confidence, esteem on the part of the recipient of care towards the carer – investments which make care synonymous with the relationship – the recipient of care enters into a relation of negative dependency. Instead of a positive investment in the recipient of care, there is a political inscription of the 'body of care' (a Body-with-Organs), mediated through the discourse of professional care which smothers and envelops (White 1991: 92). Expertise in care takes control, seeks to possess the object of its desire. As such, it cannot but re-territorialize its object according to its particular discursive technique of metaphoric representation. Only if this symbolic investment is reconstituted in the realm of the Gift can the interaction substitute control with 'becoming', a territorialized subject with a nomadic subject.

De Swaan's (1990) study of a cancer ward suggests the difficulties of contemplating a caring relationship based in generosity. Here, as de Swaan describes it, is a libidinal economy in which Gift relations are hard to achieve. The anxieties of staff caring for people who are dying are displaced: translated into medical terms. Patients' bodies are cared for, while their emotions go untended; staff do not discuss their upset with colleagues. Doctors and nurses learn not to become attached to seriously ill and dying people: the investment of care, affection and generosity by a member of staff in a patient goes 'unrewarded' when the next day the patient is dead (de Swaan 1990: 42–7). Yet, as de Swaan documents, there are examples of generosity, enabling patients to 'become'.

> To patients it means much when doctors and nurses know how to handle their wounds competently and without fear. The nurse patiently washing a dilapidated patient, changing his clothes, is also the only one who dares touch him without disgust or fear, who quietly and competently handles the body which so torments and frightens the patient ... [and who] knows how to deal skilfully with the

wounds and lumps, in doing so liberating the patients for the moment from their isolation.

(de Swaan 1990: 48)

This extract suggests how one is to understand the force of the Gift: it is constituted in an open-endedness. It stands in place of discourse, even a discourse on liberation or empowerment (for example, Malin and Teasdale 1991), which tells the Other *how* to be more free or more sexy or more something else, and of course in doing so closes down the possibilities, making the Other an appendage of the discourse, inscribed with the power of the Word. It does not say what something is, or is not: it allows, for a moment at least, a thing to become multiple, to be both something and another thing and another. Bunting offers as an example of such opening-up:

a family working with a child with special health needs. As the family members work with the child and with one another, each moves beyond the self and the present reality to the possibles that unfold. . . . The family's health is the movement toward and the expression of these possibles as they are chosen and lived.

(Bunting 1993: 14)

The final promise of postmodernism is that generosity, trust, love, affirmation, confidence give the other a chance – here and now – to be other, not more of the same. For a moment, her subjectivity is freed, and this nomad subject *becomes*. Nomadism is only ever momentary, because we are tied to language – there is nowhere else to go. But it is enough, it is how it is possible to be human.

REFERENCES

Armstrong, D. (1987) 'Theoretical tensions in biopsychosocial medicine', *Social Science & Medicine* 25:1213–18.

Bauman, Z. (1989) *Modernity and the Holocaust*, Cambridge: Polity Press.

Bond, J. (1991) 'The politics of care-giving: the professionalization of informal care', paper presented to the British Sociological Association conference, Manchester.

Braidotti, R. (1993) 'Discontinuous becomings. Deleuze on the becoming-woman of philosophy', *Journal of the British Society for Phenomenology* 24: 44–55.

Bukatman, S. (1993) 'Gibson's typewriter', in M. Derv (ed.) *Flame Wars. The Discourse of Cyberculture*, Durham, NC: Duke University Press (Vol. 92 (4) of the *South Atlantic Quarterly*).

Bunting, S. (1993) *Rosemarie Parse. Theory of Health as Human Becoming.* Newbury Park, CA: Sage.

Canguilhem, G. (1989) *The Normal and the Pathological*, New York: Zone Books.

Cixous, H. (1986) 'Sorties', in H. Cixous and C. Clement (eds) *The Newly Born Woman*, Manchester: Manchester University Press.

—— (1990) 'The laugh of the Medusa', in R. Walder, (ed.) *Literature in the Modern World*, Oxford: Oxford University Press.

Cupitt, D. (1994) *After All. Religion without Alienation*, London: SCM Press.

Deleuze, G. and Guattari, F. (1984) *Anti-Oedipus: Capitalism and Schizophrenia*, London: Athlone.

—— (1986) *Nomadology. The War Machine*, New York: Semiotext(e).

—— (1988) *A Thousand Plateaus*, London: Athlone.

Derrida, J. (1976) *Of Grammatology*, Baltimore, MD: Johns Hopkins University Press.

—— (1978) *Writing and Difference*, London: Routledge.

—— (1992) *Given Time, 1: Counterfeit Money*, Chicago: University of Chicago Press.

de Swaan, A. (1990) *The Management of Normality*, London: Routledge.

Dunlop, M.J. (1986) 'Is a science of caring possible?', *Journal of Advanced Nursing* 11: 661–70.

Foucault, M. (1970) *The Order of Things*, London: Tavistock.

—— (1976) *The Birth of the Clinic*, London: Tavistock.

—— (1979) *Discipline and Punish*. Harmondsworth: Peregrine.

—— (1984) *The History of Sexuality, Part 1*, Harmondsworth: Penguin Books.

—— (1986) *The Care of the Self*, New York: Random House.

Fox, N.J. (1993) *Postmodernism, Sociology and Health*, Buckingham: Open University Press.

—— (1995a) 'Postmodern perspectives on care: the vigil and the gift', *Critical Social Policy* 15: 107–25.

—— (1995b) 'Professional models of school absence associated with home responsibilities', *British Journal of Sociology of Education* 16: 221–42.

Gardner, K. (1992) 'The historical conflict between caring and professionalisation: a dilemma for nursing', in D.A. Gaut (ed.) *The Presence of Caring*, New York: National League for Nursing Press.

Haber, H. (1994) *Beyond Postmodern Politics. Lyotard, Rorty, Foucault*, New York: Routledge.

Hamilton, P. (1992) 'The Enlightenment and the birth of social science', in S. Hall and B. Gieben (eds) *Formations of Modernity*, Cambridge: Polity Press.

Hochschild, A.R. (1983) *A Managed Heart*, Berkeley: University of California Press.

Kleinman, A. (1988) *The Illness Narratives*, New York: Basic Books.

Malin, N. and Tensdale, K. (1991) 'Caring versus empowerment: considerations for nursing practice', *Journal of Advanced Nursing* 16: 657–62.

Mauss, M. (1990) *The Gift: The Form and Reason for Exchange in Archaic Societies*, London: Routledge.

Moi, T. (1985) *Sexual/Textual Politics*, London: Methuen.

Parse, R. (1987) *Nursing Science: Major Paradigms, Theories and Critiques*, Philadelphia: W.B. Saunders.

Plant, S. (1993) 'Nomads and revolutionaries', *Journal of the British Society for Phenomenology* 24: 88–101.

Rosenau, P.M. (1992) *Postmodernism and the Social Sciences*, Princeton, NJ: Princeton University Press.

Rushkoff, D. (1994) *Cyberia*, London: Flamingo.

Sacks, O. (1991) *Awakenings*, London: Picador.

—— (1995) *An Anthropologist on Mars: Seven Paradoxical Tales*, London: Picador.

Sedgewick, P. (1982) *Psychopolitics*, London: Pluto.

White, S. (1991) *Political Theory and Postmodernism*, Cambridge: Cambridge University Press.

WHO (1985) *Targets for Health for All*, Geneva: World Health Organization.

Wright, W. (1982) *The Social Logic of Health*, New Brunswick, NJ: Rutgers University Press.

Chapter 3

Medical sociology and modernity
Reflections on the public sphere and the roles of intellectuals and social critics

Graham Scambler

> Sociology is a subject whose insights should be available to the great mass of the people in order that they should be able to use it to liberate themselves from the mystification of social reality which is continuously provided for them by those in our society who exercise power and influence.
>
> (Rex 1974: ix)

Ever since its genesis in a pattern of thought representative of the Western Enlightenment, sociology has had its problems and its opponents. One key set of problems has issued from its earliest practitioners' commitment to a privileged, compelling and scientific account of the true nature of modernity. Not only has such an account proved elusive, but, in Kuhnian terms, sociology has enjoyed few if any stable periods of collective assent to a dominant paradigm (Kuhn 1970). Its critics have emphasized this failure to realize its putative potential and (even) to command a consensus on the means to do so. They have also caricatured its long-standing ambition to pioneer a value-neutral route towards the 'good society'.

Such criticisms now rarely unsettle sociologists, many of whom no longer see themselves as scientists or 'legislators' (Bauman 1987), feel the discipline has 'moved on' in numerous subtle ways, and in any case often question the motives of detractors. From the 1970s onwards, however, a new and more far-reaching critique of the entire Enlightenment legacy has emerged, or coalesced, under the general rubric of 'postmodernism'. According to some readings of the postmodern, for example, the sociological enterprise – at least as conceived in and framed by modernity – has been fatally undermined by the exposure and collapse of the concept of universal reason and of the family of metanarratives that have long underpinned and informed it.

This postmodern challenge has force to it, despite the internal inconsistencies found in many of its articulations. It will be argued here that many early forms of sociology were flawed precisely because of their commitment to the legislative absolutism of 'unreconstructed' Enlightenment thought. But it will also be maintained that sociology is necessarily, and morally, constrained by parameters set by a post-legislative, post-absolutist, or 'reconstructed', version of the Enlightenment tradition, and that this requires it to be critical and engaged.

The opening part of this chapter outlines the general case for a critical sociology allied to just such a reconstruction of the Enlightenment project. The second part extends the first in an attempt to show that there is also a moral imperative implicit in the critical sociological enterprise. In the third part the case and potential for critical sociology to be an agent in civil society is discussed. The fourth part focuses on the critical sociologist qua intellectual or social critic. And the fifth and concluding part illustrates some of the chapter's main themes by drawing on the domain of medical sociology.

A RECONSTRUCTED ENLIGHTENMENT PROJECT AND A CRITICAL SOCIOLOGY

The core arguments in this chapter draw heavily on the evolving work of Jürgen Habermas. Three particularly well-known themes from this work need to be rehearsed briefly before the case for a critical sociology is summarized. The first concerns Habermas's reconstruction of the Enlightenment project (Habermas 1984, 1987). The pivotal role here is accorded to his theory of communicative action. Universal reason, he maintains, must be grounded not, as in the Enlightenment of late eighteenth-century Europe, in the subject–object relations of the philosophy of consciousness, but in the subject–subject relations of communicative action. His basic insight is that people's use of language to communicate implies a common endeavour to attain consensus in a context in which all participants are free to contribute and have equal opportunities to do so. 'Reaching understanding is the inherent telos of human speech' (Habermas 1984: 287). Language-use, in short, presupposes commitment to an 'ideal speech situation' in which discourse can realize its full potential for rationality. Communicative action, or 'action oriented to understanding', is contrasted with strategic action, or 'action oriented to success', often through manipulation or coercion.

The second theme revolves around the distinction between 'system' and 'lifeworld'. Habermas's (1984) concept of the lifeworld is more ambitious than those evoked in the phenomenology of Schutz and Berger and Luckman. For him, the concept of the lifeworld is a correlate of the concept of communicative action. It 'appears in interaction as a context of relevance', conceived not in terms of consciousness but as a 'culturally transmitted and linguistically organized stock of interpretive patterns' (Outhwaite 1994: 86). Thus it may be defined as 'the intuitively present, in this sense familiar and transparent, and at the same time vast and incalculable web of presuppositions that have to be satisfied if an actual utterance is to be meaningful, i.e. valid or invalid' (Habermas 1987: 131). It is the medium or 'symbolic space' within which culture, social integration and personality are sustained and reproduced.

The lifeworld may be contrasted with the concept of system, which pertains to material rather than symbolic reproduction and is characterized by strategic rather than communicative action. The system comprises the market economy and the state apparatus and is governed by functional imperatives. Habermas daws a distinction between system and lifeworld rationalization. System rationalization leads to a growth in differentiation and complexity; that is, to an expansion of markets and of political and administrative organization. The rationalization of the lifeworld leads to an increase in the scope of communicative action and thereby to an extension of communicative rationality.

The third theme contrasts the 'logic' and the 'dynamic' of rationalization in the West. Habermas contends that modern societies have witnessed a fundamental 'uncoupling' between the economy and the state, constituting the system, on the one hand, and what he refers to as the public and private spheres of the lifeworld, on the other. These four domains or subsystems – the economy, the state, the public sphere and the private sphere – are interdependent: each is specialized in terms of its product, but each relies on the others for what it does not produce. The economy produces 'money', the state 'power', the public sphere 'influence' and the private sphere 'commitment'. These products or media are traded between subsystems. The economy, for example, relies on the state to establish and maintain legal institutions such as private property and contract, on the public sphere to influence consumption patterns, and on the private sphere to provide a committed labour force, and itself sends money into each other subsystem (Crook *et al.* 1992). The media of the subsystems are far from equivalent in their capacities however. As system and lifeworld become more clearly defined, the media, and thus subsystems, of the former come progressively to dominate the latter. It is in this context that Habermas discerns a 'colonization of the lifeworld'.

Picking up the Weberian theme of rationalization and the Marxist theme of commodification, Habermas argues that the lifeworld becomes colonized, that is, increasingly state administered or 'juridified' and commercialized. 'Possibilities for communicative action become attenuated as social participation becomes hyper-rationalized in terms of immediate and instrumental returns. Participants encounter each other as legal entities to contracts rather than as thinking and acting subjects' (Crook *et al.* 1992: 28). Rationalization in the West, in other words, has been 'selective': it has taken place in a 'one-sided, distorted and crisis-ridden way' (Roderick 1986: 133). While the dynamic of development has meant that system rationalization has outpaced the rationalization of the lifeworld, however, Habermas insists that there was nothing inevitable about this, and that the logic of development allows for further lifeworld rationalization.

Having completed this exceedingly schematic reading of certain of Habermas's ideas, it is now possible to encapsulate the case for a critical sociology, a sociology perhaps best situated in the tradition of critical social theory represented by a long and imposing line of postwar thinkers from C. Wright Mills to Habermas himself (see Hearn 1985). Five meta-theoretical theses are involved, each of which has been elaborated and defended in considerably more detail elsewhere (Scambler 1996a).

The first thesis attests that *the full ramifications of the reflexivity of high modernity for sociological practice have not been sufficiently addressed.* The reflexivity of modernity 'consists in the fact that social practices are constantly examined and reformed in the light of incoming information about those very practices, thus constitutively altering their character' (Giddens 1990: 38). This reflexivity has become extremely unsettling in its subversion of unreconstructed Enlightenment ideals of certain knowledge. Furthermore, the re-entry of sociological discourse into the contexts it analyses is pivotal; indeed, 'modernity is itself deeply and intrinsically sociological' (Giddens 1990: 43). Although the importance of reflexivity, thus defined, is widely acknowledged by sociologists, it is less apparent, as the second thesis avers, that this translates into 'appropriate' practices.

The second thesis maintains that *sociology needs to examine more critically its primary allegiance to economy and state and, via the media of money and power, system rationalization.* Given its genesis in and subsequent affinity to unreconstructed Enlightenment thinking, it is not surprising that sociology's history is one of abetting as much as resisting selective rationalization and lifeworld colonization. Moreover, it seems clear that as we move towards 2000 there remains a *primary* and *disproportionate* allegiance to a pattern of enquiry and research consonant with, or at least not effectively resistant to, the imperatives of economy and state.

The third thesis states that *sociology's principal commitment is to the rationalization of the lifeworld*, and such an overriding commitment is of course incompatible with a *primary* allegiance to system needs.

Continuing this theme, the fourth thesis asserts that *the nature of sociology's commitment to lifeworld rationalization requires its promotion and engagement in a reconstituted public sphere*. Societies like Britain are characterized by 'formal' democracy, namely, 'a legitimation process that elicits generalized motives – that is, diffuse mass loyalty – but avoids participation' (Habermas 1973: 36). By contrast, 'substantive' democracy *institutionalizes* in the public sphere of the lifeworld the fundamental norms of rational speech (although Habermas here warns against utopianism and against equating substantive democracy with any particular form of organization). If critical sociology, fated to be an actor in high modernity, is to realize its overriding commitment to lifeworld rationalization, it must *of necessity* engage with a public sphere *reconstituted* out of the residue of a 'bourgeois public sphere' once progressive and resistant to economy and state but long since 'collapsed into a sham world of image creation and opinion management in which the diffusion of media products is in the service of vested interests' (Thompson 1993: 177; see Habermas 1989).

The final thesis claims that *if sociology is to be effective in promoting and engaging in a reconstituted public sphere, alliances must arguably be built with system-based and, especially, lifeworld-based activists*. Alliances with activists from the *new social movements*, which Habermas sees as provoked by lifeworld colonization and emerging 'at the seam between the lifeworld and system in a kind of ongoing boundary dispute over the limits of systemic intrusion' (Ray 1993: 60), may be particularly felicitous. Indeed, some such movements might themselves be prototypes for 'the development of new participatory-democratic institutions which would regulate markets, bureaucracies and technologies' (Ray 1993: 62). For all that certain new social movements may currently be the most plausible agents of a reconstituted public sphere and of a further rationalization of the lifeworld, however, no self-respecting critical sociologist could be anything but pessimistic about the prospects for imminent change.

DISCOURSE ETHICS, JUSTICE AND SOLIDARITY

Habermas's (1990, 1993) discourse ethics can be interpreted as an elaboration or deepening of his theory of communicative action. As such it too remains at the formal or procedural level. It starts from a *principle of universalization* reflecting, but also departing from, that of Kant. McCarthy (1978: 326) writes: 'the emphasis shifts from what each can will without contradiction to be a universal law to what all can will in agreement to be a universal norm'. Habermas's strategy, in essence, is to socialize Kant's individualistic moral theory in such a way as to satisfy objections first mounted by Hegel (see Outhwaite 1996).

Habermas's principle of universalization is intended to compel the 'universal exchange of roles' that Mead called 'ideal role taking' or 'universal discourse'. Thus every valid norm has to fulfil the following condition:

> *All* affected can accept the consequences and the side effects its *general* observance can be anticipated to have for the satisfaction of *everyone's* interests (and these consequences are preferred to those of known alternative possibilities for regulation).
>
> (Habermas 1990: 65)

The principle of universalization should not be confused with the *principle of discourse ethics*:

> Only those norms can claim to be valid that meet (or could meet) with the approval of all affected in their capacity *as participants in a practical discourse*.
>
> (Habermas 1990: 66)

The principle of universalization has to do with *moral* questions of 'justice' and 'solidarity', which admit of formal universal resolution, while the principle of discourse ethics concerns *ethical* questions of the 'good life', which can only be addressed in the context of substantive cultures, forms of life or individual projects.

As a deontological rather than a teleological theory, discourse ethics accords priority to moral questions of justice and solidarity. Justice and solidarity are necessarily related and of the essence of communicative action. Justice, in its modern sense, refers to the 'subjective freedom of inalienable individuality'; and solidarity refers to the 'well-being of associated members of a community who intersubjectively share the same lifeworld' (Habermas 1990: 200). Morality, Habermas (1990: 200) writes, 'cannot protect the rights of the individual without also protecting the well-being of the community to which he belongs'. Rehg (1994: 245) is worth quoting at length here:

> Contrary to Descartes, one arrives at rational conviction not in isolation but only in a public space, however much a certain solitude might be necessary as one moment in this process. We thus find justice linked – at its very basis in rational autonomy – with a real dependence on others' rational autonomy. For inasmuch as my conviction about moral obligation cannot come at the expense of yours, in disregard for your inviolable right to say no, it must submit itself to the testing of the deliberating community of all those affected. Precisely the effort to convince others of the justice of a normative expectation demands that I attend empathetically to its effects on others' welfare. Both the community whose cooperative structures are at stake in moral deliberation as well as the concrete others involved in such cooperation enter into the very constitution of justice under the aegis of rational solidarity.

Habermas's claims for his analysis are formal and modest. Qua moral theory, discourse ethics aims to 'ground the moral point of view', to clarify the 'universal core of our moral intuitions' and to 'refute value scepticism'. What discourse ethics cannot and does not purport to do, its critics notwithstanding, is resolve substantive issues. 'By singling out a procedure of decision-making, it seeks to make room for those involved, who must then find answers on their own to the moral-practical issues that come at them, or are imposed upon them, with objective historical force' (Habermas 1990: 211).

What, then, of the social mechanisms and institutions most likely in practice to facilitate discourse-ethical procedures or, more generally, the 'public use of reason'? What is required, at base, is an extension of substantive democracy, which alone affords 'genuine participation of citizens in processes of will-formation', and such an extension, as indicated ealier, is conditional upon further lifeworld rationalization via a reconstitution of its public sphere.

The discussion in this second part of the chapter allows three 'elaborations' of the five meta-theses summarized in the first. The first of these is that *sociology's commitment to the rationalization of the lifeworld is a moral requirement*. It is not being maintained that all sociology (including system-driven sociology) defined here as pre- or non-critical is undesirable or without return; but it is being maintained that a critical sociology allied to a reconstructed Enlightenment project is under an inescapable and prepotent moral compulsion to decolonize and further rationalize the lifeworld.

The second elaboration states that *the moral character of sociology's commitment to lifeworld rationalization entails a commitment, too, to the formation of 'real institutional procedures' approximating to the rational intersubjective will-formation idealized in discourse ethics.* It has been argued that justice and solidarity have an 'internal relation' to communicative action. If this is so, and if the core tenets of Habermas's theory of communicative action are tenable, then it follows that a critical sociology allied to a reconstructed Enlightenment project is also committed to the pursuit of what Rehg (1994: 248) terms 'real institutional procedures' with potential to realize the justice and solidarity implicit in the ideal speech situation in practical discourse. This, in turn, necessitates working for the development of substantive democracy in the public sphere of the lifeworld.

And finally, *sociology's moral commitment to lifeworld rationalization is exclusive of any particular vision of the good life.* Sociology cannot anticipate any particular vision of the good life without betraying either a utopian or, worse, a totalitarian impetus. Rather, a critical sociology, possibly extended to subsume what Giddens (1990) calls models of 'utopian realism', would often be a pivotal or telling resource for participants in a discourse-ethical procedure.

CRITICAL SOCIOLOGY, CIVIL SOCIETY AND THE PUBLIC SPHERE

It has been noted that the public sphere of the lifeworld generates 'influence', a conception Habermas inherited from Parsons. Habermas regards the public sphere as a 'warning system' with 'sensors' that, though unspecialized, are sensitive throughout society. He writes:

> From the perspective of democratic theory, the public sphere must, in addition, amplify the pressure of problems, that is, not only detect and identify problems but also convincingly and *influentially* thematize them, furnish them with possible solutions, and dramatize them in such a way that they are taken up and dealt with by parliamentary complexes.
>
> (Habermas 1996: 359)

He adds that political influence supported by public opinion is only translated into political power – 'into a potential for rendering binding decisions' – when it affects the behaviour of voters, legislators, officials and so on.

The expressions 'public sphere' and 'civil society' are often used as synonyms, but Habermas (1996: 367) differentiates the two and gives the latter a more specific designation. Civil society, for him, consists of those 'more or less spontaneously emergent associations, organizations and movements that, attuned to how societal problems resonate in the private life spheres, distil and transmit such reactions in amplified form to the public sphere'. Its core comprises a network of associations that institutionalize 'problem-solving discourses on questions of general interest'. He continues: 'These "discursive designs" have an egalitarian, open form of organization that mirrors essential features of the kind of communication around which they crystallize and to which they lend continuity and permanence.' This network of associations is of course overshadowed in a public sphere of the lifeworld dominated by 'mass media and large agencies, observed by market opinion research, and inundated by the public relations work, propaganda, and advertising of political parties and groups' (Habermas 1996: 367).

It is apparent that civil society has a limited scope for action (see Cohen and Arato 1992). A robust civil society can only develop in a liberal political culture; its actors can acquire influence, but not political power; and the effectiveness of politics is in any event severely constrained in modern – functionally differentiated – societies. Certainly civil society is 'no macrosubject' able to 'bring society as a whole under control and simultaneously act for it' (Habermas 1996: 372). Nevertheless, Habermas contends, the social movements, citizen initiatives and forums, political and other group associations that make up civil society can 'under certain circumstances' acquire influence in the public sphere which extends to the political domain.

It will be helpful here to draw on three models of how new and pressing issues emerge and fare, advanced by Cobb and colleagues (Cobb *et al.* 1976). They distinguish between:

1 *the inside access model* – where the initiative is generated and pursued by office-holders or political leaders, while the broader public is either excluded altogether or able to exercise only scant influence;
2 *the mobilization model* – where the initiative is again taken within the political system, but where the support of a mobilized public sphere is required to effect change;
3 *the outside initiative model* – where it is a mobilized public sphere, or the pressure of public opinion, that promotes an issue to the point of salience and concern in the political system.

Of the outside initiative model, Cobb and associates (1976: 132) write:

> The outside initiative model applies to the situation in which a group outside the government structure 1) articulates a grievance, 2) tries to expand interest in the issue to enough other groups in the population to gain a place on the public agenda, in order to 3) create sufficient pressure on decision makers to force the issue onto the formal agenda for their serious consideration. This model of agenda building is likely to predominate in more egalitarian societies. Formal agenda status . . . however, does not necessarily mean that the final decisions of the authorities or the actual policy implementation will be what the grievance group originally sought.

Habermas (1996) argues that it is in fact on the 'civil social periphery' that many of the great issues of the recent past initially assumed significance. He lists, for example, the spiralling nuclear arms race; the risks involved in the peaceful use of atomic energy, in other large-scale technological projects and in scientific experimentation (e.g. genetic engineering); the ecological threats involved in an 'over-strained' natural environment, leading, for example, to acid rain, water pollution and species' extinction; the progressive impoverishment of the Third World and the problems of the world economic system; issues arising from feminism or enhanced migration and the associated problems of multiculturalism. Hardly any of these issues were raised *first*, he claims, by 'exponents of the state apparatus, large organizations, or functional systems'. Rather, they were broached by 'intellectuals, concerned citizens, radical professionals, self-proclaimed "advocates", and the like'. From this 'outermost periphery', they force their way into newspapers and universities. Subsequently:

> They find forums, citizen initiatives, and other platforms before they catalyze the growth of social movements and new subcultures. The latter can in turn dramatize contributions, presenting them so effectively that the mass media take up the matter. Only through their controversial presentation in the media do such topics reach the larger public and subsequently gain a place on the 'public agenda'.
> (Habermas 1996: 381).

Protracted campaigning and mass protests, even civil disobedience, may be required before an issue can progress 'via the surprising election of marginal candidates or radical parties, expanded platforms of "established" parties, important court decisions, and so on, into the core of the political system' (Habermas 1996: 381).

Returning to sociology's necessary, and moral, ties to lifeworld rationalization, it bears repetition that its historical system affiliations, cemented by commissioned research monies and 'McDonaldized' criteria for employment and promotion (Ritzer 1993), are currently such that many of its practitioners not only work under the aegis of the selective rationalization of economy or state, but also communicate almost exclusively to (other) system or 'established intellectuals' (Eyerman and Jamison 1991). The central theme of this chapter is that sociologists are rationally and morally obliged, in line with a reconstructed Enlightenment project, to reflexively pursue the decolonization and enhanced rationalization of the lifeworld *as their first priority*; and that this, in turn, requires their commitment to: substantive democratization, via the institutionalization of discourse-ethical procedures in civil society and the public sphere; and addressing and publicizing issues of concern in the lifeworld (analogous to, for example, the recent phenomenon of 'popular epidemiology' [see Brown 1992, 1995]). It is not enough merely to project research findings into a Popperian (1972) 'third world'. Meeting this obligation, with its attendant commitments, demands consideration of 'alliances of interest' with other system and, especially, 'movement intellectuals' and activists in the public sphere. Such alliances may be forged in the context of either the mobilization or, more likely, outside initiative models of Cobb and colleagues.

CRITICAL SOCIOLOGISTS AS INTELLECTUALS OR CRITICS

The potential for institutionalizing discourse-ethical procedures in civil society and the public sphere – the potential, that is, for creating what is often termed 'deliberative democracy' (see Fishkin 1991) – has been queried on a number of grounds. The impediments seem formidable indeed. Numerous commentators have highlighted, for example, the deep and conspicuous complexity and pluralism of modern societies.

More concretely, Bohman (1996: 110) identifies three basic types of 'deliberative inequalities': *power asymmetries*, which affect access to the public sphere; *communicative inequalities*, which affect the ability to participate and to make effective use of available opportunities to deliberate in the public sphere; and *political poverty*, which makes it unlikely that 'politically impoverished' citizens can participate in the public sphere at all. He argues that deliberation 'without corrections for inequalities' will always have elitist tendencies in practice, 'favouring those who have greater cultural resources (such as knowledge and information) and who are more capable of imposing their own interests and values on others in the public arena' (Bohman 1996: 111–12). After the manner of Habermas, and with no less caution, Bohman sees a role for social movements here. A social movement, he avers, can have a significant impact on deliberative inequalities:

First, it is a mechanism for pooling the resources, capacities and experiences of various persons and groups, and it gives coherent expression and unified voice to their shared problems and grievances. Second, solidarity within these informal networks permits pooling of resources and information and thus the creation of public goods within the movement as a way to compensate for resource inequalities and political poverty. The organization of the movement itself also gives it a voice, putting it in dialogue with other actors and institutions who recognize their grievances as public problems or expand the pool of their public reasons. Small acts of contestation can then be generalized into protests and become a public challenge to the existing distribution of deliberative resources in institutions. Once given powerful public expression, the movement's grievances can be publicly recognized as legitimate and made part of the public agenda of decision-making institutions.

(Bohman 1996:137)

Bohman also offers some reflections on the role of intellectuals or 'critics'. This is not the occasion to review the sociological literature on intellectuals. As Brym (1980) notes, they have conventionally been portrayed in modernity in one of three ways: as spokespersons for a particular class interest; after Mannheim, as 'free-floating' or detached from any particular class interest; or as constituting a class in their own right. More recently, Bauman (1987) has offered a distinctive – some would say postmodern – reading. Intellectuals, according to this view, have lost – or been liberated from – their legislative role; 'unwanted by the contemporary state', they have a chance to develop their discourses 'unhindered by power considerations of the type that formerly held them in thrall'. They can become interpreters. They can offer up their ideas to whoever will listen, 'so to speak, without strings' (Varcoe and Kilminster 1996: 231). It is 'notoriety' now which is the measure of public significance. Intellectuals, as interpreters, must:

compete with sportsmen, pop stars, lottery winners, as well as terrorists and serial killers. In this competition they have no great hope of winning; but to compete they must play the game of notoriety according to its rules – that is, adjust their own activity to the principle of 'maximal impact and instant obsolescence'. At bottom it is 'selling/rating potential' that counts.

(Bauman 1995: 239)

In terms of this chapter, the sociologist may be said to be critical insofar as his or her work is directed primarily towards the decolonization and further rationalization of the lifeworld, and an intellectual insofar as he or she is *an active agent in civil society and the public sphere*. These definitions suggest a post-legislative intellectual role, associated with a reconstructed Enlightenment project, which is nevertheless not (merely) interpretive. Interestingly, while there is much here that Bauman would doubtless baulk at, his recent reflections on the possible – if improbable – 'recomposition' of the 'intellectual configuration' (see Balandier, *Le Monde* 22 October 1993) incorporate a favourable reference to Jamison and Eyerman's (1994: 210) comments on the work of fifteen noteworthy 'thinkers' in the USA in the 1950s:

> These radical witnesses were . . . partisans of critical process, seeing their task, indeed, the main task of the intellectuals, not to formulate truths but to help others to share in the collective construction of truth. Their ambition was to catalyze dialogic understanding in the general public. . . . Theirs was a commitment to arguing in public, to opening up and keeping open spaces for what has been called critical discourse.

Bohman utilizes the Heideggerian terms 'disclosure' and 'world disclosure' to denote the opening up of novel possibilities of human freedom and transformative agency. 'Disclosure designates radical change in the ordinary interpretation of the world – just what is needed for innovation in public deliberation' (Bohman 1996: 213). Bohman defines disclosure primarily in terms of its impact on the audience, so it follows that numerous different forms of expression, and even such phenomena as visual images, new technologies, art, historical events and so on, may be disclosive. More specifically, he identifies four elements of disclosure. First, the disclosure opens up new possibilities of dialogue and recovers the openness and plasticity essential for learning and change. Second, the disclosure is not a disclosure of truth, but is rather prior to truth and concerns 'what makes truth possible'. Third, the disclosure is often 'indirect', as a result of conditions of social and cultural restrictions. And fourth, in disclosing a world relevant to public deliberation, the disclosure 'identifies the proper role of social critics:

criticisms point to new possibilities, but always relative to the limits of existing possibilities of meaning and expression' (Bohman 1996: 213). The role of the critic or intellectual, according to Bohman, is to point out new patterns of relevance. He elaborates:

> In disclosing new possibilities, critics are not simply announcing a new truth or a new form of justice; they are addressing an audience and expanding what it considers relevant to deliberation. The ultimate test comes in the reflection on these new possibilities in public deliberation: the practical question of how we should live. The disclosive capacity of a culture is therefore not only a precondition for truth but also, and perhaps more important, a precondition for freedom. As in the case of learning, disclosure indicates a necessary condition for the autonomy of an agent within a cultural context, that is, an open and 'dialogical' relation to the conditions of joint public activity. Such an open relation permits reflective agents to change these conditions, even if one piece at a time. All critics open up the fields of meaning and action of a culture by introducing new themes or facts; but radical critics, by doing so, do not merely interpret 'worlds' – they change them.
>
> (Bohman 1996: 228–9)

It is no part of the argument of this chapter that *all* sociologists should become active players or agents in the public sphere, that is, should double-up as intellectuals or critics in Bohman's sense. But Bohman's account does suggest that some of their number, in pursuit of prepotent objectives spelled out earlier, might effectively go beyond the forging of alliances of interest with other establishment or movement intellectuals or activists to precipitate disclosures themselves.

ILLUSTRATIONS FROM MEDICAL SOCIOLOGY

In illustration of the general argument outlined and extended here, reference has previously been made to medical sociology's system ties constraining work on both the health reforms embodied in the NHS and Community Care Act of 1990 and social-class-related health inequalities (see Scambler and Goraya 1994a, 1994b; Scambler 1996a). It was suggested that *disproportionate* attention has been devoted, respectively, to the 'fine print' of the 1990 Act, to the neglect of a transparently flawed package of changes; and to the contribution of behavioural risk factors to social-class-related health inequalities, to the neglect of material and structural factors. It was maintained that this pattern of enquiry and research is consonant with, or at least not effectively opposed to, the functional imperatives of economy and state. It was further contended that many sociologists have become either witting agents of 'manipulation' in the lifeworld or unwitting agents of 'systematically distorted communication'; in short, their work serves strategic action and lifeworld colonization rather than communicative action and lifeworld rationalization (Habermas 1984, 1987; Scambler 1987).

In this section some of these same arguments are rehearsed in a different area of investigation, namely, research into 'health-related quality of life' (Scambler 1996b). This brief discussion is subsequently used to highlight some pertinent general features of contemporary medical sociology.

Arguably, research on health-related quality of life has a long and strong pedigree in medical sociology. What is novel is the emphasis on quantification. The catalyst for much, although by no means all, of this newly quantitative research is interest in the outcomes of medical interventions, as is reflected in this extract from the statement on 'Aims and Scope' for the journal *Quality of Life Research*:

> Researchers in every clinical field are becoming increasingly aware of the importance of quality of life measurements in estimating the health effects of treatments. Until recently, objective biological outcomes, such as the prolongation of life, remained the basis for the evaluation of any new therapy. However, the emergence and widespread application of new sophisticated treatments has made obvious the fact that quality of life has become an essential and perhaps the only important parameter of interest to the patient.

'Outcomes research' has certainly yielded a sophisticated and interesting return and, in the process, enhanced sociological appreciation of the day-to-day impact of a range of diseases and treatments on people's lives. Its rationale seems clear and unobjectionable: it promises increasingly subtle, valid and reliable measures of general and disease-specific quality of life, incorporating 'the patient voice', and with the potential to inform, evaluate and even determine, aspects of medical management and service delivery.

It might reasonably be objected that outcomes research is not yet subtle enough to realize its full pragmatic potential; but the critique sketched here is different in kind. The basis of the critique is that the sociological return on outcomes research is fortuitous given that this programme of research is itself in large part the outcome of system

imperatives, part and parcel of a continuing process of system rationalization and lifeworld colonization. The rationale for outcomes research
might in this sense be described as a rhetorical 'gloss': this well-funded
research programme is in reality driven first and foremost by the system
requirement to legitimate the increasingly explicit rationing of health
care.

Perhaps this is most obvious in relation to aggregate measures like
Quality Adjusted Life Years (QALYs). Constructed in strict accordance
with the presuppositions and principles of health economics, QALYs
afford a mechanism for translating putative voices from the lifeworld
into notational forms appropriate for system needs. In effect, these
voices are transmuted into functional reifications of the patient voice.
This process of transmutation was explicated some years ago by Ashmore
and colleages (1989: 100–1), who are worth quoting at some length:

> We are never given direct access to the reasoning practices of
> patients or ordinary people in relation to the issues as they might
> define them. This is very clear in the case of people's judgements of
> quality of life and the indices of quality adjusted life years. This
> material is always presented in tabular or graphical form. Con-
> sequently, in this text, we are never concerned with any individual
> person's actual evaluations but with aggregate evaluations prepared
> by economists or by their colleagues. It is quite misleading, therefore,
> to suggest that QALYs can bring the preferences of the general public
> directly to bear upon health care policy.

They continue:

> It is the value produced by the expert and given meaning in terms of
> the expert's analytical assumptions which is to be used as the basis for
> policy and as a guide for practical action. In this case, it is the econo-
> mist alone who is allowed to speak on behalf of potential patients as a
> collectivity, even though no individual members of the collectivity
> may endorse the values proposed by the economist.

The charge might again be levelled that some medical sociologists
engaged in research on health-related quality of life are, at best, unreflex-
ive agents of systematically distorted communication.

This intentionally brief and focused account provides opportunities
for a number of more general observations linking with themes adum-
brated earlier. First, it should be acknowledged that health-related quality of life is an important topic for investigation in its own right, and that
quantitative approaches are probably under- rather than over-employed

in this context by contemporary British medical sociologists. Moreover, many medical sociologists involved in quantitative work in this area have sought to distance themselves from the perspectives and impetus of health economists.

But, second, it equally requires acknowledgement that, when it does occur, the use of techniques of quantification by medical sociologists or others directly to reify, or indirectly to assist in the reification of, the patient voice is questionable on a number of counts: the process of reification itself is intrinsically undesirable; such work necessarily entails the subsumption of a multiplicity of patient assessments in a single or 'typical' expert one; and it lends itself directly or indirectly to enhanced system rationalization and lifeworld colonization through its – generally non-coincidental – relevance to system or functional decision-making around health care rationing.

This is not to suggest, third, that health care rationing is new or avoidable; that old-style 'implicit' rationing ('rationing by muddling through' [Ham 1995]) is preferable to alternative and more 'explicit' forms of rationing; or that medical sociologists should play no part in deliberations on rationing. On the contrary, it is consistent with themes developed in this chapter to insist that medical sociologists should re-cognize a commitment to promote and contribute to the public use of reason around such issues (sometimes as social critics or intellectuals, authors or facilitators of what Bohman calls 'disclosures').

Fourth, survey solicitations of public opinion are inadequate substi-tutes or proxies for public deliberation. Consonant with the findings of the Oregon initiatives (Oregon Health Services Commission 1991), British surveys have tended to indicate a public propensity to accord high priority to such items as treatments for children with life-threatening illness and special care and pain relief for the terminally ill, and low priority to such items as infertility treatment and treatments for people aged 75 or more with life-threatening illness (Bowling 1996). But tapping, publicizing and noting public opinion or preferences in this fashion, although illuminating in its way, has little to do with deliberative democracy, which Bohman (1996: 27) defines as 'a dialogical process of exchanging reasons for the purpose of resolving situations that cannot be settled without interpersonal coordination and cooperation'.

Fifth, it bears reiteration that medical sociologists' capacity to con-tribute to the public use of reason around rationing as for other issues is contingent upon the institutionalization of discourse-ethical procedures in the public sphere, and that their commitment extends to substantive democratization itself. The potential for effective alliances of interest with other system/establishment or lifeworld/movement intellectuals and activists (or even for their own disclosures) may be considerable in relation to issues like the rationing of health care. As anticipated earlier, such alliances are perhaps most likely to arise in the context of the mobilization of outside initiative models of Cobb and associates.

CONCLUSION

This chapter extends an argument developed elsewhere for an adequately grounded reflexive and critical sociology allied to the project of modernity and oriented to the decolonization and rationalization of the lifeworld through active engagement in civil society and the public sphere (Scambler 1996a). Through reference to Habermas's discourse ethics, it has been suggested that this task represents a moral imperative, entailing a formal commitment to the pursuit of principles of justice and solidarity internally related to discourse-ethical procedures. It follows too that a critical sociology is committed to the removal of Bohman's triad of deliberative inequalities, namely, power asymmetries, communicative inequalities and political poverty; and that it cannot therefore remain neutral in the face of relevant stratified structures and practices associated with class, gender, ethnicity and age. This said, aside arguably from a purely formal commitment to the general good of autonomous cooperation, sociology, while pertinent in various ways to substantive considerations of goods and values, remains independent of any particular vision of the good life. The argument remains programmatic and requires formal and substantive elaboration in the light of ongoing debate (see, for example, White 1995; Rasmussen 1996).

It is appropriate to close with a disclaimer. While it *has* been maintained that sociology has become muted and distracted by its system ties, it has *not* been argued here that all system-driven sociology, including some outcomes research within medical sociology, is intrinsically undesirable, nor that what might be defined here as pre- or non-critical sociology is of no value. Moreover, an extraordinary and sociologically naive optimism would be required to anticipate imminent and effective action towards a reconstituted public sphere characterized by what Rehg (1994: 248) calls a 'concrete rational solidarity'.

The chapter concludes with an apposite quotation from colleagues who also draw on a Habermasian perspective, in their case to analyse barriers to social movements in health:

If the expertise of both professional and lay experts is to be tapped,

the validity of their different forms of knowledge has to be recognized *and then carried into the public sphere for debate.*
(Williams *et al.* 1995: 129; emphasis added)

REFERENCES

Ashmore, M., Mulkay, M. and Pinch, T. (1989) *Health and Efficiency: A Sociology of Health Economics*, Milton Keynes: Open University Press.

Bauman, Z. (1987) *Legislators and Interpreters: On Modernity, Postmodernity and Intellectuals*, Cambridge: Polity Press.

—— (1995) *Life in Fragments: Essays in Postmodern Morality*, Oxford: Blackwell.

Bohman, J. (1996) *Public Deliberation: Pluralism, Complexity and Democracy*, Cambridge, MA: MIT Press.

Bowling, A. (1996) 'Health care rationing: the public's debate', *British Medical Journal* 312: 670–4.

Brown, P. (1992) 'Popular epidemiology and toxic waste contamination: lay and professional ways of knowing', *Journal of Health and Social Behavior* 33: 267–81.

—— (1995) 'Popular epidemiology, toxic waste and social movements', in J. Gabe (ed.) *Medicine, Health and Risk*, Oxford: Blackwell.

Brym, R. (1980) *Intellectuals and Politics*, London: Allen & Unwin.

Cobb, R., Ross, J. and Ross, M. (1976) 'Agenda building as a comparative political process', *American Political Science Review* 70: 126–38.

Cohen, J. and Arato, A. (1992) *Civil Society and Political Theory*, Cambridge, MA; MIT Press.

Crook, S., Pakulski, J. and Waters, M. (1992) *Postmodernization: Change in Advanced Society*, London: Sage.

Eyerman, R. and Jamison, A. (1991) *Social Movements: A Cognitive Approach*, Cambridge: Polity Press.

Fishkin, J. (1991) *Democracy and Deliberation: New Directions in Democratic Reform*, New Haven: Yale University Press.

Giddens, A. (1990) *The Consequences of Modernity*, Cambridge: Polity Press.

Habermas, J. (1973) *Legitimation Crisis*, London: Heinemann.

—— (1984) *Theory of Communicative Action, Vol. 1. Reason and the Rationalization of Society*, London: Heinemann.

—— (1987) *Theory of Communicative Action, Vol. 2. Lifeworld and System: A Critique of Functionalist Reason*, Cambridge: Polity Press.

—— (1989) *The Structural Transformation of the Public Sphere: An Inquiry into a Category of Bourgeois Society*, Cambridge: Polity Press.

—— (1990) *Moral Consciousness and Communicative Action*, Cambridge, MA: MIT Press.

—— (1993) *Justification and Application: Remarks on Discourse Ethics*, Cambridge: Polity Press.

—— (1996) *Between Facts and Norms: Contributions to a Discourse Theory of Law and Democracy*, Cambridge: Polity Press.

Ham, C. (1995) 'Health care rationing', *British Medical Journal* 310: 1,483–4.

Hearn, F. (1985) *Reason and Freedom in Sociological Thought*, London: Allen & Unwin.

Jamison, A. and Eyerman, R. (1994) *Seeds of the Sixties*, Berkeley: University of California Press.

Kuhn, T. (1970) *The Structure of Scientific Revolutions*, 2nd edn, Chicago, IL: University of Chicago Press.

McCarthy, T. (1978) *The Critical Theory of Jürgen Habermas*, Cambridge: Polity Press.

Oregon Health Services Commission (1991) *Health Care in Common*, Salem, OR: Oregon Health Decisions.

Outhwaite, W. (1994) *Habermas: A Critical Introduction*, Cambridge: Polity Press.

Outhwaite, W. (ed.) (1996) *The Habermas Reader*, Cambridge: Polity Press.

Popper, K. (1972) *Objective Knowledge: An Evolutionary Approach*, Oxford: Clarendon Press.

Rasmussen, D. (ed.) (1996) *The Handbook of Critical Theory*, Oxford: Blackwell.

Ray, L. (1993) *Rethinking Critical Theory: Emancipation in the Age of Global Movements*, London: Sage.

Rehg, W. (1994) *Insight and Solidarity: The Discourse Ethics of Jürgen Habermas*, Berkeley: University of California Press.

Rex, J. (1974) *Sociology and the Demystification of the Modern World*, London: Routledge & Kegan Paul.

Ritzer, G. (1993) *The McDonaldization of Society: An Investigation into the Changing Character of Contemporary Social Life*, Thousand Oaks, CA: Pine Forge Press.

Roderick, R. (1986) *Habermas and the Foundations of Critical Theory*, London: Macmillan.

Scambler, G. (1987) 'Habermas and the power of medical expertise', in G. Scambler (ed.) *Sociological Theory and Medical Sociology*, London: Tavistock.

—— (1996a) 'The "project of modernity" and the parameters for a critical sociology: an argument with illustrations from medical sociology', *Sociology* 30: 567–81.

—— (1996b) 'Why do medical sociology? An excursus on Habermas's discourse ethics and lifeworld rationalization', *Medical Sociology Working Paper 1*, London: Unit of Medical Sociology, UCL.

Scambler, G. and Goraya, A. (1994a) 'The people's health: Habermas, the public sphere and the role of social movements', *British Medical Anthropology Review* 2: 35–43.

Scambler, G. and Goraya, A. (1994b) 'Movements for change: the new public health agenda', *Critical Public Health* 5: 4–10.

Thompson, J. (1983) 'Rationality and social rationalization: an assesment of Habermas's theory of communicative action', *Sociology* 17: 278–94.

Varcoe, I. and Kilminster, R. (1996) 'Addendum: culture and power in the writings of Zygmunt Bauman', in R. Kilminster and I. Varcoe (eds) *Culture, Modernity and Revolution: Essays in Honour of Zygmunt Bauman*, London: Routledge.

White, S. (ed.) (1995) *The Cambridge Companion to Habermas*, Cambridge: Cambridge University Press.

Williams, G., Popay, J. and Bissell, P. (1995) 'Public health risks in the material world: barriers to social movements in health', in J. Gabe (ed.) *Medicine, Health and Risk*, Oxford: Blackwell.

Chapter 4

Issues at the interface of medical sociology and public health

Richard Levinson

Four decades ago, Robert Straus (1957) warned that sociologists 'in' medicine were behaving like chameleons, in danger of losing their identifying colours by overadaptation to medical environments. Whereas sociologists 'of' medicine made medicine the subject of social enquiry, examining its norms, power, professional dynamics and structure, sociologists 'in' medicine appeared to be in service to the medical profession, carrying out research within a framework of medical values and assumptions that were accepted uncritically. For example, sociologists investigated ways of making patients more compliant with physician orders rather than examining how those patients came to be viewed as 'problems' or developed knowledge designed to prevent behaviours defined as 'pathological' by medicine (e.g. extra-marital pregnancies or alcohol consumption) rather than asking how the profession of medicine became an institution for the social control of deviance.

Twenty years after Straus's cautionary note, Gold (1977) demonstrated, through an examination of medical sociology publications, that sociologists largely adopted a medical value system in their work. Gold argued that a 'medical bias' should be a matter of some concern not only because the implicit and uncritical acceptance of medicine's social definitions affects sociology's integrity as an independent academic enterprise, but because it shapes social policy as well (Gold 1977: 165).

There is also a sociology 'in' and 'of' public health and the same concerns are relevant. A sociology 'of' public health helps define the field, how its functions are related to the political economy and the social definition of public health problems. It provides a lens for viewing the public health profession and largely explains the orientation of sociologists 'in' public health practice. Sociologists at the 'interface' of public health, examining social aetiology, have linked the health of populations to social structure. Given the nature of public health, as seen through a sociology 'of', sociologists 'in' public health practice are reluctant to address the structural causes described by those at the 'interface', decontextualizing them and re-attributing aetiology to individual behaviours.

SOCIOLOGY 'OF' PUBLIC HEALTH

A Committee for the Study of the Future of Public Health, assembled by the Institute of Medicine of the National Academy of Sciences, reported that the central mission of public health is to assure the existence of conditions in which people can be healthy by organizing community efforts aimed at preventing disease and promoting health (Institute of Medicine 1988: 41). Public health agencies, often components of government, carry out those functions alone or with the collaboration of private (for-profit and not-for-profit) organizations.

The specific functions of public health agencies are said to include the assessment and identification of health problems through surveillance of the population's health and by research on disease causation. Public health is expected to mobilize effort and resources to address health problems through policies and programmes, including prevention and health promotion interventions. Finally, it assures that the services required for the promotion or preservation of health are received and when they are not, either facilitates access to them or directly offers the services (Institute of Medicine 1988: 43).

Public health activities are not carried out in a social vacuum, however. They are subject to the same pressures from powerful interests reflecting the political economy as are other government or state-sponsored programmes. Well-established interests that are generally content with the status quo contribute to the shaping of both the definition of public health problems and the policies and programmes in response to them.

For example, in the United States, where the practice of medicine is largely private, organized medicine condemned as 'municipal socialism' the efforts by public health departments during the 1920s to deliver free health care and medicine to indigent urban populations (Starr 1982: 186). Public health agencies accommodated private medicine's demands by concentrating on screening populations for health conditions and referring detected problems to private practitioners (Starr 1982: 181–6). In general, health services ascribed to public health in capitalist societies are those for which there is no, or a limited, private marketplace.

Not only in the delivery of services does public health acquiesce to powerful established private interests, but it defines problems so as not to threaten established institutional arrangements. Sociologists at the 'interface' of public health have identified social conditions that are at the root of a population's health status. They are not new discoveries, nor are the insights unique to sociology. In 1848, Rudolf Virchow, a pathologist who developed the field of cellular biology, commented on the association between a typhus epidemic in Upper Silesia and existing social conditions (Taylor and Rieger 1985). His proposed remedy for the epidemic included political reforms to address social inequity and powerlessness, unemployment, poverty and lack of education (Waitzkin 1981).

The role of social conditions in health was reinforced more recently by McKeown (1979) who found that most of the decline in mortality over the eighteenth and nineteenth centuries in England and Wales resulted from improvements in hygiene and nutrition that made populations less vulnerable to infection rather than from medical measures. As Levin (1987) suggests, a small increase in the population's education or economic level will have a greater impact on health than all health resources combined. Nevertheless, public health has continued to concentrate on changing individual behaviours and exposures to pathology rather than targeting the conditions influencing those behaviours and exposures.

'Germ theory' guided the development of both medicine and public health in the twentieth century as interventions targeted the micro-organisms producing disease with newly discovered 'magic bullets' of immunization and antibiotics. With a focus on 'germs', the socio-economic context of exposure to the micro-organisms was often lost (Tesh 1988: 34–40). Public health moved from an emphasis on environmental sanitation, aligned with engineering, to the prevention of diseases in individuals, associated with medicine. Although many recognized that major public health problems, such as tuberculosis and venereal diseases, were associated with malnutrition, poor housing conditions, hazardous work sites and urban squalor, public health moved further away from its advocacy of social reform to narrow its focus in more politically acceptable directions, emphasizing personal hygiene, prevention and medical examinations with subsequent treatment (Starr 1982: 192).

The orientation of epidemiology, the 'Mother Science' of public health (Terris 1985), also helped narrow the focus. Epidemiology, as the 'scientific core' or 'glue' holding public health together (Institute of

Medicine 1988: 41), rarely considers broader social questions or community involvement with disease (Shy 1997). Epidemiology has tended to focus on immediate causes of illness or risk factors, such as establishing a link between smoking and lung cancer rather than helping to understand how and why cigarette smoking in the West grew so much over the century, just as it is now increasing in developing nations (Brandt 1997). Epidemiology finds determinants in individuals rather than in populations (Rose 1985) and is rarely used to understand disease as a result of the way society, or its socio-economic forces, is organized. Shy (1997) charges epidemiology with the 'bio-medical fallacy' of inferring that risk factors for disease in individuals can be added together to understand the causes of disease in populations.

A sociology 'of' public health helps to explain why the narrow focus is preferred in public health practice and why the field has tended to overlook the health consequences of social, political and economic structures and policies. To the extent that public health serves to preserve the existing social institutions and their power arrangements, its function might best be understood as one of social control. Public health is among the various social welfare programmes that enable the current social order to continue while minimizing public opposition (Piven and Cloward, 1971).

Medical sociologists and their social science colleagues at the 'interface' of public health, typically in academic settings, have generated considerable knowledge about how the social structure serves as the root cause of much disease and disability. Social and behavioural scientists 'in' public health practice, however, often redefine the causes of disease and disability, attributing them to individual behaviours or isolated environmental exposures as more politically acceptable explanations. Consequently, their health promotion interventions are principally designed to target individual risk behaviours. The following is a review of some contributions by medical sociologists at the 'interface', findings that are often transformed by their colleagues 'in' public health practice.

SOCIOLOGY AT THE 'INTERFACE' OF PUBLIC HEALTH: THE QUEST FOR SOCIAL AETIOLOGY

Social scientists have documented presumably causal associations between social conditions and the health of populations. The search for social aetiology has identified causes that could be, but typically are not,

:ts of public health intervention. As Turshen notes: 'health and ιre the products of the way society is organized, of the way ιce is produced as well as surplus and the way subsistence and surplus are distributed among the members of society' (1989: 24). Three interrelated causes are socioeconomic status or social class, the relative distribution of wealth and socially constructed gender roles.

Social class and health

The inverse association between morbidity and mortality and social class or socioeconomic status (SES), often indicated by income, educational attainment and occupational prestige, is well established (Syme and Berkman 1976; Dutton 1986; Pappas *et al.* 1993; Anderson and Armstead 1995). Davey *et al.* (1992), for example, examined the height of obelisks in the Victorian burial grounds of Glasgow, Scotland, for individuals who had died between 1800 and 1920. Age at death was significantly older for individuals with taller grave markers, whose families were presumably wealthier. Lower SES is associated with lower life expectancy, higher overall mortality rates, higher rates of infant or pre-natal mortality (Pappas *et al.* 1993; Adler *et al.* 1994), greater prevalence of mental disorders (Kessler *et al.* 1994) and higher rates of mortality for each of the fourteen major causes of death contained in the International Classification of Diseases (Illsley and Mullen, 1985). Even within the British Civil Service, Marmot *et al.* (1984) noted that as the rank increased, the risk of death from cardiovascular disease diminished.

The inverse association between social class and mortality or morbidity is not fully explained by a greater prevalence of risk behaviours or poorer access to health services among lower SES populations. (Haan *et al.* 1989). Nor is it explained by social selection, whereby poor health results in a failure to achieve upward social mobility or results in a downward 'drift' in affluence (Pappas *et al.* 1993). Something about the conditions of life associated with low income, lower educational attainment and/or occupational prestige appears to play a causal role.

Among the conditions damaging the health of lower SES populations are the pathological effects of unemployment. Brenner's (1976) research in several countries finds rising rates of psychiatric institutionalization and mortality from various diseases associated with cycles of unemployment. Individual-level research indicates that involuntary loss of employment such as during an economic recession results in diminished health status including increased prevalence of somatization, depression and anxiety (Kessler *et al.* 1987).

Not only is the lack of employment problematic for health, so are the work conditions of the employed. Low-income work is often characterized by higher levels of 'job strain', high demands with low decision latitude or personal control. Such occupational conditions are associated with an increased risk of coronary heart disease (Karasek *et al.* 1988) and elevated rates of hypertension (Schnall *et al.* 1992). Of course, unintentional injuries and hazardous exposures are more prevalent in low-paying manufacturing or extractive industries (Freund and McGuire 1995: 65–9).

So pervasive is the association between SES and health that Link and Phelan (1995: 85–6) consider SES or social class to be a 'Fundamental Cause'. SES is associated with the incidence of health risk behaviours, social conditions and exposure to environmental hazards that increase the risk of death, disease and disability such that it must be understood as a primary risk factor, however distal it may be to the actual illness event (Link and Phelan 1995).

Distribution of wealth

Roemer (1985: 41–52) found the distribution of wealth, as measured by the Gini coefficient, and general levels of affluence, as measured by per capita Gross Domestic Product, to be strong independent predictors of a nation's health status. More recently, Wilkinson (1992) reported that the association between national mortality rates and the average standard of living is weaker in technologically developed countries than in less developed and less affluent nations. There is a stronger relationship, however, between the distribution of income and life expectancy in the developed industrialized nations such as those in the Organization for Economic Cooperation and Development (OECD). Among the OECD nations, countries with the smallest income differentials between rich and poor reported the highest life expectancy at birth. If the USA or Britain had income distributions that were as equitable as Japan, Sweden or Norway, they could add two years in average life expectancy (Wilkinson 1992: 1083).

The parallels between income distributions and health have been followed over time. In 1970, the income distributions of Britain and Japan were comparable and at the centre of the OECD range. Since that time, Japan's income distribution narrowed dramatically whereas Britain's widened. Correspondingly, Japan's life expectancy at birth moved far ahead of Britain's and mortality differentials between social classes narrowed in Japan while they widened in Britain (Wilkinson, 1992: 1083). Similarly, the Gini coefficient increased in the USA over the past thirty years, reflecting greater inequalities in income distribution, just as the gap in age-adjusted mortality between rich and poor has grown (Pappas *et al.* 1993).

The health status of a population is also affected by the country's position in the world economic system. Wimberley (1990), in a study of sixty-three underdeveloped countries, found that greater multinational corporate penetration, associated with increased income inequality, resulted in increased rates of infant mortality over time. Among the reasons why multinational corporate investment may distort development in the Third World, and thus undermine the health of populations, is that it tends to displace domestic firms, obstructs progressive domestic political processes contrary to core economic interests and sometimes results in the diversion of land from food production for domestic use while displacing poor farmers (Wimberley 1990: 76).

The interrelationship between the world economy, local labour markets and the health of populations may also be reflected in AIDS and its transmission in central and southern Africa (Hunt, 1989). The pattern of industrialization during and since colonization was based largely on a migrant labour system for males working in mines, railroads, primary production and on plantations. This led to prolonged family separations and, with the depletion of males in rural areas, some deterioration in rural agriculture and subsequent migration of unmarried women to urban areas. With limited employment opportunities for women in urban settings, many were attracted to prostitution. The migration to urban slums escalated with large-scale takeovers of fertile land to produce foods for export and a push toward mechanization and monoculture (Loewenson 1988).

An urban labour force of men long separated from families and numbers of single women available as prostitutes, contributed to an explosion of sexually transmitted diseases in the years before AIDS was recognized. As men periodically returned to families that remained in rural villages, they brought with them the diseases so prevalent in urban environments such as tuberculosis and STDs (Doyal 1981). The labour patterns, reflecting in part the position of those nations in a world economic system, provided the social conditions for the rapid transmission of HIV virus and AIDS epidemic. Thus, the socioeconomic conditions of populations within and between nations, with their related economic inequities, are reflected in health status.

Gender roles

Surveys indicate that women have higher morbidity and health services use than men while age-adjusted mortality rates are higher for men than women (Verbrugge 1989). Women's higher rates of morbidity include less serious, self-limiting acute illnesses whereas the prevalence of life-threatening chronic diseases such as ischemic heart disease and atherosclerosis are greater among men. According to Verbrugge (1989), social conditions and gender role cultural norms account for much of the difference in morbidity and mortality.

Higher morbidity rates for women have been associated with cultural norms of 'nurturant role demands' (Gove and Hughes 1979; Gove 1984). Expectations that women should be the principal caregivers for their children, spouses and elderly parents, that they are responsible for maintaining the household and should provide for the social and medical health of family members, regardless of employment status, can create chronic stress and strain. It also makes it difficult for women to care for their own physical, social and psychological needs (Gove and Hughes 1979; Gove 1984). Bird and Fremont (1991) found that time spent in some gender-typed roles, including housework and work at lower wages, accounted for most of the differences in morbidity rates between men and women. That is, when men and women had comparable experiences, morbidity rates were comparable, and even a bit higher, in men (Bird and Fremont 1991).

Patterns of age-specific mortality in men may also reflect social and cultural conditions. Durkheim (1951) noted the importance of social integration, particularly through family involvement as a parent or spouse. Using data from the US National Center for Health Statistics, Gove (1973) reported that married persons exhibited lower mortality rates for virtually all causes of death in which psychological conditions or behaviours played a substantial role. Thus, marriage was associated with lower mortality from homicide and suicide, cirrhosis of the liver, cancer of the respiratory system and conditions that benefit from careful attention such as hypertension and tuberculosis. The advantage associated with marriage was greater for men than women.

According to Umberson's (1987) findings, the health advantages of marriage and parental status are linked to the reduced incidence of behaviours placing people at risk for morbidity and mortality. The internalization of norms for more conventional behaviour and external sanctions associated with marriage and parenthood presumably account for a more orderly lifestyle and fewer health risk behaviours, e.g. substance abuse, drinking and driving, etc. (Umberson 1987). Since risk behaviours are more prevalent in this culture among men, and because men appear to benefit more from the culturally patterned nurturing roles of a spouse (wife), the protection of marriage for health is greater among men.

Structure and social aetiology

Medical sociologists at the interface of public health and sociology have examined social aetiology and documented that the patterns of disease are caused, to a considerable extent, by structure and culture. Although poverty, relative deprivation, the organization of labour, or gender roles appear to be distal causes of disease and disability, they should be considered in the promotion of health (Link and Phelan 1995). For public health practitioners to have a significant impact on the health of populations, they must at some point address the social origins of morbidity and mortality.

SOCIOLOGY 'IN' PUBLIC HEALTH

Examining the activity of sociologists and behavioural scientists 'in' public health, we witness a redefinition of social aetiology. Fundamental social causes tend to be overlooked, as poor health status is viewed as the consequence of individual behavioural choices or unhealthy life styles.

Medical sociologists, as they practise public health through the design and evaluation of community health promotion programmes, generally target individual risk behaviours for change, thus decontextualizing health status. Public health practitioners rarely address the reasons for the exposure or vulnerability to exposures because that requires addressing the fundamental causes and would therefore threaten established economic and political interests (Tesh 1988).

Some public health practitioners go further with assumptions that personal health behaviours are discrete and independently modifiable, that anyone can decide to change, that all have the capacity to act on their decisions to alter behaviours and that people have a personal responsibility to live well. Becker (1993) notes that this ideology contradicts what we empirically know about the major determinants of health and prevention and essentially 'blames the victim'. Health habits are acquired from social situations and supported by powerful cultural and structural forces. Intervention on an individual level is generally ineffective without concomitant attempts to alter the broader political, economic and structural components of society that produce and support poor health (Becker 1993; Link and Phelan 1995).

Despite its shortcomings, a focus on 'lifestyle' fits well with the politics of public health. The Canadian Health Ministry's document *A New Perspective on the Health of Canadians* (Lalonde 1974) set the stage for the contemporary emphasis on getting people to make healthy choices. A short time later the US Surgeon General produced a document with a similar approach to public health entitled *Healthy People* (USDHEW 1979). Here the role of public health was to address individual risk behaviours such as dietary improvements, stopping smoking, stress reduction, reduced alcohol and drug consumption and increased physical activity. Not only could the population grow healthier, but health expenditures could be reduced.

Medicalization

The term 'medicalization' refers to a process by which illness becomes socially constructed (Conrad and Schneider 1992). Certain behaviours or conditions are given medical meanings and thus medical practice becomes the appropriate vehicle for their elimination or control. Deviant behaviours such as heavy consumption of alcohol, the use of certain illicit substances, gambling or domestic violence become defined as pathological and, as either disease or disease symptoms, are seen as the legitimate problems of medicine to understand and treat (Barsky 1988). In addition, conditions of life such as childbirth, menstruation and menopause have, over time, been defined as problematic health conditions appropriate for medical intervention (McCrea 1983; Reissman 1983; Scambler and Scambler 1993; Figert 1996).

A similar process occurs in the social construction of problems appropriate for public health. In this case, behaviours or conditions that stem from cultural or structural origins are redefined as weaknesses or diseases of individuals and subject to intervention. Community violence growing out of deprivation, cultural values and the availability of weapons becomes reconfigured as a problem to be addressed by boosting individual self-esteem, or teaching conflict negotiation (Prothrow-Stith 1991). AIDS in central and southern Africa, linked to economic conditions and the labour market (Hunt 1989), is addressed by public health programmes to promote condom use and distribute information about viral transmission. Malnutrition in poor underdeveloped nations is understood as a problem to be remedied by food supplements or a Green Revolution rather than changing land ownership patterns and agribusiness production for export (George 1977; Tesh 1988: 64). Individuals are warned to avoid the risks of exposure to toxic waste when the racial and economic composition of a community are strong predictors of where commercial hazardous waste facilities are constructed (Monhai and Bryant 1992).

Design of community public health promotion interventions

Public health interventions designed to promote health and prevent disease generally reflect how problems are defined. Primarily, although not exclusively, they target individual risk behaviours. A model community health intervention, emulated around the world, began in 1972 in North Karelia, a rural area in eastern Finland. The project addressed the high rates of cardiovascular disease mortality through a better control of hypertension, reduction of smoking and diets designed to lower the intake of saturated fats (McAlister et al. 1982). A number of health promotion actions included improvements in secondary prevention services (screening for hypertension and follow-up treatment), dissemination of health information, persuasive messages to motivate dietary changes, and training to improve skills anticipated to result in behavioural changes that would reduce health risks. The project also included some attempts to alter the social environment of residents such as increasing the availability of low-fat food products and the prevention of smoking in certain public areas (McAlister et al. 1982).

After five years, there was little evidence of a reduction in cardiovascular mortality (Wagner 1982), although some improvements were detected ten years into the programme (Tuomilehto et al. 1986). There were significant reductions in the prevalence of hypertension, smoking and mean levels of cholesterol. It is unclear, however, whether the healthier patterns of behaviour can be sustained beyond the intervention programmes.

Subsequent large-scale community interventions in the USA reported a similar impact on health risk behaviours and some change in health outcomes (Blackburn et al. 1984; Lasater et al. 1984). For example, the Stanford 3-Community Study and Stanford 5-City Multi-Factor Risk Reduction Projects examined the effects of communication through the mass media combined with various community programmes on such factors as blood pressure, salt consumption, plasma cholesterol, fat content of diet, cigarette use and weight control (Flora et al. 1989; Farquhar et al. 1990). During and shortly after the interventions in the 3-Community Study, there was a modest impact on some risk behaviours, particularly when the communication was combined with programmes directly contacting individuals (Flora *et al.* 1989). In the 5-City Study, the results were comparable to the Karelia intervention (Farquhar *et al.* 1990). After 30–64 months of education, there were statistically significant net reductions in community averages favouring the experimental intervention in plasma cholesterol, blood pressure, resting pulse rate and smoking reduction (Farquhar *et al.* 1990). Although the authors claim that changes are 'potentially sustainable' and 'may diffuse as they are woven into the fabric of the community' (Farquhar *et al.* 1990: 363), the evidence for this is, as yet, unclear.

Becker (1993) observes that many of the gains from behavioural changes are exaggerated or overestimated. For example Taylor *et al.* (1987) estimate the additional time of life resulting from lifelong cholesterol dietary reduction for average individuals between the ages of 20–60 to be 3 days to 3 months. Kaplan's (1985) meta-analysis of five studies suggested that any potential reduction in mortality associated with heart disease because of diet was offset by increases in deaths from other causes and thus life expectancy remained unchanged. Some wonder whether the benefits of alarms targeting individual behaviours such as dietary health risks are greater than the 'epidemic of apprehension' they may be creating (Thomas 1983; Barsky 1988).

Without altering the social conditions, it is difficult to change behaviours, many of which are shaped by, or adaptive to, those conditions. Interventions focusing on behaviours alone often fail to sustain changes (Link and Phelan 1995). Addressing fundamental causes, however, requires considering changes in the social structure, not an inviting prospect to those in public health practice. Powerful institutions content with current political and economic arrangements will resist surveillance and change. Public health agencies have limited capacity and autonomy to target established political and economic forces. As political entities, they are subject to those forces. Perhaps as a consequence of this situation, public health practice has given relatively little thought and attention to the development of programmes and policies that address fundamental structural causes of disease and disability. Public health may claim that its attempts are ineffective because resources are lacking, but their impotence also stems from an incapacity to address the root causes.

SUMMARY

Medical sociologists and their colleagues in the social and behavioural sciences interact with public health in different roles. Investigations at the interface of sociology and public health identify how social aetiology involves the social structure, culture or life conditions. Through a sociological perspective, public health functions as an institution of social control, preserving the political–economic system by ameliorating some of its damage to the population's health. Thus medical sociologists within public health decontextualize health problems and redefine their aetiology, undoing sociology's principal contribution to the field. More proximal causes of morbidity such as individual lifestyles or health risk behaviours become the targets of community interventions.

If public health is understood to be part of a quest for 'social justice', its structure limits the achievement of those ends. Sociology 'of' and at the 'interface' of public health helps explain the limitations and why those 'in' public health generally overlook the social inequities that threaten the population's well-being.

REFERENCES

Adler, N.E., Boyce, T., Chesney, M.A. *et al.* (1994) 'Socioeconomic status and health: the challenge of the gradient', *American Psychologist* 49(1): 15–24.

Anderson, A.B. and Armstead, C.A. (1995) 'Toward understanding the association of socioeconomic status and health: a new challenge for the biopsychosocial approach', *Psychosomatic Medicine* 57(2): 213–25.

Barsky, A.J. (1988) 'The paradox of health', *New England Journal of Medicine* 318(7): 414–18.

Becker, M.H. (1993) 'A medical sociologist looks at health promotion', *Journal of Health and Social Behavior* 34(1): 1–6.

Bird, C.E. and Fremont, A.M. (1991) 'Gender, time use and health', *Journal of Health and Social Behavior* 32(2): 114–29.

Blackburn, H., Leupker, R.V., Kline, F.G. *et al.* (1984) 'The Minnesota Health Program: a research and demonstration project in cardiovascular disease prevention', in J.D. Matarazzo, S.M. Weiss, J.A. Herd, N.E. Miller and S.M. Weiss (eds) *Behavioral Health: A Handbook of Health Enhancement and Disease Prevention*, New York: John Wiley.

Brandt, A. (1997) 'The rise and fall of the cigarette', Harvey Young Lecture, Emory University (9 April).

Brenner, M.H. (1976) 'Estimating the social costs of economic policy: implications for mental and physical health and criminal aggression', Paper No. 5 Reported to the Congressional Research Service of the Library of Congress and Joint Economic Committee of Congress, Washington, DC: US Government Printing Office.

Conrad, P. and Schneider, J. (1992) *Deviance and Medicalization: From Badness to Sickness*, Philadelphia, PA: Temple University Press.

Davey, S.G., Carroll, D., Rankin, S. *et al.* (1992) 'Socioeconomic differentials in mortality: evidence from Glasgow graveyards', *British Medical Journal* 305(12): 1554–7.

Doyal, L. (1981) *The Political Economy of Health*, Boston: South End Press.

Durkheim, E. (1951) *Suicide: A Study in Sociology*, trans. A. Spaulding and G. Simpson, New York: The Free Press.

Dutton, D.B. (1986) 'Social class, health and illness', in L. Aiken and D. Mechanic (eds) *Applications of Social Science to Clinical Medicine and Health Policy*, New Brunswick, NJ: Rutgers University Press.

Farquhar, J.W., Fortmann, S.P., Flora, J.A. *et al.* (1990) 'Effects of a communitywide education on cardiovascular disease risk factors', *Journal of the American Medical Association* 264(3): 359–65.

Figert, A.E. (1996) *Women and the Ownership of PMS*, New York: Aldine de Gruyter.

Flora, J.A., Maccoby, N. and Farquhar, J.W. (1989) 'Communication campaigns to prevent cardiovascular disease: the Stanford community studies', in R. Rice and C. Atkin (eds) *Public Communication Campaigns*, Beverly Hills, CA: Sage.

Freund, P.E.S. and McGuire, M.B. (1995) *Health, Illness and the Social Body*, Englewood Cliffs, NJ: Prentice-Hall.

George, S. (1977) *How the Other Half Dies: The Real Reasons for World Hunger*, Montclair, NJ: Allanheld Osmun.

Gold, M. (1977) 'A crisis of identity: the case of medical sociology', *Journal of Health and Social Behavior* 18(2): 160–8.

Gove, W. (1973) 'Sex, marital status and mortality', *American Journal of Sociology* 79(1): 34–44.

—— (1984) 'Gender differences in mental and physical illness: the effects of fixed roles and nurturant roles', *Social Science and Medicine* 19(1) : 77–91.

Gove, W. and Hughes, M. (1979) 'Possible causes of the apparent sex differences in physical health: an empirical investigation', *American Sociological Review* 44(1): 126–46.

Haan, M.N., Kaplan, G.A. and Syme, S.L. (1989) 'Socioeconomic status and health: old observations and new thoughts', in J.P. Bunker, D.S. Gomby and B.H. Kehrer (eds) *Pathways to Health: The Role of Social Factors*, Menlo Park, CA: Kaiser Family Foundation.

Hunt, C.W. (1989) 'Migrant labor and sexually transmitted disease: AIDS in Africa', *Journal of Health and Social Behavior* 30(4): 353–73.

Illsley, R. and Mullen, K. (1985) 'The health needs of disadvantaged client groups', in W.W. Holland, R. Detels and G. Knox (eds) *Oxford Textbook of Public Health*, Oxford: Oxford University Press.

Institute of Medicine (1988) *The Future of Public Health*, Washington, DC: National Academy Press.

Kaplan, R.M. (1985) 'Behavioral epidemiology, health promotion and health services', *Medical Care* 23(5): 564–83.

Karasek, R., Theorell, T., Schwartz, J. *et al.* (1988) 'Job characteristics in relation to the prevalence of myocardial infarction in the US Health Examination Survey (HES) and the Health and Nutrition Examination Survey (NHANES)', *American Journal of Public Health* 78(8): 910–18.

Kessler, R., House, J.S. and Turner J.B. (1987) 'Unemployment and health in a community sample', *Journal of Health and Social Behavior* 28 (1): 51–9.

Kessler, R., McGonagle, K., Zhao, S. *et al.* (1994) 'Lifetime and twelve-month prevalence of DSM-III-R psychiatric disorders in the United States: results from the National Comorbidity Survey', *Archives of General Psychiatry* 51(1): 8–19.

Lalonde, M. (1974) *A New Perspective on the Health of Canadians*, Ottawa: Canadian Health Ministry.

Lasater, T., Abrams, D., Artz, L. *et al.* (1984) 'Lay volunteer delivery of a community-based cardiovascular risk factor change programme: The Pawtucket Experiment', in J.D. Matarazzo, S.M. Weiss, J.A. Herd, N.E. Miller, and S.M.Weiss (eds) *Behavioral Health: A Handbook of Health Enhancement and Disease Prevention*, New York: John Wiley.

Levin, L.S. (1987) 'Every silver lining has a cloud: The limits of health promotion', *Social Policy* 27(1): 57–60.

Link, B.G. and Phelan, J. (1995) 'Social conditions as fundamental causes of disease', *Journal of Health and Social Behavior*, extra issue: 80–94.

Loewenson, R. (1988) 'Labour insecurity and health: an epidemiological study in Zimbabwe', *Social Science and Medicine* 27(7): 733–41.

McAlister, A., Puska, P., Salonen, J.T. *et al.* (1982) 'Theory and action for health promotion: illustrations from the North Karelia Project', *American Journal of Public Health* 72(1): 43–50.

McCrea, F.B. (1983) 'The politics of menopause: the "discovery" of a deficiency disease', *Social Problems* 31(1): 111–22.

McKeown, T. (1979) *The Role of Medicine: Dream, Mirage or Nemesis*, Oxford: Blackwell.

Marmot, M., Shipley, M.J. and Rose, G. (1984) 'Inequalities in death-specific explanations of a general pattern?' *Lancet* I(11): 1003–6.

Monhai, P. and Bryant, B. (1992) *Race and the Incidence of Environmental Hazards: A Time for Discourse*, Boulder, CO: Westview Press.

Pappas, G., Queen, S., Hadden, W. *et al.* (1993) 'The increasing disparity in mortality between socioeconomic groups in the United States, 1960 and 1986', *New England Journal of Medicine* 329(2): 103–9.

Piven, F.F. and Cloward, R.A. (1971) *Regulating the Poor*, New York: Random House.

Prothrow-Stith, D. (1991) *Deadly Consequences*, New York: HarperCollins.

Reissman, C.K. (1983) 'Women and medicalization: a new perspective', *Social Policy* 14(1): 3–18.

Roemer, M.I. (1985) *National Strategies for Health Care Organization*, Ann Arbor, MI: Health Administration Press.

Rose, G. (1985) 'Sick individuals and sick populations', *International Journal of Epidemiology* 14(1): 32–8.

Scambler, A. and Scambler, G. (1993) *Menstrual Disorders*, London: Routledge.

Schnall, P., Schwartz, J., Landsbergis, P. *et al.* (1992) 'Relation between job strain, alcohol and ambulatory blood pressure', *Hypertension* 19(3): 488–94.

Shy, C.M. (1997) 'The failure of academic epidemiology: witness for the prosecution', *American Journal of Epidemiology* 146(6): 479–84.

Starr, P. (1982) *The Social Transformation of American Medicine*, New York: Basic Books.

Straus, R. (1957) 'Nature and status of medical sociology', *American Sociological Review* 22(2): 200–4.

Syme, L.S. and Berkman, L.F. (1976) 'Social class, susceptibility, and sickness', *American Journal of Epidemiology* 104(1): 1–8.

Taylor, R. and Rieger, A. (1985) 'Medicine as social science: Rudolf Virchow on the typhus epidemic in Upper Silesia', *International Journal of Health Services* 15(3): 547–59.

Taylor, W., Pass, T.M., Shepard, D.S. *et al.* (1987) 'Cholesterol reduction and life expectancy: a model incorporating multiple risk factors', *Annals of Internal Medicine* 106(4): 605–14.

Terris, M. (1985) 'The public health profession', *Journal of Public Health Policy* 6(1): 7–14.

Tesh, S.N. (1988) *Hidden Arguments: Political Ideology and Disease Prevention Policy*, New Brunswick, NJ: Rutgers University Press.

Thomas, L. (1983) 'An epidemic of apprehension', *Discover* 4(1): 78–80.

Tuomilehto, J., Geboers, J., Salonen, J.T. *et al.* (1986) 'Decline in cardiovascular mortality in North Karelia and other parts of Finland', *British Medical Journal* 293(9): 1068–71.

Turshen, M. (1989) *The Politics of Public Health*, New Brunswick, NJ: Rutgers University Press.

Umberson, D. (1987) 'Family status and health behaviors: social control as a dimension of social integration', *Journal of Health and Social Behavior* 28(3): 306–19.

United States Department of Health Education and Welfare (USDHEW) (1979) *Healthy People: The Surgeon General's Report on Health Promotion and Disease Prevention 1979*, Washington, DC: Public Health Service Publication no. 79–55071.

Verbrugge, L.M. (1989) 'The twain meet: empirical explanations of sex differences in health and mortality', *Journal of Health and Social Behavior* 30(3): 282–304.

Wagner, E.H. (1982) 'The North Karelia Project: what it tells us about the prevention of cardiovascular disease', *American Journal of Public Health* 72(1): 51–2.

Waitzkin, H. (1981) 'The social origins of illness: a neglected history', *International Journal of Health Services* 11(1): 77–103.

Wilkinson, R.G. (1992) 'National mortality rates: the impact of inequality?', *American Journal of Public Health* 82(8): 1082–84.

Wimberley, D.W. (1990) 'Investment dependence and alternative explanations of Third World mortality: a cross-national study', *American Sociological Review* 55(1): 75–91.

Chapter 5

Explaining health inequalities
How useful are concepts of social class?

Paul Higgs and Graham Scambler

That there is a link between social class and health is accepted by most medical sociologists, even if the nature of the link is disputed. The influential collation of data and 'ruling' in favour of such a link by Black and colleagues (Townsend and Davidson 1992) has subsequently been supported and given further substance by a continuing flow of large- and small-scale empirical studies. In fact, a decade after the *Black Report* was published, Davey Smith and associates (1990; Blane *et al.* 1990) were able to affirm that class-related health inequalities had in all probability increased rather than diminished in the interim, a conclusion in line with Black's own assessment (1993; see also Whitehead 1992).

In some ways paradigmatic of recent work in this area are the 'Whitehall studies' of Marmot and his team (see Marmot *et al.* 1991). Epidemiological rather than sociological in intent, design and mode of analysis, these studies have played a significant part in consolidating the view that class is important in the genesis and reproduction of health inequality; they have relied, however, on identifying particular circumstances and behaviours that are 'subsumed' by social class and which are thought to have special salience for health. These studies consequently demonstrate the weakness of not theorizing class. Wadsworth (1997), in a comprehensive survey of the literature, outlines a large number of factors and processes that could account for social inequalities in health; some of these relate to lifestyle and behavioural factors and some to the nature of the life events gone through by the successive generations studied. Problems of providing an explanatory account continually emerge leaving it difficult to see how any general synthesis can be reached.

Bartley and colleagues (1997) also point to the importance of understanding the effect of inequalities over the course of individuals' lives and in particular at 'socially critical periods' such as the transition to parenthood or job loss. By paying particular attention to these, policy-makers might be able to ameliorate some of the negative effects on health created by inequalities in income but even with this in mind they are left discussing the importance of the welfare state as a safety net for the poorest, rather than explicitly discussing how these critical periods are linked to class.

At the close of a report in 1986 on 'social inequalities in mortality', Marmot aptly remarked on the different implications of research find-ings for epidemiology, public health and sociology. Of sociology he wrote: 'No doubt for sociology, the need is to understand the general social structural causes of differences in health behaviour and mortality' (1986: 32). While this remark might be criticized for an undue emphasis on health behaviour, it was nevertheless a timely reminder that sociology had a *distinctive* contribution to make but has so far failed to deliver. In our view sociology's contribution before and since has been somewhat disappointing, for three strongly related reasons: first, sociologists have been too content to follow epidemiological agendas and initiatives; sec-ond, they have tended to deploy 'abstracted' (Wright Mills 1970) or 'systematic empiricist' (Willer and Willer 1973) methodologies, one effect of which has been to severely limit the sociological return on their research investment; and third, the concepts of class they have relied on have too often been crude and inadequately theorized. Sociologists' work in this area, we would suggest, has been insufficiently sociological.

Our object in this chapter is to proffer neither another review of cur-rent empiricist research on class and health inequalities, nor another critique of assorted neo-positivisms, both of which are plentiful, but rather to reflect on the ramifications of ongoing pivotal sociological debates about class in the mainstream of the discipline for the future consideration of health inequalities. One of our reasons for doing so is to restore the political nature of class to the debate about inequalities. This implicit political debate has already been commented upon by Klein (1991) and underlines the need to understand these questions as connected to wider concerns. Bury (1997) points out:

> There is little point, for example, in collecting detailed evidence about physical characteristics of individuals, say the colour of their eyes or hair, unless it has some relevance to life chances, including health. Evidence about the attributes of people only matters to epi-demiologists and sociologists at least, if they have *social* significance. It is, in the present context, the outcome of influences of *social position* on *health status* that matters, and invoking the term

'inequalities' frequently rests on the assumption that modern societies are characterised by *social hierarchies* . . . which structure and to some extent determine people's lives.

(Bury 1997: 48–9)

In the opening section we focus on arguments that researchers of health inequalities have been overly dependent on under-theorized or outmoded notions or measures of class; this charge is premised on a lack of sophistication. In the second section we look at the increasingly popular contention that, however conceptualized or measured, class no longer has the explanatory power it had during the heyday of industrial capitalism; this charge is sometimes premised on a putative transition to post-industrial capitalism or, more radically, to a new era of post-modernity. In the third section we offer some general comments on the continuing significance of class. And finally, arising from these comments, we suggest some possible lines of investigation for the future.

A LACK OF SOPHISTICATION?

The charge of insufficient sophistication typically takes one of two forms. These are conveniently encapsulated in the distinction between 'class theory' and 'class analysis'.

Class theory

According to Pakulski and Waters (1996: 10), 'class theory', of which neo-Marxist versions are the most prominent, embraces the four propositions of 'economism' (i.e. class is a fundamentally economic phenomenon); 'groupness' (i.e. classes are real features of social structure rather than mere statistical aggregates or taxonomic categories); 'behavioural and cultural linkage' (i.e. class is causally linked to consciousness and identity); and 'transformational capacity' (i.e. classes are potential actors in economic and political arenas). Similar criteria were raised by Mann (1974) over two decades previously in his attempt to delineate the problems of totalizing class in a combined ontological and political way.

From the perspective of class theory, thus defined, ranging from Marx and Engels through Lukács and Poulantzas to contempories like Wright (see, for example, Wright's [1985] 'principal assets model'), most studies of class-related health inequalities to date appear empiricist and superficial. There has, for example, been little attempt to theorize class, or even to take it seriously as a phenomenon in its own right. Rather, medical sociologists, first, have been content to regard crude measures of occupational status like the Registrar General's as an expedient proxy for social class (for criticisms see Jones and Cameron 1984; Nichols 1996; and Macintyre 1997); and, second, have aped the reductionism of epidemiologists by trying to 'explain class away' by means of empiricist manoeuvres featuring 'class-constitutive' or 'class-associated' factors like educational attainment, marital and employment status, family size, household income, quality of housing and patterns of lifestyle and behaviour.

For the class theorist, empiricist research is intrinsically flawed and a poor substitute for sociological engagement. It is not of course atheoretical, since all observations about the natural and social worlds presuppose commitment to a cluster of theories. Rather, this theoretical commitment is implicit and unaddressed. To a neo-Marxist it is demonstrably a commitment to a distorted view of the social world. Wright (1985) offers an influential example of a rival explicit and more sophisticated theory of class. Drawing on Roemer's theory of exploitation, he extends the concept of class to a range of 'principal assets' that operate in parallel with the means of production. Two types of assets have special significance for contemporary capitalism. The use of the term 'organizational assets' arises from the idea that it is possible to control productive resources without owning them. 'Credentialized skills' also permit exploitation by rendering some forms of labour scarce and allowing workers to expropriate surplus through monopolistic control.

Wright's principal assets model cross-classifies property ownership with organizational assets and credentialized skills. The fundamental division is still that between owners and non-owners of the means of production, but owners are internally differentiated according to the extent to which they exploit others' labour (large employers, small employers and the petty bourgeoisie), and non-owners on the basis of organizational assets and credentialized skills (yielding nine classes of non-owner, eight of which are non-proletarian 'intermediate' classes). One consequence of Wright's scheme of twelve class locations is that the 'bourgeoisie' and 'proletariat' account for fewer than half the members of the labour force of any advanced capitalist society (Pakulski and Waters 1996).

Gubbay (1997), taking a more orthodox Marxist position, criticizes Wright for overloading his schema with additional classes by making the notion of exploitation 'weakly relational' insofar as he minimizes the importance of direct economic exploitation through the creation of surplus value. Gubbay argues that, over the course of his work, Wright has failed to utilize an adequate theory of exploitation. This has made it difficult for him to relate his analysis to capitalist dynamics and has led him to move from notions of domination to neo-Weberian ideas of market relationship. As an alternative Gubbay posits a more conflict-based approach:

> The research programme of Marxist class analysis consists of exploration of how surplus value is created and pumped around the system by interacting classes and fractions of classes, and investigation of the conditions which foster or hinder these processes, associated tensions which the system itself generates and the consequences thereof for conflict and cooperation between and within classes.
>
> (Gubbay 1997: 84)

Class analysis

If the propositions of class theory indicate a 'hard' concept of social class, 'class analysis' may be said to be characterized by a 'soft' concept. Class analysis, often defined as neo-Weberian and perhaps best epitomized by the 'Nuffield programme' (Crompton 1996a), accepts multidimensional bases for stratification. If it privileges class, it also grants 'autonomous causal capacity' to gender, ethnicity, religion, political arrangements and even to individual preferences. 'It simply seeks to establish the impact of class on these and other arenas' (Pakulski and Waters 1996: 15).

Insofar as he focuses on markets and life chances, Weber might be judged to have offered a stratification rather than a production theory of class. To many, Goldthorpe's class scheme reflects this Weberian equation of 'market situation' with 'class situation' (Goldthorpe, 1987; Erikson and Goldthorpe 1992). Noting the predominance of corporate rather than individual employers, he contends that, small employers apart, all are now employees. Employees are divided according to the extent to which they exercise delegated authority or special knowledge and expertise. Additional allowance is made for skill levels and for location in industry or agriculture. The result is a scheme of eleven classes, allowing for reductions to seven-, five- and three-class versions.

Crompton (1996b), who identifies the employment-based class schemes of Wright and Goldthorpe as the two most influential programmes of recent years, emphasizes that while Wright's scheme is explicitly grounded in Marxist theory, Goldthorpe's is only loosely based on a neo-Weberian rationale. Indeed, Goldthorpe has taken pains to deny that the construction of his scheme has any theoretical antecedents (Goldthorpe and Marshall 1992). Be this as it may, and independently of the question of its 'gender-blindness' (Stanworth 1984), it remains clear that the scheme developed and used by him offers a degree of sophistication conspicuously absent from the Registrar General's mechanisms for allocating class membership.

A LACK OF EXPLANATORY POWER?

While debates surrounding the status and existence of social class have been contentious for a long time, a growing orthodoxy in sociology has deemed social class to be redundant as a tool of social investigation. Taking their cues from varieties of post-structuralist and postmodernist thought this orthodoxy is now so entrenched that it has become what one commentator, borrowing from the work of Thomas Kuhn, has deemed 'normal science' (Callinicos 1995). From this perspective it is important to get away from modernist notions such as class and replace the focus of theorizing with a concern for complexity, difference and identity. Turner sums up this position:

> The role of social theory is to comprehend the infinitely complex and changing relations between scarcity and solidarity, and in particular how scarcity is produced out of abundance and solidarity out of conflict. The conviction remains, however, that class theory and analysis, far from aiding the search for comprehension, has become its fetter.
>
> (Turner 1996: 261)

Pakulski and Waters go further and argue that approaches utilizing class are inconsistent, empirically suspect and cannot explain changes in the structure of work, globalization, identity politics and the decomposition of the welfare state. They write:

> It is merely fideistic, to use Gramsci's term, to take the view that the class structure forms the dominant power grid, and is the key mechanism in structuring life chances, but that we cannot see it clearly because class formation or structuration is impaired. If structures do not manifest themselves and if there is no evidence that they are operational, then there is little point in clinging to the concepts that reference them. Most sociologists will accept that structures are historical, that they are formed and that they inevitably expire. Let

class also rest in peace, respected and honoured, but mainly relevant
to history.

(Pakulski and Waters 1996: 152)

Some theorists have drawn back from this total dismissal and have
adapted class analysis to what they regard as a significantly changed
world. From a recognizably neo-Weberian perspective, for example,
Esping-Anderson (1993) posits a model of a post-industrial class structure which he argues derives from post-Fordist work principles and
allows for the growing salience of gender, race and age. His scheme
consists of four occupation-based classes and a fifth 'outsider' or surplus
population group, which he regards as a significant new factor in
post-industrial society. This fifth group is a product of labour market
change and welfare policies, both of which encourage, for example, the
formation of sectors of the long-term unemployed or early-retired.

For some theorists, however, class, at least as conventionally conceived
(i.e. along neo-Marxist or neo-Weberian lines), simply no longer has the
explanatory potential it possessed a generation or more ago. Postmodern thinkers frequently espouse this view, although they may have
little else in common. Bradley (1996: 67) has distinguished three tendencies within postmodernist thought. The first combines a postmodern
account of culture with orthodox Marxist or neo-Marxist class theory.
The second maintains that postmodern culture heralds an end to class
inequalities. And the third holds that class remains relevant but now
requires to be conceptualized more in terms of consumption than
production.

Jameson (1991) represents the first of these tendencies. He combines
an account of cultural change with an analysis of globalizing capitalism.
He remains vague, however, about class groupings, suggesting that we
may well be between two capitalist epochs and that class outcomes
cannot yet be predicted. Beck (1992: 87) has given expression to the
second tendency, arguing that long-established class communities and
ties are yielding to 'a social surge of individualization', and goes on to
argue that the most important questions are not related to the distribution of resources but rather that of risks. Pursuing the same theme,
Crook and colleagues (1992: 111) anticipate a decline in the salience of
class as society becomes more individualized and the media play more
part in exhorting people to identify with particular 'symbolically simulated communities' as represented by various consumer groups. They see
future forms of stratification as 'fluid and chaotic' (see also Pakulski and
Waters 1996).

In many respects Bauman (1992) typifies the third tendency, maintaining that the core relation between capital and labour has altered, with capital now engaging labour in the role of consumers rather than producers (see for example his *Freedom*, 1988). According to this view, the 'new poor', another version of Esping-Anderson's outsider or surplus population group, are not part of the labour reserve but 'permanently displaced'. This has not led, as might be expected, to social unrest because most people are seduced by the glamour of the new consumerism. The state may yet, however, have to take repressive measures to keep the new poor in order, for example, by extending policing and surveillance and contracting citizenship rights. As Bradley (1996: 69) puts it, 'seduction and repression become the twin axes of class domination'.

A common theme among postmodernists hinges on the concept of identity and warrants a further comment. Since the break up of stable class communities and ties, it is argued, class is no longer a potent source of identity. Consumer identities may be replacing class identities. In fact, identities tend to have a multitude of constituents, and to be adapted by individuals more or less continuously in line with personal choice. In Bradley's (1996: 25) terminology, class has become a more 'passive identity': people now rarely define themselves or act in terms of class membership. Seductive as this notion is, we should be aware of Warde's conclusion that such consumption-based notions of identity have been unduly exaggerated by the strongest of postmodernist theses. He concludes: 'personal, and even more social, identity is still more readily achieved through non-commodified processes, the outcome of social learning from family, friends, occupational groups, religious associations and clubs for enthusiasts' (Warde 1997: 203).

ASPECTS OF THE THEORETICAL DEFICIT

It is our contention that the increasingly vigorous and far-reaching debates on social class taking place in mainstream sociology, selections of which we have briefly summarized, are highly pertinent to any consideration of the present under-theorization of class in medical sociology. Before we elaborate on this deficit, however, two preliminary observations are in order.

The first has to do with discontinuity. It is necessary to acknowledge the rapid and accelerating processes of change that have characterized Britain since the mid-1970s. These have been most discernible in the cultural domain and are perhaps most readily captured by the rhetoric of the postmodern; but they are not only cultural. As well as newly fragmented identities, with class perhaps a more passive constituent than hitherto, new patterns of labour, often incorporating 'flexible' post-Fordist work principles, have become commonplace, and gender, ethnicity and age have come to rival class in some commentators' perspectives on Britain's social strata.

The second concerns continuity. The accelerating pace of – especially cultural – change has arguably occasioned a neglect of continuity. It is certainly pertinent to note, for example, that empiricist and/or more sophisticated research programmes in Britain have pointed to continuing and apparently class-patterned post-war inequalities, not only in health but also in attainment in comprehensive secondary education (Heath and Clifford 1996); sustained class patterns of voting at general elections (Marshall *et al.* 1988; Goldthorpe 1996); and a high degree of stability in relative rates of intergenerational class mobility (Erikson and Goldthorpe 1992; see also Westergaard 1995).

Bearing these observations in mind, we have five general points to make on theorizing class. It is axiomatic, first, that even if class has become a more passive identity of late, it does not follow that it no longer has any theoretical purchase. As Scott (1996: 2) puts it: 'While people in their everyday lives may, indeed, now be less likely to identify themselves in "class" terms, this does not mean that class relations, *as objective realities*, have disappeared' (our emphasis). There is in any case poll evidence from Gallup that growing numbers of people think 'class struggle' a reality in Britain: the proportion has risen consistently from around a half in the mid-1960s to 76 per cent in the 1996 poll (Deer 1996).

Our second point precisely concerns the nature of class relations 'as objective realities', and invokes the work of Bhaskar (1989; see also Collier 1994). In line with his transcendental realism, and his transformational and relational models of social activity and society respectively, Bhaskar asserts a real ontological difference, if also a mutual ontological dependence, between *people* and *society*, the latter being defined, after Marx, in terms of a 'network of relations': 'people are not relations, societies are not conscious agents' (Collier 1994: 147). Acknowledging a debt to Giddens (1979), he writes:

> Society is both the ever-present *condition* (material cause) and the continually reproduced *outcome* of human agency. And praxis is both work, that is, conscious *production*, and (normally unconscious) *reproduction* of the conditions of production, that is society. One

could refer to the former as the *duality of structure*, and the latter as
the *duality of praxis*.

(Collier 1989: 34–5)

Society as the condition of action and society as its outcome both
belong to the subject-matter of sociology.
People no more work to reproduce the capitalist economy, writes
Bhaskar, than they marry to sustain the nuclear family.

Yet it is nevertheless the unintended consequence (and inexorable
result) of, as it is also a necessary condition for, their activity. Moreover, when social forms change, the explanation will not normally lie
in the desires of agents to change them that way, though as a very
important theoretical and political limit, it *may* do so.

(Bhaskar 1989: 35)

In our view class might profitably be interpreted relationally within a
framework of the type devised by Bhaskar. Sociologists, of course, are
obliged to operate in an 'open system'; they cannot secure even artificial
'closures' of the kind found in laboratory experiments. As Bhaskar rightly observes, however, sociologists can (a) enquire into open systems in
the same way as the concrete or applied natural sciences do; (b) find a
partial analogue to experiment; and (c) find something to compensate
for its absence (Collier 1994: 162). It is not class relations but rather
their *effects* that offer themselves for study.

Our third point about class relations is a more substantive one. There
is a degree of clarity on the circumstances at the 'bottom' and, to a lesser
extent, the 'top' of the British spectrum of class relations. Complicating
this picture, however, is the debate about the existence or not of an
'underclass' consisting of a sizeable outsider or surplus population of
people materially, and perhaps culturally, chronically adrift. Borrowing
from debates current in the USA, where there has been much concern
regarding the position of the predominantly black residents of inner
city ghettoes, influential researchers such as those involved with the
Nuffield project (Marshall *et al.* 1995) have been keen to refute the
existence of an underclass on the grounds that the opinions of this group
do not differ markedly from those of individuals in the lowest social
classes. This unsatisfactory way of refuting the existence of an underclass
has been commentated on by Morris and Scott (1995), but the importance of a more theoretical approach is emphasized by Wright
(1995) who points to the importance of examining the question from
the point of view of what an underclass is expected to do in relation to

the rest of society. Here he draws an analogy with the native American Indians who became the victims of genocide during the nineteenth century because there was little interest in incorporating them into the formal economy. In a similar way, in more recent times, an underclass is perceived as having limited usefulness in terms of the wider economic system and therefore becomes an issue for social policy and containment. Their position may be variously attributed to the growth of long-term unemployment; the decline in industrial jobs; women's changing labour market position; the collapse of established working-class communities; and attempts to dismantle the welfare state (Bradley 1996: 50), but the effect is to see them as a problem and this in turn becomes the focus of their relationship to the wider society.

Less often remarked upon, and indeed less conspicuous, is the persistence in Britain of a power elite. Most eloquent here has been Scott who, in answer to the question 'Who rules Britain?', writes: 'Britain is ruled by a capitalist class whose economic dominance is sustained by the operations of the state and whose members are disproportionately represented in the power elite which rules the state apparatus' (1991: 151). The capitalist class, increasingly dependent on a system of impersonal capital resulting from the growth of institutional property holdings, is composed of entrepreneurial capitalists, 'passive' rentiers and executive capitalists, together with an 'inner circle' of 'finance capitalists with directorships in two or more very large enterprises in the system of impersonal capital' (Scott 1991: 89–90). Scott estimates the size of this class at 0.1 per cent of the adult population, some 43,500 individuals.

A fourth point, of special pertinence to the fortunes of Britain's outsiders and rulers, is the untenability in high modernity of analysing class relations in Britain within the confines of British society alone. It is now unequivocally accepted, for example, as world-system theorists like Wallerstein and others maintain has long been the case (see Chase-Dunn 1989) that an international or *global* perspective is required to comprehend the 'system of impersonal capital' obtaining in any given nation-state. This point has become as commonplace in the theoretical literature as it has been neglected in empirical research.

The fifth point is that there seems to have been something of a convergence of late among proponents of class on the related issues of its conceptualization and operationalization. This is not to say either that neo-Marxist and neo-Weberian class theories are no longer distinguishable, or that each has surrendered entirely to the putative requirements of class analysis; rather, it is to suggest a common inadequacy or flaw across many, if not all, class schemata. This flaw arises, we believe, out of a misguided attempt to 'map' too many aspects of an increasingly complex and subtle pattern of social differentiation on the sole basis of occupational data.

While it has long been customary for occupation-based schemata to exclude reference to an underclass or ruling/capitalist class, it seems increasingly difficult too to explicate and defend their theoretical rationales for delineating other or 'intermediate' class strata. Often, it seems, occupation-based class schemata reflect less a precise attempt to delineate and/or address class strata ('interpreted relationally'), than an imprecise attempt to assimilate and synthesize what Scott (1996), from his neo-Weberian perspective on stratification, terms people's class, status and command situations. In consequence, many occupation-based class schemata seem to differ surprisingly little from those advanced by theorists of a 'post-class society' (witness, for example, Pakulski and Waters's [1996] focus on 'status attainment' in their model of a 'status-conventional society').

This is not the place to make good general and outstanding deficiencies in sociological theorizations of class, nor do we have the requisite expertise to do so. But these brief and selective remarks do, we believe, raise some key issues, not least for medical sociology. It has been claimed, in summary: that subjective perceptions of class can and frequently do vary independently of objective class realities; that there is a strong but as yet largely unexamined case for interpreting objective class realities relationally; that the salience of an underclass and, to a greater extent, of an inconspicuous ruling/capitalist class for Britain's social strata has been neglected; that a global rather than a national perspective is a precondition for understanding patterns of social and class differentiation in Britain; and that too many, and too many under-theorized, expectations have been, and continue to be, invested in occupation-based class schemata in research on social and class differentiation. With these claims in mind, we now return to the topic of class-related health inequalities.

SOME POINTERS FOR RESEARCH ON CLASS-RELATED HEALTH INEQUALITIES

The initial 'pointer' concerns the need for sociologists to develop a more comprehensive *macro*-perspective on health inequalities. If there remain solid grounds for retaining and building on theories of class in Britain, and arguably for continuing to characterize Britain as a class society, then this theorizing should inform and be informed by research purporting to link class and health inequalities. Not only should neo-Marxist theories like Wright's (extending to relational theories) and neo-Weberian theories like Goldthorpe's be recruited to this cause, but more attention should be paid both to other dimensions of stratification like status and command, and to other telling social factors such as gender, ethnicity and age, and to their interactions with class. To this cocktail, too, should be added theorizations of late twentieth-century structural and cultural change, particularly in the realms of lifestyle and distinction.

Coupled with the need for a more ambitious macro-theoretical perspective is the need for more innovation and precision in empirical but not empiricist research. This is emphatically *not* a matter of deploying more abstruse techniques of abstracted or systematic empiricism in the hope of some fortuitous inductive return. It concerns the harnessing of both quantitative and qualitative means to test macro- (and derivative middle-range) theories of linkages between class relations, accessible only through their effects in open systems, and health inequalities. Such research, in short, must be grounded in, and address, substantive theory; theoretical sophistication is as important as, and must precede rather than issue from, sophistication in the collection, processing and analysis of data.

A fuller consideration of class relations, including the – arguably changing – nature of their interaction, not only with status and command but also gender, ethnicity and age, and a reconsideration in this light of the postulated link between class relations and health inequalities, might produce 'unexpected' results. While new research might corroborate and proffer theoretical grounds for commonplace empirical or empiricist affirmations of linkage, it might instead uncover equivalent or more potent linkages with alternative factors, such as differentiation by status or command. Many published studies, too, including those yielding large data sets, offer rich sources for innovative secondary analysis. Enhanced sophistication of theory and method in open systems requires open minds.

A further pointer emerges from the distinction between objective class realities and subjective perceptions of these realities. It has already been noted that these can vary independently of each other, and that the divergence between the two can be considerable. This may have important implications for health inequalities. It has been found, for example, that objective work conditions are not always matched by subjective perceptions of those conditions, and that it can be the latter rather than the former that predispose to poor health outcomes (Stansfeld *et al.* 1995). There is a need, then, for more investigation both of the conditions under which objective class relations might directly produce health inequalities, and of the potential for subjective perceptions to mediate such associations.

Not surprisingly, the growing body of work on interventions to reduce health inequalities also suffers from the under-theorization of class. As Whitehead (1995) usefully observes, such interventions may occur at any of four 'policy levels': strengthening individuals; strengthening communities; improving access to essential facilities and services; and encouraging macro-economic and cultural change. While most work has predictably occurred at the first level, there have been some effective engagements at each in Britain and elsewhere. There have been successes too for 'strategic approaches', which operate simultaneously across a number of different levels. Class has potential relevance for each policy level as well as for strategic approaches, but its pertinence to macro-economic and cultural change warrants a special comment.

According to Whitehead (1995: 52), there is evidence that key policy requirements at the fourth level include: income maintenance policies that afford adequate financial support for those who fall into poverty; education and training policies that help prevent poverty in the longer term; and more equitable policies for taxation and income distribution. In a challenging reflection on 'unheathy societies', Wilkinson (1996) cites both empirical and empiricist research favouring the thesis that egalitarian societies – that is, societies with narrower income differences – tend to have greater social cohesion. He goes on to illuminate some of the 'psychosocial pathways' through which income inequality and lack of social cohesion can adversely affect the health of the people. Although Wilkinson makes little reference to class in his macro-analysis of health inequalities, it is clear that, insofar as class remains salient in Britain, there is a strong case for the invocation of theories of class to refine our understanding and explanations of health inequalities and to inform our attempts to reduce them.

The final pointer returns to the idea of a ruling or capitalist class in Britain. It is remarkable to us that the – admittedly, overwhelmingly and systematically empiricist – British literature linking class and health inequalities so diligently ignores this class. It seems axiomatic that its influence extends not only to conditions – such as the extent of rising relative poverty and of income inequality (Townsend 1996) – instrumental for health inequalities in Britain, but to state-sponsored policies supposedly targeted at reducing them.

In the course of arguing that Britain has a ruling class, Scott (1991: 124) writes: 'A ruling class exists when there is both political domination and political rule by a capitalist class.' After the manner of Wright Mills (1959), he contends that this requires that there be 'a power bloc dominated by a capitalist class, a power elite recruited from this power bloc, and in which the capitalist class is disproportionately represented, and that there are mechanisms which ensure that the state operates in the interests of the capitalist class and the reproduction of capital'. If a power bloc is to endure, then it must attain 'consciousness' and 'coherence' and a capacity for 'conspiracy': 'it must evolve some awareness of common interests and concerns, it must achieve some degree of solidarity and cohesion, and its leading members must be capable of pursuing some kind of coordinated policy of action to further these interests' (Scott 1991: 122).

Research programmes purporting to corroborate or illuminate links between class and health inequalities can hardly proceed with credibility without sustained analysis of the typically covert but decisive role of the 'power bloc dominated by the capitalist class' which, through an amalgam of consciousness, cohesion and a capacity for conspiracy, 'rules' in Britain. This necessarily involves examining the potential of this small but potent class to define and underwrite, first, aspects of social – including class – differentiation, and, second, government policies bearing on health inequalities. For example, although the 'gap' between government rhetoric on health inequalities, on the one hand, and its funding of research and health policies and service reforms, on the other, has often been commented on (e.g. Francome and Marks 1996), little attention has been paid either to the salience of the capitalist class with regard to the extent and continuance of this gap, or to the probability of a deepening 'crisis of legitimation' for any government intent on its closure (Habermas 1973). Only rarely are such pivotal issues mentioned, let alone afforded any prominence, in otherwise wide-ranging discussions of social class and health inequalities.

CONCLUSION

Our intention in this chapter has been to interrogate the nature of medical sociology's contribution to the understanding of linkages between class and health inequalities. We have argued that medical sociologists have missed opportunities, partly by failing to devise their own distinctive research agendas, and partly by neglecting the investigations and debates on stratification and class in the mainstream of their discipline. There are, of course, exceptions, but they are disappointingly few and far between.

We have epitomized key aspects of mainstream thinking on class, embracing 'class theory', 'class analysis' and what might be termed the 'postmodern perspective'. We then offered some brief remarks of our own on social class in Britain, and, in light of these, suggested some potentially rewarding avenues of enquiry. There are two themes under-lying these suggestions, and some of the preceding discussion, that we wish to highlight by way of conclusion.

The first identifies the under-theorization of class in medical sociology as a primary problem. It is a lack of socio-theoretical sophistication, we believe, which has contributed most to sociology's failure to deepen, or even to enliven, the vast published literature on class and health inequalities. This under-theorization of class has, predictably enough, gone hand-in-hand with a continuing and outmoded neo-positivistic orientation to the conduct of research. While neo-positivistic sociology is not necessarily without return, its limitations have long been exposed (see especially the Willers's [1973] devastating critique of J. S. Mill's canons of scientific enquiry).

The second theme is substantive and concerns the poorly documented 'ways' of the ruling or capitalist class in Britain, and the relevance of these for class divisions in society in general, the class character of health inequalities, and the ability of governments to intervene pragmatically in (even) national, regional and local marketplaces and elsewhere to ameliorate or reduce health inequalities.

If this chapter provokes some debate on the need for explicit theory-driven research, incorporating – among other things – an examination of the salience of 'rulers' for the differential health of the 'ruled', then it will have served its purpose.

REFERENCES

Bartley, M., Blane, D. and Montgomery, S. (1997) 'Health and the life course: why safety nets matter', *British Medical Journal* 314: 1194–6.
Bauman, Z. (1988) *Freedom*, Milton Keynes: Open University Press.
—— (1992) *Intimations of Postmodernity*, London: Routledge.
Beck, U. (1992) *Risk Society: Towards a New Modernity*, London: Sage.
Bhaskar, R. (1989) *The Possibility of Naturalism*, 2nd edn, Hemel Hempstead: Harvester Wheatsheaf.
Black, D. (1993) 'Deprivation and health', *British Medical Journal* 307: 163–4.
Blane, D., Davey Smith, G. and Bartley, M. (1990) 'Social class differences in years of potential life lost: size, trends and principal causes', *British Medical Journal* 301: 429–32.
Bradley, H. (1996) *Fractured Identities: Changing Patterns of Inequality*, Cambridge: Polity Press.

Bury, M. (1997) *Health and Illness in a Changing Society*, London: Routledge.
Callinicos, A. (1995) 'Postmodernism as normal science', *British Journal of Sociology* 46: 734–9.
Chase-Dunn, C. (1989) *Global Formation: Structures of the World Economy*, Oxford: Blackwell.
Collier, A. (1994) *Critical Realism: An Introduction to Roy Bhaskar's Philosophy*, London: Verso.
Crompton, R. (1996a) 'The fragmentation of class analysis', *British Journal of Sociology* 47: 56–67.
—— (1996b) 'Gender and class analysis', in D. Lee and B. Turner (eds) *Conflicts about Class: Debating Inequality in Late Industrialism*, London: Longman.
Crook, S., Pakulski, J. and Waters, M. (1992) *Postmodernization*, London: Sage.
Davey Smith, G., Bartley, M. and Blane, D. (1990) 'The Black Report on socio-economic inequalities in health 10 years on', *British Medical Journal* 301: 373–7.
Deer, B. (1996) 'Still struggling after all these years', *New Statesman* 23 August: 12–14.
Erikson, R. and Goldthorpe, J. (1992) *The Constant Flux*, Oxford: Clarendon.
Esping-Anderson, G. (ed.) (1993) *Changing Classes*, London: Sage.
Francome, C. and Marks, D. (1996) *Improving the Health of the Nation: The Failure of the Government's Health Reforms*, London: Middlesex University Press.
Giddens, A. (1979) *Central Problems in Social Theory*, London: Macmillan.
Goldthorpe, J. (1987) *Social Mobility and Class Structure in Modern Britain*, 2nd edn, Oxford: Clarendon.
—— (1996) 'Class and politics in advanced societies', in D. Lee, and B. Turner (eds) *Conflicts about Class: Debating Inequality in Late Industrialism*, London: Longman.
Goldthorpe, J. and Marshall, G. (1992) 'The promising future of class analysis: a response to recent critiques', *Sociology* 26: 381–400.
Gubbay, J. (1997) 'A Marxist critique of Weberian class analysis', *Sociology* 31: 73–90.
Habermas, J. (1973) *Legitimation Crisis*, London: Heinemann Educational.
Heath, A. and Clifford, P. (1996) 'Class inequalities and educational reform in twentieth-century Britain', in D. Lee, and B. Turner (eds) *Conflicts about Class: Debating Inequality in Late Industrialism*, London: Longman.
Jameson, F. (1991) *Postmodernism, or the Cultural Logic of Late Capitalism*, London: Verso.
Jones, I. and Cameron, G. (1984) 'Social class analysis – an embarrassment to epidemiology', *Community Medicine* 6: 37–46.
Klein, R. (1991) 'Making sense of inequalities: a response to Peter Townsend', *International Journal of Health Services* 21: 241–57.
Macintyre, S. (1997) 'The Black Report and beyond: what are the issues?', *Social Science & Medicine* 44: 723–45.
Mann, M. (1974) *Consciousness and Action among the Western Working Class*, London: Macmillan.
Marmot, M. (1986) 'Social inequalities in mortality: the social environment', in

R. Wilkinson (ed.) *Class and Health: Research and Longitudinal Data*, London: Tavistock.

Marmot, M., Davey Smith, G., Stansfeld, S., Patel, C., North, F., Head, J., White, I., Brunner, E. and Feeney, A. (1991) 'Health inequalities among British civil servants: the Whitehall II study', *The Lancet* 337: 1387–93.

Marshall, G., Newby, H., Rose, D. and Vogler, C. (1988) *Social Class in Modern Britain*, London: Hutchinson.

Marshall, G., Roberts, C. and Burgoyne, C. (1995) 'Social class and the underclass in Britain and the USA', *British Journal of Sociology* 47: 22–44.

Morris, L. and Scott, J. (1995) 'The attentuation of class analysis: some comments on Marshall, Roberts and Burgoyne, "Social class and the underclass in Britain and the USA"', *British Journal of Sociology* 47: 45–55.

Nichols, T. (1996) 'Social class: official, sociological and Marxist', in R. Levitas and W. Guy (eds) *Interpreting Official Statistics*, London: Routledge.

Pakulski, J. and Waters, M. (1996) *The Death of Class*, London: Sage.

Scott, J. (1991) *Who Rules Britain?* Cambridge: Polity Press.

—— (1996) *Stratification and Power: Structures of Class, Status and Command*, Cambridge: Polity Press.

Stansfeld, S., North, F., White, I. and Marmot, M. (1995) 'Work characteristics and psychiatric disorder in civil servants in London', *Journal of Epidemiology & Community Health* 49: 48–53.

Stanworth, M. (1984) 'Woman and class analysis: a reply to John Goldthorpe', *Sociology* 18: 159–70.

Townsend, P. (1996) *A Poor Future*, London: Lemos & Crane.

Townsend, P. and Davidson, N. (eds) (1992) *The Black Report*, London: Penguin.

Turner, B. (1996) 'Capitalism, classes and citizenship', in D. Lee and B. Turner (eds) *Conflicts about Class: Debating Inequality in Late Industrialism*, London: Longman.

Wadsworth, M. (1997) 'Health inequalities in the life course perspective', *Social Science & Medicine* 44: 859–69.

Warde, A. (1997) *Consumption, Food and Taste*, London: Sage.

Westergaard, J. (1995) *Who Gets What? The Hardening of Class Inequality in the Late Twentieth Century*, Cambridge: Polity Press.

Whitehead, M. (1992) *The Health Divide*, 2nd edn, London: Penguin.

—— (1995) 'Tackling inequalities: a review of policy initiatives', in M. Benzeval, K. Judge, and M. Whitehead (eds) *Tackling Inequalities in Health: An Agenda for Action*. London: King's Fund.

Wilkinson, R. (1996) *Unhealthy Societies: The Afflictions of Inequality*, London: Routledge.

Willer, D. and Willer, J. (1973) *Systematic Empiricism: A Critique of a Pseudo-Science*, Englewood Cliffs, NJ: Prentice-Hall.

Wright, E. (1985) *Classes*, London: Verso.

—— (1995) 'The class analysis of poverty', *International Journal of the Health Services* 25: 85–100.

Wright Mills, C. (1959) *The Power Elite*, New York: Oxford University Press.

—— (1970) *The Sociological Imagination*, Harmondsworth: Penguin.

Chapter 6

Gender, health and the feminist debate on postmodernism

Annette Scambler

It is probably from within medical sociology that one of the strongest critiques of postmodern feminist projects can be mounted. In this chapter I will be arguing that, while the *tools* of postmodernist discourse have often deepened and enriched debates around issues of gender and the subordination of women under patriarchy, the postmodern feminist project itself is fundamentally flawed. It is logically flawed in negating the concept of grand narratives whilst postulating its own, namely, that only '*petit*' narratives are now possible. The postmodern standpoint also undermines the concept of patriarchy, although this has not allayed feminist interest and, for some, an all-embracing adoption of its key tenets. Lyotard's condemnation of metanarratives, for example, is typically presented not only as necessary, but also as desirable:

> big stories are bad, little stories are good. . . . Narratives are bad when they become philosophies of history. Grand narratives have become associated with a political programme or party while little narratives are associated with localized creativity.
>
> (Sarup 1993: 146)

Postmodern discourse is most antagonistic to the concept of a feminist movement, it might be argued, when it focuses on the deconstruction of the notion of 'woman' and when, relatedly, it privileges individuals over groups. The resultant focus on individual empowerment fragments and diminishes the concept of power by denying commonality. The concept of 'woman' is denied validity because it is said to be constructed within a patriarchal discourse characterized by dichotomies and opposites. Woman has been created as opposite to man in this discourse, but has also been created inferior. While there is no doubt that patriarchal discourse has led to a particular construction of womanhood (and manhood), what is problematic is that, once the social genesis of patriarchal discourse has been exposed, there remain 'underlying realities' to contend with. Male and female biology retains its difference, for example, and many complex and gendered social structures survive their deconstruction.

Thus, when postmodernists move on from the notion that womanhood is defined in patriarchal discourse to assert that women can therefore deconstruct the old and construct a new woman, it is appropriate to add, 'only within parameters'. When the argument moves further to suggest that each woman can construct her own individual concept of womanhood, since the existing model is a figment of the male imagination, then, sociologically, other difficulties arise: humans, regardless of sex, exist in relation to societies and cultures, and have multiple connections to other people as well as histories and futures. These interconnections suggest that general, even grand, theories are not impossible and, indeed, that they can provide significant insights into the human condition. After all, it was not long ago that women were sociologically invisible. Are postmodernists really trying to say that our understanding of the gendering of society is not much richer for such insights?

What made the feminist movement successful in the earlier part of the second wave was the way it was grounded at grassroots level. Of course mistakes were made, but even these often took it forward by promoting an understanding of difference among women as well as commonality. But what the postmodern wave must not forget is that it was the commonality that made possible their critique of meaning. It was an attempt at connecting rather than dividing women. The postmodern project within feminism has the potential not only to be deconstructive but also destructive.

In this chapter I will consider first the relationship between feminist thinking and the postmodern. The focus will then switch to issues of health. Central will be notions of the 'normal' in mental health and the effects of the social and economic position of women on their general health status. It will be argued that the tools of postmodernism open up debate, but that they are limited in their wider impact in the health domain.

FEMINIST THINKING AND THE POSTMODERN

Difference among women has led many feminist theorists to embrace postmodern thought. Why did difference come to be so important to feminists? At the beginning of the second wave of feminism, in the

1960s and 1970s, feminists felt united in their aims to free women from their subordination. They wanted equality with men in terms of education, job opportunities and income. They believed that equality would come about when power was shared equally with men within the existing social structure. Coming from the liberal tradition, they were concerned that individual women should attain the same rights as individual men and, although they did assume a level of sisterhood, this tended to be instrumental and to occur only while reforms were being fought for and attained. In the main, then, liberal feminists followed mainstream social philosphy in pursuit of civil equality with men (Mill 1970; Friedan 1974; Wollstonecraft 1975; Byrne 1978).

In Europe and in America, as the inadequacies of the liberal philosphy of gradual change became more and more apparent with its failure to secure anything approaching full equality, alternative philosophies gained ground. In Britain, Marxist-feminists began to focus on the problems facing women who wanted equality in a capitalist system which was using them as cheap paid labour, as unpaid reproducers of the next labour force and as carers of the existing male workers (Rowbotham 1973; Barratt 1980). They demanded fundamental changes to the economic infrastructure.

By the late 1960s, radical feminism, especially in the USA, was advocating a quite different approach. Instead of focusing on a lack of equal opportunities, as the liberal feminists had done, or on the forces of capitalism, as the Marxists had done, radical feminists defined men as constituting the problem: women were controlled *as a group* by men *as a group*. Men held power in society and used it in their interests. Women were systematically excluded from power and had no option but to function as subordinates within a patriarchal structure (Daly 1973; Dworkin 1974, 1983; Firestone 1970; Millet 1970; Rich 1976).

Other, broadly socialist, feminists took up this idea and began to structure their theory around both patriarchal and capitalist power bases (Hartmann 1979; Ehrenreich 1976; Easton 1974). Some saw capitalism as a patriarchal form of social organization, while some later theorists, like Sylvia Walby, saw two independent forces operating on women: sometimes they acted in concert, and sometimes in opposition. Both, however, resulted in the suppression of females (Walby 1986).

As the feminist movement matured so discord and fractioning began to appear. Two particular groups were prominent here. Black feminist groups emanating initially from the USA began to argue that feminism was basically white and middle class (Davis 1971). Although the movement was slower to emerge in Britain, groups such as the Southall Black

Sisters, founded in 1979, began to operate independently of their white 'sisters', but were still largely middle class. Working-class women in all sectors of society were slow to join the feminist movement. They were motivated by *class* issues, and agitated from within socialism. For example, miners' wives organized to fight the establishment over pit closures, and, although these groups of women had a strong internal solidarity, their fundamental alliance was with working-class men and predominantly male unions, against the middle classes.

Women in the different strands of feminism began to focus on different aspects of women's situation. While liberal feminism tended to support the family but wanted women to have more rights within it and more access to jobs and child care, white radical and Marxist/socialist feminists began to see the family as a key source of oppression. Black women, on the other hand, were integrating two different forces of oppression in their analyses and had to contend with the fact that the family, while it may act as a source of subordination within patriarchy, was also a source of support for black women against white oppression. And white oppression obviously included oppression by white *women*. So black women began to see their needs as very different from white women and began to argue that one feminism was not possible (Omolade 1980; hooks 1981; Lorde 1984).

At the same time the gay women's movement was focusing its attention on sexuality and on forging a special link with authentic femaleness. Discord arose between heterosexual women and the lesbian groups. Women who wanted to bear and care for children began to feel threatened, and factions appeared at the women's conferences. Gradually it became apparent that the women's movement was in danger of disunity and fragmentation.

Thus it could be maintained that the women's movement towards the end of the second wave was ripe for the assimilation of a new theoretical initiative, postmodernism. But there is another issue to add into the equation. In Europe there was a surge of individualism, which in Britain was consolidated from 1979 by the new Thatcher regime. This mirrored the more institutionalized individualism fundamental to the political and social philosophy of the USA. The further demise of the social was imminent. Mrs Thatcher insisted there is no such thing as society, which is just an aggregation of individuals. The emphasis was on the rights of the individual and *empowerment*.

It is part of the argument of this chapter that there is a strong association between the ideology of individualism and the growth of feminisms of difference, notwithstanding the fact that much individualist philosophy is in conflict with those difference philosophies which centre heavily on class, race, sexuality, religion and so on, which have a *social* basis. On the whole, the postmodern theorists from within feminism fitted neatly into the individualist ethos. Perhaps, given the factionalizing of feminism, it was the appropriateness of the *timing* of the rise of post-modernism that led some feminists to commit the cardinal 'female' sin of throwing the baby out with the bath-water. The new ideas were exciting and seemed (even) more liberating than the old.

The significance of empowerment for individual women has been taken up by postmodern feminisms to help women to forge their own identities, careers and pathways through life. There is nothing wrong with the concept of empowerment *per se*, and we shall see later how important this concept has been for women in relation to health issues. But while the empowerment thesis has been crucial for establishing a critique of the social in relation to women and health, it is not sufficient. Gains in empowerment for individual women tend to come at the expense of others, usually other women. Moreover, individual empowerment depoliticizes in a fundamentally anti-feminist way. In employment women use other women as child-carers and cleaners, and those of the Western world are involved in the indirect exploitation of Third World women, even while arguing for *their* empowerment.

In order to understand the problems of the postmodern it is import-ant to grasp how the project of modernity assimilated the female. It is clear that the effects of modernity on women have been contradictory since the Enlightenment. The liberal philosphers who sought to sweep away the old superstitions and establish the new secular view of reality created a scientific and rational framework of ideas challenging the existing Christian order and prevailing ideas about *man*, nature and society. Knowledge became progressive, universal and objective, as opposed to the distorted vision of the 'common-sense' 'intuitive' tradi-tion. Against the old hierarchical order of the feudal estate, the Enlighten-ment spread the notion of universal citizenship for all and a privileging of knowledge over nature.

What this meant in reality was the projection of masculine ways of conceptualizing as normal. It consolidated the existing understanding that women were not inherently logical or rational since they were inescapably bound by their reproductive ties to nature and could not therefore elevate their understanding to the level of men. The essential character of womanhood was informed by common-sense and intuitive approaches to understanding. And all this could now be backed up by the new scientific methods which were being created to make sense of the new social order, and later justified by the theories of doctors like Freud.

When the concept of citizenship was proclaimed to give equal status to all people, it was assumed that only those who were capable of full rational use of free will should be considered able to exercise the rights of such freedom. And women did not fit the original criteria. While all men, regardless of class, gained some citizenship rights, even if these were largely hypothetical, women, as a group, were judged biologically ill-equipped to exercise pure uncontaminated reason. And since the concept of citizenship was bound to the public sphere where women were largely absent or without influence, the 'problem' of women in relation to citizenship did not present as one to be surmounted.

So liberal theory, for all its lauded egalitarianism, managed to incorporate a patriarchal view of women. Phillips writes of patriarchy creeping in by the backdoor (Phillips 1992: 215). She suggests that early liberals like Locke did *not* reject all forms of 'natural authority', but incorporated them by locating them in the private sphere and separating that from the public sphere of government. He saw political authority as comprising free and equal beings who had vested their authority in a ruler to regulate their lives. But he also saw fathers as having a natural authority over their children and husbands their wives. He went on to infer that, if women were naturally subordinate in the family, they were not 'consenting adults', and it was men who became the citizens of Locke's state, and they who should control the public sphere (Phillips 1992: 215).

As Phillips also points out, J.S. Mill, while rejecting the idea that women should be excluded from public affairs because of their role as wives and mothers, nonetheless expected women to choose to stay in the private sphere. And Carol Pateman (1987: 116) argues: 'Mill's acceptance of a sexually ascribed division of labour or the separation of domestic from public life, cuts the ground from under his argument for enfranchisement . . . how can wives who have "chosen" private life develop a public spirit?'

And it all fitted neatly together. Women were 'citizens', but their natural sphere of operation was in the domestic. Common sense, intuition and empathy were not harmful if kept within the confines of the home and environs of the children. But such ways of thinking and feeling must not be allowed to contaminate the rational world of the 'public'. So women were never full partners in the liberal movement but were used by the modern project as adjuncts to males. And industrial capitalism was able to make full use of the ambiguity of women's status by 'capitalizing' on her role in the unpaid private sphere of work and by a partial and subordinate assimilation into the paid public arena.

This is why the liberal feminist movement was doomed to failure. Women were never full citizens, even at an abstract level. The whole social structure was designed around a philosophy which marginalized them, which is why the notion of patriarchy and its structural power was such an important insight for feminism. It helped to explain women's subordinate position in both civil society and the marketplace. Those insights do not need to be discarded in our effort to assimilate any gains from postmodernism.

Kate Soper (1991) examines the problems of theoretical consistency which postmodernism faces when it presents itself as a form of critical theory. Postmodernist thought promises to deconstruct the established notion of identity 'and its binary grid of oppositional concepts', and to direct us to 'a future in which we might be freed from the tyranny of constructed identities' (Soper 1991: 100). However, Soper argues, while it is doing this it subverts itself by using the meaning structure of the old in order to construct the new. One particularly insidious move is apparent in its commitment to:

> a logic of difference which is theoretically incompatible with the logic of democracy, while continuing implicitly to rely on the latter for its critical force. . . . For why should we 'respect' or 'preserve' the plurality of social actors . . . unless we think it is right that they should be represented, and that in treating different persons or groups as different we are treating them more equally.
>
> (Soper 1991: 100)

She asks postmodernists to show their hand. While negating the possibility of political movements, she suggests, they appear to rely on democratic principles in order to promote their own. In relation to the postmodernist deconstruction of identity and the privileging of difference, she says:

> There is a risk, in short, that under cover of the very respectable request that we acknowledge difference, we justify as forms of self-expression what we ought to denounce as modes of greed, narcissism and egoism which are all too little considerate of the basic needs of others; or that in challenging the political collective as a false form of humanism we grant legitimacy to what are actually very disquieting forms of tribalism. . . . In other words, to grant all the rope to 'discourse' and none of it to 'reality' is to put the noose round those

cardinal values of equality and democracy in whose name all serious struggle against oppression must be conducted.

(Soper 1991: 107–8)

The position adopted here is somewhat similar to that of Sylvia Walby (1997), who insists that we need a structural, but not structuralist, theorization of gender. While we draw on the insights of discourse we do not need to abandon the 'elegant causal' in order to assimilate difference. As she points out, we can still use the notion of patriarchy while analysing the different forms it takes, and the different structures and practices it employs. A strong modernism, reinforced by the insights of discourse analysis, offers both an appreciation of difference *and* a structural theory of a patriarchy which is pervasive but chameleon-like in its effects.

POSTMODERNISM, GENDER AND HEALTH

One of the key issues when considering the health of women is the emphasis which has been placed on her psychological frailty or her emotionalism, which displaced the emphasis on her propensity to wickedness incorporated into the doctrinal teachings of the Christian Church throughout Europe and salient well into the nineteenth century (Ehrenreich and English 1979). Indeed the propensity to evil was assimilated into the new philosophy in the weakened but still destructive form of moral failing. This can be illustrated by an episode in the 1870s. Several women working with sewing machines presented with a cluster of symptoms which we would have no hesitation, now, in relating to lack of light or air, excessively long hours of work, repetitive strain injury or malnutrition. They were in fact diagnosed as suffering from the results of immoral behaviour as they enjoyed the 'erethrism' caused by the up and down movement of the treadles on the sewing machines (Down 1867, quoted in Scambler and Scambler 1993).

This pervasive ideology concerning the essence of womanhood sat very uneasily with the newer Victorian middle-class ideal of the angel in the home. This later stance set women on a pedestal as caretakers of family values in the homes of the rapidly growing business classes. They held this position precariously since any deviation would expose their hidden but still dangerous moral frailty. As Ehrenreich and English show, any deviant behaviour on the part of these women was dealt with through the new medical treatments which incorporated such measures as public humiliation or, in the event of excesses of sexuality or recalcitrant behaviour, more radical approaches such as the removal of the clitoris or the ovaries (Ehrenreich and English 1978). These ideas did not disappear with the turn of the century but emerged in Edwardian times in the form of the moral hygiene movement, where women were castigated for their role in promoting promiscuity among men, and new and punitive rules relating to prostitution. Men's behaviour was seen as reactive to women's immoral advances (Bland 1982).

Feminist analyses from the 1960s revealed how men have been able to control women's sexuality and to construct images of woman requiring her conformity. Further work showed how models of women's behaviour and mental health had been formed in line with a patriarchal ethos. Theorists like Juliet Mitchell (1974) began to structure their thinking in relation to the ideas of the psychoanalytic school, using Freud as a starting point. From this sort of analysis feminists began to form an understanding of how socialization within a gendered society could create males and females with deeply internalized gendered beliefs relating to how they should feel and behave, nurture and reproduce, and conduct sexual relations. Increasingly the women working in this area began to reformulate the underlying tenets of psychoanalytic constructions of women to incorporate a less phallocentric approach. Chodorow (1978), for example, within the confines of 'object relations theory', refocuses the psychoanalytic analysis away from the primacy of the father to the mother–daughter relationship. She creates a triangular relationship in which girls *don't* give up the mother for the father, but grow up sexually attached to the father and emotionally attached to the mother. So for women, Chodorow suggests that heterosexual relationships are experienced in a triangular way with men becoming emotionally secondary for women because they were never the first love object. Because women need a third person in the relationship, having a baby completes the triangle and women continue to want to mother.

While this school of thought was making important inroads, other feminists in Europe had been more overtly immersed in post-structuralist/postmodernist forms of thought. They began to ponder the identity of women from another angle, that of language and the construction of meaning itself. They began to explore the way in which women were excluded from language and defined within it. Those combining the psychoanalytic with the postmodern began to consider the entry of women into language and how this might affect their identity in relation to men. Postmodernists began to deconstruct the notion of woman itself, and the whole project of feminism was thrown into confusion.

Luce Irigaray contends that what she calls the 'male imaginary' has dominated the West from the time of the Greeks (Irigaray 1985: 25). She has been heavily influenced by the psychoanalytic school and by Lacanian analysis of women's entry into language. According to Irigaray, Freud's woman possesses:

> few of the qualities that characterise the liberal humanist subject: her ego is underdeveloped, her sense of justice flawed and she has little autonomy. She is left, effectively, in a state of infantile dependency. She is more prone to illnesses that compromise any aspirant subject-hood she may have; for example masochism.
>
> (Assiter 1996: 69)

For Irigaray, ways of conceptualizing women have become framed in 'phallocentric' logic, and her project is to deconstruct such logic. Because of this, for Irigaray and many others, the imperative for femin-ists is to create a female symbolic, because the source of her oppression is a symbolic order dominated by a male imaginary which depends on 'the identification of subjectivity with rationality and the exclusion of the female as "other"' (Assiter 1996: 31). However, there is a problem: because we are caught in this phallocentric logic we cannot actually define woman at all. To do so would be to enter the logic and to 'con-ceptualise the relationship between the sexes in terms of polarity and opposition', for the dualities are always created from the male imaginary and the woman is only created as other to men and therefore as 'lack' in relation to the male subject (Assiter 1996: 31)

In Irigaray's thinking, therefore, the postmodern project is to discover the feminine, and in order to do this Enlightenment reason must be subverted and its philosophies deconstructed to expose its masculine nature. While Lacanian analysis uses the mirror image to suggest that woman is a distorted vision of man, contaminated by lack because she is *not* man, and not able to be conceived differently because all we know is a 'masculine feminine', Irigaray says there *may* be a non-phallic female but it cannot be defined because to do so is merely to recreate the phallic female through the medium of the phallocentric logic immersed in the symbolic. Quoting from Tong's (1992: 227) interpretation of Irigaray:

> To claim that the feminine can be expressed in the form of a concept is to allow oneself to be caught up, again, in the system of 'masculine representation' in which women are trapped in a system of meaning which serves the auto-affection of the (masculine) subject.

Irigaray uses the concept of the speculum to capture men's narcissistic identification of everything they see as a reflection of the masculine. This use of the speculum, according to one interpretation, suggests the mirror image in the visual penetration of the speculum inside the vagina (see Tong 1992: 227). Within the context of medical sociology, Irigaray's use of imagery is particularly apposite. At a theoretical level, the concept of specularization helps to illuminate a symbolic order. At the level of mundane reality, it is a concrete symbol of patriarchy at work in controlling women's bodies, and, as various feminists have suggested, in furthering their dependence on the medical profession for definitions of their health and well-being, and for its expertise in reproduction and childbirth. But Irigaray's imagery can be used to greater effect. Indeed we have a perfect example of the mirror image from the realms of medieval anatomy, where one illustrated text demonstrates how the female reproductive system is envisaged inside the body. What we are offered is a mirror image, or negative, of the external male genitalia: the very same, but hidden from view (Open University, U205, 1985).

Analyses of the male symbolic and its deconstruction of the meanings applied to woman, her psyche and behaviour, add depth to sociological analyses of women's position in a patriarchal social structure. They show how deep-seated the gendered identity may be, and how understandable the theories of the Victorian doctors were in relation to their female patients. But while women of Victorian and later eras may have had their identities constructed in circumstances not of their choosing, it is clear that they have also been able to 'break through' the phallocentric construction of their mental health, even if unable to do anything about their subordinate position in the social structure (Gilman 1973). The insights of the deconstructive method make it easier to identify complex lines of causation within the patriarchal power structure.

Remaining with the issue of mental health, a large scholarship now exists, including the work of people like Busfield (1986), Chesler (1972), Ehrenreich and English (1978), Miles (1991) and Penfold and Walker (1984), who all suggest that women's psyches have been constructed as inferior to men's within the gender dichotomy. So women emerge as labile, emotional, inconsistent, illogical, irrational, caring, sensitive and so on, compared with men's logical, rational, competitive and focused natures. Those attributes of the male psyche are highly valued in (patriarchal) society, and relate significantly to those required by a public sphere infused with capitalist thinking. Women's core attributes leave them dubiously placed in the public arena but support the needs of the domestic sphere admirably.

It has been convincingly argued that the whole of medicine is contaminated by gendered stereotypes (Oakley 1984; Roberts 1985; Blake 1990; Allen 1994). Penfold and Walker (1984) trace the image of woman from Aristotle's claim that 'the female is a female by virtue of a certain lack of qualities', through the Judeo-Christian symbolism of woman as Adam's Rib, 'responsible for the fall of mankind from perfect innocence, destined to suffer, but able to produce the male redeemer', to Freud's contention that: 'she is largely without moral sense, inclined to be less ethically rigorous, have less perception of justice, is more subject to emotional bias and unable to contribute to culture' (Penfold and Walker 1984: 84). Even feminism itself has been interpreted as an illness. Penfold and Walker (1984: 85) cite Rheingold, a Freudian psychologist writing in the 1960s and 1970s, who insisted that:

> anatomy decrees the life of a woman . . . when women grow up without dread of their biological functioning and without subversion by feminist doctrines, and therefore enter upon motherhood with a sense of fulfillment and altruistic sentiment, we shall attain the goal of a good life and a secure world in which to live it.
>
> (Rheingold 1964: 114)

Many theorists, including Chesler (1972), Miles (1991) and Rawlings and Carter (1977), suggest that women have been made social scapegoats: society's ills are laid on their shoulders and when they are miserable or try to rebel they are labelled as mentally ill. This was the rationale behind the opening of the Women's Therapy Centre in London. Penfold and Walker (1984) make clear that feminist therapy has been developed from a very wide body of experience across the spectrum of feminist scholarship, from novelists like Atwood and Lessing to philosphers like de Beauvoir and sociologists like Ehrenreich, Oakley, Mitchell and Rowbotham. While the influence of the postmodern is obvious in the deconstruction of the traditional psychoanalytic method, it is unable to progress logically to a feminist therapy to replace the flawed one generated by the male symbolic. If the category of 'woman' is denied and a theory of patriarchy is impermissible, it becomes problematic to establish a form of treatment enabling women to counter the male symbolic and a disproportionate reliance on male practitioners.

The principles underlying the Women's Therapy Centre were those of the old models of egalitarianism, with collective rather than hierarchical structures, and a stress on the equal sharing of resources, power and responsibility. However, at the same time the focus was on therapeutic strategies which were centred around maintaining and enhancing each individual woman's power and responsibility – i.e. individual empowerment. It was pointed out that such therapy was often traumatic for women because it could mean that difficult decisions might need to be made about the nature of domestic relationships or family structures in order for the source of the distress to be neutralized. But the philosophy of the feminist structure was to provide the woman with all the group support she needed while she was attempting to make changes. The Centre held that the situation women find themselves in is related to the broader aspects of patriarchal structures, and that the Centre would *never* attempt to resocialize women to accept a subordinate position. The significance of the whole social picture was never lost using this approach.

It seems very obvious that the feminisms which emerged from the project of modernism have not only changed the course of that project dramatically this century, but have themselves now been transformed by the postmodern stance. But all these changes do not amount to the demise of the modern; rather, they confirm its continuance. Consider, for example, the feminist attempt to set up separate and special health facilities for women. They have been faced with a dilemma. Since the NHS has been instrumental in the subordination of women at all levels, should services for women not be set up outside it? But women would have to pay for such services, and that, as Doyal and Elston (1986) emphasize, is not possible for many women.

POSTMODERNISM, BIOLOGY AND THE BODY

When reflecting on postmodernism and the health of women, at least two separate sets of factors need to be explored: those relating to the individual female body, pyche, illness and disease; and those that look beyond the individual to the social, toward the patterning of experience and the social structuring of morbidity and mortality among 'women'. In relation to the former, the insights of deconstruction can facilitate the exploration of how experiences affect the identity of each woman and how empowerment might improve her ability to alter or control those experiences or to change her self-image. Consider childbirth, for example: the postmodern approach has illuminated the way in which obstetricians have constructed pregnancy and childbirth, creating a double medical emergency out of an event normal to the category 'woman' (see Oakley 1986; Tew 1990).

When it comes to wider societal issues, however, such as the propensity for women to suffer from repetitive strain injury, or for young mothers to smoke to alleviate stress, or for women to suffer from domestic violence or rape or sexual harassment at work, or genital mutilation, then a little more than a theory of identity or a study of how one might define these categories of experience is required. The causal factors underpinning, for example, patterns of violence or rape need to be elicited. This is done in an attempt to alleviate the trauma created by the violence and to change the situation for *all* women *in the context of a given normative social order*. And such work presupposes acknowledgement of a gender dichotomy.

In the present postmodernist climate, any attempt to return to the primacy of the body is likely to result in charges of determinism and essentialism. Foucault's work on the social construction of the body has had a strong impact on feminist ways of conceptualizing the female body, even though, as Gatens (1992: 131) points out, his theories concentrated on the construction of *male* bodies (another example of patriarchy at work). One might almost, it seems, conceptualize the Foucauldian body as an exemplar of virtual reality, with the abstract body created by particular discourses far removed or disconnected from the (grounded) biological and social realities lived in the whole 'person'.

Modernist feminists, who still celebrate the capacity of women's bodies to nurture and reproduce, often seem to be vilified as unsophisticated theorists. At a psychological level this is understandable, since forms of biological determinism have invariably worked to women's detriment. One theorist who does focus on the biological and wants to retain the sex–gender distinction is Alison Assiter in *Enlightened Women* (1996). The comment by Elizabeth Wilson on its cover is significant: she calls it a 'brave' and 'intellectually rigorous book which goes against the grain of current orthodoxies in the interest of a political project – feminism – that we should not discard'.

Assiter argues that there is a distinction to be made between (socially constructed) gender and (biological) sex. The sex side, she says, is characterized by a 'minimal notion of the body; by the set of minimally necessary factors that enable us to identify a particular body as male or female' (1996: 125). These are not unchanging, but may be altered by psychological or social manipulation, and may vary in quantity in different males and females. 'There is, however, a minimally necessary set of bodily or biological features present in every female, features the presence of which enables us to identify the person as female', including 'some combination of chromosomes, hormones, genitalia and secondary sex characteristics'. This forms the 'real essence' or the nature of the kind 'female' in something closely akin to a 'Lockean sense' (Assiter 1996: 125).

Assiter argues for a kind of essentialism about women which is not fixed by nature. In support of her arguments for a sex–gender distinction she refers closely to the work of Stoller (1984), who studied the relation between sex and gender identity in a large number of people with indeterminate sex characteristics. He demonstrates to her satisfaction that the distinction is a meaningful one, and that the minimal body is significant in influencing social and psychological identity. While she accepts the richness that Foucauldian analysis has added to recent feminism, she is wary that, if we go too far down the constructivist road, we might lose sight of the underlying biological reality or essence.

Assiter goes on to argue for a universalist basis for feminism. She says there *are* features which all women share, and that there has been a 'universal self-identification as masculine or feminine on the basis of the possession of a particular type of sexed body'. She suggests that a refocusing on nature and on the importance of the minimal biological body provides at least a basis for a shared identity among women (Assiter 1996: 127).

Another theorist who wants to retain the biological in feminist theory is Lynda Birke (1992). She advocates a feminism which does *not* marginalize the biological but incorporates it. She, too, is not happy with the tendency in some forms of feminist thinking towards a denial of ourselves as biological beings. She identifies two key problems in the move to reduce the biological to an issue of discourse. First, while it is appropriate to reject the gendered way in which gene theories have tended to reinforce inequalities between men and women, we must not fall into the trap of denying the power of genetics. Male and female bodies *are* genetically different.

Second, Birke feels that much of feminism, because of the traditional association of women with nature in the male symbolic, has tended to go along with the relegation of animal behaviour to the realm of biology, while stressing that human behaviour is shaped by culture, and is therefore changeable. In her view, prevailing notions in Western culture, especially, suggest that: 'animals are basically bodies with little in the way of minds; we are minds busily denying that we have bodies' (Birke 1992: 73). But, as she points out, while we might want to say that our ideas and experiences of menstruation are socially constructed, few of us would be prepared to say the same thing about the bleeding itself.

Birke focuses firmly on the interactive model of the human and its development by using the concept of 'transformative change' as a continuous process through life, with the biological interacting with the social and natural environments. She wants to see the body put firmly back into feminist theory at more than the level of discourse.

What this line of thought emphasizes is that what you are now – your biological body, your experiences – is the product of complex transformations between biology and experiences in your past. And those transformations happening now will affect any such transformations in the future. Biology, in this view, does have a role: but it is neither a base to build on, nor determining.

(Birke 1992: 75)

This is a dynamic approach, unlike the more static concept of biological determinism. Within medical sociology it can be made harmonious with the form of discourse which emerges from Foucault's thinking, as, indeed, can Assiter's approach, but it does allow for an essence to remain, linking the personal and socially constructed to the biological. Significantly, these theorists allow for patriarchal power within the social, but in movement with biological change in a symbiotic relationship to create distinctive patterns of maleness and femaleness. This is a fully embodied form of thinking at the level of the whole person. It opens up the theoretical possibility of such symbiotic transformations being carried forward from one generation to the next.

ISSUES OF WOMEN'S HEALTH

Lesley Doyal's book, *What Makes Women Sick?* (1995), is an impressive resource for a modernist approach to the health of women. She stresses that she rejects both crude universalism and crude difference theories. Her focus is on 'common difference', that is, on commonalities in women's situations. Her decision to stay with the structural theories of class, race and gender places her firmly in a modernist perspective and allows her to explore inequalities of health status and experience across the generalized category of woman. She points out that there are marked differences in the health of women from different racial backgrounds and classes, but indicates that the greatest differences are those which separate the majority of women in developed countries from the majority of Third World women who are living in countries with a low per capita income. In these countries life expectancy is relatively short, the fertility rate is high and women in the paid labour force are relatively sparse. It is here, too, that we find great class and gender inequalities, and little state provision of health and welfare services.

In her analysis Doyal is careful to outline the dangers of understating cultural variation in relation to concepts of health and sickness, but employs another useful dichotomy, that involving disease (the objective category) and illness (the subjective one). Using this dichotomy, she can allow for both difference and commonality across cultures, respecting the cultural relativity of illness while measuring the social distribution of death and disease. She uses TB as an example, to illustrate how physiological manifestations and responses to tested clinical treatments in women show sufficient similarity to be measured as commonalities in order that the health status of different groups can be compared. But she is careful to point out that the comparisons are more difficult with mental health problems where objective signs are frequently lacking. Her approach to problems of mental health in women is to look for evidence of 'a reduction in their capacity to successfully participate in their culture', or for a disabling of cognitive or emotional capabilities (Doyal and Gough 1991). It is these disabling factors which Doyal feels one can compare between societies and across the commonality of women.

Pregnancy and childbirth provide pertinent case material. There are large differences between rich and poor countries, notably in relation to rates of maternal mortality. Using Doyal's data, in all developed countries maternal mortality is very infrequent, less than 5 per 100,000 live births, while in South Asia it is more than 650 and in Africa around 600 (United Nations 1991: 56). If we include fertility rates and explore lifetime risks of dying of pregnancy-related causes, we find that women in Africa have a risk of 1 in 23, while in the developed countries it is 1 in 10,000 (Rooney 1992). Reproductive deaths are a uniquely female experience, but are also closely related to economic and class factors across the globe. A modernist orientation is required to explore these issues for *all women*, and to explain the differences in mortality among women as well as between men and women.

While conditions of poverty and deprivation are at the heart of many of the health problems of both men and women in Third World countries, this is not the only reason for women's specific experiences. Their health status also relates directly to the patriarchal nature of the societies in which they live. In South Asia, for example, about 75 per cent of births have no trained health worker in attendance, while the figure for Africa is 62 per cent (United Nations 1991: 58). Doyal makes clear that women in the Third World typically have less access to medical care than men, despite their greater need. Rural women are particularly badly served. She suggests 'a particular reluctance to invest in the health of women and girls' in many Third World countries (Doyal 1995: 14).

Indeed, there is substantial evidence of structured patriarchy in many Third World countries, resulting in overt discrimination against girls and women in access to food, material resources, education and health care. In South Asia research has shown that the excess of female deaths in childhood and the childbearing period is related to just such discrimination. Women eat last after men and male children and frequently eat lower-status foods. Female infanticide is still a fairly common occurrence, but it would appear that 'chronic neglect' of female babies is a more usual cause of death (Unicef 1990; World Health Organization 1992)

It is evidence like this which indicates that it is naive and premature to dismantle the theory of patriarchy as a potent source of control over women's life experiences. While girl children in the developed world do not typically experience infanticide, and while women there infrequently die in childbirth, they do experience gender-related health hazards arising from patriarchy. They are likely to be subjected to domestic violence, rape and sexual harassment, which carry with them a combination of physical and psychological traumas. They have been subject to control of their reproductive capacity in a range of ways, from the denial of abortion to the court-ordered Caesarean. Their menstrual needs have been the source of discrimination at work and in medical care (see Scambler and Scambler 1993).

FEMALE CIRCUMCISION

Female circumcision, or, more accurately, genital mutilation, is one of those issues which has caused fierce debate among feminists. Those who accept a structural form of patriarchy see this as an issue for all women and as an attack on the bodily and mental integrity of women as a whole, somewhat akin to torture. Nor is it rare, even in the West. In its mildest form it involves cutting off the prepuce or hood of the clitoris. A second form, called excision or clitoridectomy, involves the partial or total removal of the clitoris, combined with a partial or total removal of the labia minora and majora. This form does not include closing the vulva. The most invasive form of mutilation, which has been termed Pharaonic circumcision, involves removal of the whole clitoris, all the labia minora and majora and the closing of the vulva by sewing it together. A small hole is left for the passing of urine and menstrual blood. The practice takes place in varying forms in twenty-five African countries, Asian countries including Malaysia and Pakistan, Brazil, Peru, eastern Mexico, some southern states in the USA and in second and further generations of girls in many Western nations. It takes place among Christians as well as Muslims and other religious groups, but many sources stress that there is nothing in either the Bible or the Koran or in other religious texts to advocate it (Hicks 1993). Its cause may be religious, as in Muslim belief, or to ensure chastity or control sexuality. Its use in Britain and the USA in the nineteenth century, for the control of 'excess sexuality' as a medical problem, has already been mentioned. Earlier, in Britain, chastity belts performed an equivalent function, and some feminists have called Freudian analysis of female sexuality a form of psychoanalytic castration.

It has been estimated that genital mutilation affects between 85 million to 140 million women worldwide, and that more than 10,000 children in Britain alone are at risk of female circumcision (Boulton 1993; World Bank 1993). It is performed at all ages, from babies through to older women, on whom it may be performed if the men are going away or to war. Typically, it is performed on girls between the ages of 5 and 12. The health-related effects are wide and significant. Complications which occur immediately after the procedure include haemorrhaging, infection, pain, scarring and bleeding of adjacent organs, and problems caused by restricted menstrual flow. Problems which may persist throughout women's lives include urine retention, pelvic infections and chronic stomach pain (Minority Rights Group 1980; Koso-Thomas 1987; Boulton 1993). AIDS is also a risk because of the frequent use of the same blade for more than one operation.

Before marriage a woman has to be reopened, and typically this is done without anaesthetic, although it sometimes occurs through tearing during sexual intercourse itself. Women may suffer repeated trauma during intercourse, and tearing and other problems during childbirth (Lightfoot-Klein, 1989). However, despite the problems, women ask to be re-sewn after giving birth because of the cultural pressures to do so. Through this one practice of patriarchal control women suffer physical, sexual and psychological damage. And it is most frequently the women themselves who perform the operation on the young girls. But if they do not they are unmarriageable and without a viable future.

In many countries such procedures have been ruled illegal. Infibulation has been outlawed in many countries, although there are ways to avoid the ban. In Sudan, while female circumcision was made illegal in 1946, it is acceptable to practise *sunna*, the mildest form. In Egypt a similar law was passed in 1959, but the practice is still endemic. In the UK it was made illegal in 1985 in the 'Prohibition of Female Circumcision Act'. In France there is no specific law against female circumcision but prosecutions under an Act prohibiting violence against children have led to jail sentences (Gumbel 1994). However, in 1994, a judge gave a suspended sentence to an African woman who performed the procedure on small babies, on the grounds that 'it was not France's place to interfere with the traditions of immigrants, and that the parents saw the operation on their children as "an act of love"'(Gumbel 1994). The procedure is common in France among Malians, Sengalese, Gambians and Mauritanians who live there. It has led to at least four deaths in the last ten years, and many long-term health problems. It would appear that doctors in France often fail to report excisions found during routine examinations because of fear of being branded racist (Gumbel 1994).

Several stories about circumcision hit the British newspaper headlines in the mid-1990s. In 1993 there was an outcry after a female councillor in Brent, herself circumcised, attempted to have female circumcision legalized and made available on the NHS. Ms Nyaga argued that the act was spiritual – a rite of passage from childhood to adulthood – and should be available to those who want to carry on their traditions (Boulton 1992). One consultant obstetrician, Mary Macaffray, who practised at Northwick Park Hospital, and who has cared for circumcised African women from Somalia and the Sudan, is quoted as saying: 'We have found in some cases that the memory of the operation is so strong that no safe amount of anaesthetic allows us to approach the vaginal area of the woman during delivery without causing her considerable distress' (Boulton 1993). In November 1993, a London doctor was asked to appear before the General Medical Council, charged with performing multiple female circumcisions (Dyer 1993). In Britain, as in France, health workers, including doctors and social workers, have been reluctant to intervene for fear of being branded racist. Forward International, in a 1991 survey, looked at the practice among some minority families of sending their daughters back to their countries of origin for 'holidays' in order to have the circumcision carried out, and found that ten out of sixty-five social service departments surveyed reported intervening in suspect cases (Dyer 1993). In London there are at least two groups working towards awareness about circumcision. These are the FORWARD group (The Foundation for Women's Health and Development), founded to promote the health of women and children from Africa, and LBWHAP (the London Black Women's Health Action Project). Several such groups have been funded by regional health authority grants. They see their brief as trying to educate women to bring about reform from within their cultural groups and societies because the practices are so entrenched and rarely discussed between men and women. But it is just this sort of problem which makes patriarchal practices so insidious. They are hidden in the ideological make-up of cultures and parade in so many guises that they are often difficult to bring to the surface, let alone dismantle. The medical and social service establishments in Britain, however, are beginning to move on the issue, and an advertisment appeared in March 1996 for a Somali woman to coordinate a project into the effects of genital mutilation on Somali women and girls for Newham Council in London (Newham Council 1996). Organizations such as Forward International are attacking this, and other health problems for women, at a global level.

Doyal suggests that, while health and health care was a major issue for feminists of the second wave in the developed countries of North America, Europe, Australia and New Zealand, its political importance declined when grassroots feminism did (Doyal 1995: 197). She suggests that its focus for action then moved to the Third World. Health issues for women have gone off the agenda in the developed world, but the nature of the protest has changed and diversified, becoming more 'incorporated', and related to green issues or to eco-feminism, while 'new' issues of particular relevance to women in Third World countries have moved into the spotlight.

What is exciting at the moment in the women's health movement is that there is activity at just about every level from very localized action groups to internationally coordinated conferences. Reproductive rights, on a very broad base, continues to be a key issue, but more general issues relating to access to food, hygiene, housing and clean water are also at the heart of female-centred health action groups. These are similar, in many ways, to the concerns of the eco-feminists (see, for example, Cox 1992).

It is difficult, when one learns the extent of the practice of female circumcision and the range of medical problems created by it, to keep patience with those who still retain a relativist stance and argue that women, as a whole, have no basis to interfere with the practices of cultures other than their own. If one makes an analysis at any level of power on the subject of genital mutilation, one can find sufficient evidence to support the contention that patriarchal power exists at a global level. What is needed is a strong and integrated global feminist movement with the health and well-being of *all* women as its focus, so that the efforts of all the fragmented groups working for the needs of their own women can be strengthened and supported. The Newham advertisement was a drop in the ocean in its brief for the women of Somalia. What is now needed is a new world movement: a third wave of feminism which can incorporate the tools of the postmodern without absorbing its philosophy, and emerge from the the fragmentation of the dying embers of the second wave with renewed strength. The postmodern movement has given us difference, but it has failed to negate the project of modernity for feminism.

There is currently a strong women's health movement which is concerned with the physical, pychological and general well-being of women, and is in a key position to trigger a global regeneration of feminism – a third wave. Women's health is close to the heart of patriarchal practice and illustrates well the diversity in the manifestations of patriarchy. Women's health is also of strategic importance to the social. Women, as well as being the reproducers and having the status of their health reflected in their offspring, still, globally, have the major responsibility for the health and well-being of themselves, their children, whole families and communities (Doyal 1995). At the heart of the concern of most women throughout the world is not the problem of the integrity of their identity, but the problems of daily living. That is not to say that worries about identity have no part in a women's movement, just that they should not be allowed to subvert or distort a vision that challenges and seeks to destroy the world-wide exploitation and subordination of over half the population of the world.

We could do worse than encourage the development of societies where some of the devalued traits of the deconstructed woman of the postmodern might take precedence in the promotion of the health of *all* citizens, where a caring, sensitive, empathic, nurturing and loving community might be part of a health movement at both social and individual levels. In this respect, judgement might be reserved as to whether the world of individual narcissism, which seems to have so powerful a pull on some contemporary feminists, has anything to do with health at all.

Capitalist and patriarchal structures exist, and will continue to do so for some considerable time, and we will not be able to construct a new woman or fundamentally change the life experiences of existing women, especially in the dimension of health, unless we have a united feminism which can see the broader picture as well as the detail, and can continue to attack the prevailing male power structure at all levels, including the very nature of the male symbolic.

By way of conclusion, it might be suggested that a major part of the problem with the postmodern project is that it somehow manages to disembody the concept of woman when it reduces it to the structure of the male symbolic, even when it is focusing on it corporeally. The mental has been privileged over the notion of embodiment at the expense of the very real problems of dealing with the gritty subjects of conception, childbirth and childrearing, not just as individual experiences of women but as requirements for the social to persist. The focus on identity and individual empowerment tends to gloss over these issues.

REFERENCES

Allen, I. (1994) *Doctors and their Careers*, London: Policy Studies Institute.
Assiter, A. (1996) *Enlightened Women: Modern Feminism in a Postmodern Age*, London: Routledge.
Barrett, M. (1980) *Women's Oppression Today: Problems in Marxist Feminist Analysis*, London: Verso.
Birke, L. (1992) 'Transforming biology', in H. Crowley and S. Himmelweit (eds) *Knowing Women: Feminism and Knowledge*, Cambridge: Polity Press/ Open University.
Blake, C. (1990) *Charge of the Parasols: Women's Entry to the Medical Profession*, London: The Women's Press,
Bland, L. (1982) ' "Guardians of the race" or "Vampires upon the nations's health"? Female sexuality and its regulation in early twentieth-century Britain', in E. Whitelegg, A. Arnot, E. Bartels, V. Beechey, L. Birke, S. Himmelweit, D. Leonard, S. Ruehl and M.A. Speakman (eds) *The Changing Experience of Women*, Oxford: Martin Robertson with the Open University.
Boulton, A. (1993) 'Calls for female circumcision on the NHS sparks storm', *Observer* 14 February.
Busfield, J. (1986) *Managing Madness: Changing Ideas and Practice*, London: Unwin & Hyman,
Byrne, E. (1978) *Women and Education*, London: Tavistock.
Chesler, P. (1972) *Women and Madness*, New York: Doubleday.
Chodorow, N. (1978) *The Reproduction of Mothering: Psychoanalysis and the Sociology of Gender*, Los Angeles: University of California Press.
Cox, C. (1992) 'Eco-feminism', in G. Kirkup and L. Smith Keller (eds) *Inventing Women: Science, Technology and Gender*, Cambridge: Polity Press/ Open University.
Daly, M. (1973) *Beyond God the Father: Towards a Philosophy of Women's Liberation*, Boston: Beacon Press.
Davis, A. (1971) 'The black woman's role in the community of slaves', *Black Scholar* 3(4).
Down, J. (1867) 'Influence of the sewing machine on female health', *British Medical Journal* 12 (January): 26–7.
Doyal, L. (1995) *What Makes Women Sick: Gender and the Political Economy of Health*, London: Macmillan.
Doyal, L. and Elston, M.A. (1986) 'Women, health and medicine', in V. Beechey and E. Whitelegg (eds) *Women in Britain Today*, Milton Keynes: Open University Press.
Doyal, L. and Gough, I. (1991) *A Theory of Human Need*, London: Macmillan.
Dworkin, A. (1974) *Woman Hating: A Radical Look at Sexuality*, New York: E.P. Sutton.
—— (1983) *Right-Wing Women*, New York: Coward-McCann.
Dyer, C. (1993) 'Doctor's "illegal circumcisions"', *Guardian* 22 November.

Easton, B. (1974) 'Socialism and feminism 1: Toward a unified movement', *Socialist Revolution* 4(1): 59–67.

Ehrenreich, B. (1976) 'What is socialist feminism?' *Win* 3 June: 4–7,

Ehrenreich, B. and English, D. (1978) 'The sick women of the upper classes', in B. Ehrenreich (ed.) *The Cultural Crisis of Modern Medicine*, New York: Monthly Review Press,

—— (1979) *For Her Own Good: 150 Years of the Experts' Advice to Women*, London: Pluto Press,

Firestone, S. (1970) *The Dialectic of Sex*, New York: Bantam Books.

Friedan, B. (1974) *The Feminine Mystique*, New York: Dell (originally published in 1963).

Gatens, M. (1992) 'Power, bodies and difference', in M. Barrett and A. Phillips (eds) *Destabilizing Theory: Contemporary Feminist Debates*, Cambridge: Polity Press,

Gilman, C. Perkins (1973) *The Yellow Wallpaper*, Old Westbury, NY: The Feminist Press,

Gumbel, A. (1994) '"Female circumcision", women freed amid outcry', *Guardian* 17 September.

Hartmann, H. (1979) 'Capitalism, patriarchy and job segregation by sex', in M. Blaxall and B. Reagan (eds) *Women and the Workplace*, Chicago: University of Chicago Press,

Hicks, E. (1993) *Infibulation: Female Mutilation in Islamic North Eastern Africa*, New York: Transaction Publishers.

hooks, b. (1981) *Ain't I a Woman? Black Women and Feminism*, Boston: South End Press.

Irigaray, L. (1985) *This Sex Which Is Not One*, Ithaca, NY: Cornell University Press.

Koso-Thomas, O. (1987) *The Circumcision of Women: A Strategy For Eradication*, London: Zed Press.

Lightfoot-Klein, H. (1989) *Prisoners of Ritual: An Odyssey into Female Genital Circumcision in Africa*, New York: Haworth Press.

Lorde, A. (1984) *Sister Outsider: Essays and Speeches*, New York: The Crossing Press.

Miles, A. (1991) *Women, Health and Medicine*, Milton Keynes: Open University Press.

Mill, Harriet Taylor (1970) 'Enfranchisement of women', in John Stuart Mill and Harriet Taylor Mill, *Essays On Sex Equality*, ed. A. Rossi, Chicago: University of Chicago Press.

Millet, K. (1970) *Sexual Politics*, Garden City, NY: Doubleday.

Minority Rights Group (1980) *Female Circumcision, Excision and Infibulation*, S. Mclean MRG, report no. 47, London: MRG.

Mitchell, J. (1974) *Psychoanalysis and Feminism*, Harmondsworth: Penguin.

Newham Council (1996) Newham Social Services advertisement for a 'Somali Female Genital Mutilation Project Co-ordinator', *Guardian* March.

Oakley, A. (1984) *The Captured Womb*, Oxford: Blackwell.

—— (1986) 'The limits of professional imagination', in A. Oakley, *Telling the Truth about Jerusalem*, Oxford: Blackwell.

Omolade, B. (1980) 'Black women and feminism', in H. Eisenstein and A. Jardine (eds) *The Future of Difference*, pp. 247–57, Boston: G.K. Hall.

Open University U205 Course Team (1985) *Medical Knowledge, Doubt and Certainty*, Milton Keynes: Open University Press.

Pateman, C. (1987) 'Feminist critiques of the public/private dichotomy', in A. Phillips (ed.) *Feminism and Equality*, pp. 103–126, Oxford, Blackwell.

Penfold, P. and Walker, G. (1984) *Women and the Psychiatric Paradox*, Milton Keynes: Open University Press.

Phillips, A. (1992) 'Feminism, equality and difference', in L. McDowell and R. Pringle (eds) *Defining Women: Social Institutions and Gender Division*, Cambridge and Milton Keynes: Polity Press and Open University. Reprinted from A. Philips (ed.) *Feminism and Equality*, pp. 1–23, Oxford: Blackwell, 1987.

Rawlings, E. and Carter, D. (1977) 'Values and value change in psychotherapy', in E. Rawlings and D. Carter (eds) *Psychotherapy for Women: Treatment Towards Equality*, Springfield, IL: Charles C. Thomas.

Rheingold, J. (1964) *The Fear of Being a Woman*, New York: Grune & Stratton.

Rich, A. (1976) *Of Woman Born: Motherhood as Experience and Institution*, New York: W.W. Norton.

Roberts, H. (1985) *Patient Patients: Women and their Doctors*, London: Pandora Press.

Rooney, C. (1992) *Antenatal Care and Maternal Health: How Effective Is It? A Review of the Evidence*, Geneva: World Health Organization.

Rowbotham, S. (1973) *Women's Consciousness, Man's World*, Harmondsworth: Penguin.

Sarup, M. (1993) *An Introductory Guide to Post-Structuralism and Postmodernism*, 2nd edn, Hemel Hempstead: Harvester Wheatsheaf.

Scambler, A. and Scambler, G. (1993) *Menstrual Disorders*, London: Tavistock/Routledge.

Stoller, R. (1984) *Sex and Gender: The Development of Masculinity and Femininity*, vol. 1, London: Maresfield Reprints.

Soper, K. (1991) 'Postmodernism and its discontents', *Feminist Review* 39 (Winter): 97–108.

Tew, M. (1990) *Safer Childbirth? A Critical History of Maternity Care*, London: Chapman and Hall.

Tong, R. (1992) *Feminist Thought: A Comprehensive Introduction*, London: Routledge. 1st edn Westview Press Inc., USA, 1989.

Unicef (1990) *The State of the World's Children 1989*, Oxford: Oxford University Press.

United Nations (1991) *The World's Women 1970–1990: Trends and Statistics, Social Statistics and Indicators*, Series K, no. 8, New York: United Nations.

Walby, S. (1986) *Patriarchy at Work: Patriarchal and Capitalist Relations in Employment*, Cambridge: Polity Press.

Walby, S. (1997) *Gender Transformations*, London: Routledge.

Wollstonecraft, M. (1975) *A Vindication of the Rights of Women*, ed. C. Poston, New York: W. W. Norton.

World Bank (1993) *World Development Report 1993: Investing in Health*, Oxford: Oxford University Press,

World Health Organization (1992) *Women's Health: Across Age and Frontier*, Geneva: World Health Organization.

Chapter 7

In search of the 'missing body'
Pain, suffering and the (post)modern condition

Simon Williams and Gillian Bendelow

In recent years, sociological theory has undergone something of a revolution. Previously banished to the margins of sociological discourse, the body is now firmly on the research agenda having exorcized the ghost of socio-biology. Emotions, too, look set to assume centre-stage, as part and parcel of a critical attack on the Western dualist legacies of the past and the notion of the disembodied, rational actor. Alongside current debates over class, consumption and risk, together with the recent arrival of postmodernist/post-structuralist thought, this suggests a climate of considerable intellectual ferment and uncertainty at the turn of the twenty-first century.

Always seen as the 'poor relation' or 'Cinderella' of contemporary social theory, the sociology of health and illness is proving a particularly fertile terrain upon which to fashion some of these evolving debates, both theoretically and empirically. From the social construction of biomedical knowledge to the phenomenological experience of pain, illness, disability and death, sociological approaches to health and disease throw into critical relief deep ontological questions concerning the nature and status of human embodiment.[1] This, coupled with other recent debates surrounding consumption and risk, the new genetics, the role of emotions and the postmodernist critique of health, highlight once again the fruitful links and mutually informing relations between sociological theory and medical sociology.

It is against this theoretical backdrop that the present chapter is located. Taking as its point of departure the contested nature of contemporary sociological theorizing around the body, health and illness, we critically assess postmodernist accounts of pain, suffering and the 'fabricated' subject. As we argue, while postmodernist attempts to deconstruct essentialism, mind–body dualism and interior–exterior notions of the self are indeed important, they nonetheless result in an ultimate dissolution of the body itself as a shifting, unstable, (inter)-textual effect. Bodies, in other words, become elusive, de-materialized, incorporeal entities through a postmodern bracketing of ontological questions (i.e. the search for underlying 'essences') and a prioritization instead of a relativist epistemological stance. In order to recover this 'missing' body, our own approach, in contrast, seeks to combine what may be termed a foundationalist (i.e. realist) ontology with a social constructionist (i.e. relativist) epistemology of pain and emotions, unified through a corporeal notion of the 'mindful' body. Contra the postmodernist/post-structuralist prioritization of the 'social', the argument here is for a subtle and sophisticated dialectical relationship between the immediate embodiment of disease as brute materiality and its meaning-laden character as human experience; one in which narrative and culture play a crucial mediatory role (Kleinman 1988). In taking this position, we aim to show how transcendence of the dualist legacies of the past, and the championing of emotions, is possible without recourse to a postmodernist de-materialization of the body and a decentring of the subject.

The first section of the chapter takes up these issues through a brief sketch of the postmodernist/post-structuralist position on pain and the body (without organs), together with some critical reflections on the relative merits of these perspectives from our own particular viewpoint. Having done so, we then proceed to a critical exploration of pain as an embodied structure of ongoing *lived* experience; one which crucially involves emotions as gendered modes of being-in-the-world. The relationship between the pre-linguistic and symbolic aspects of pain are addressed in the next section through a consideration of the mediatory role of narrative and culture in the (re)construction of human suffering as a meaningful experience. Finally, in the concluding part of the chapter, we again return to the problems of postmodernism, this time in relation to an ethics of caring and responsibility regarding pain, suffering and the human condition. It is to the first of these issues that we now turn.

PAIN AND THE (POST)MODERN CONDITION: WHO DESIRES A BODY WITHOUT ORGANS (BwO)?

As suggested above, the emergence of postmodernism and post-structuralism calls into question many of the previously held tenets and cherished beliefs of modernist Western thought through its decentring of the Cartesian rationalist subject, its championing of desire, and its commitment to *différance*, 'otherness' and 'becoming'. Underlying this position is a deep distrust of grand/master narratives or transcendent interpretations, an abandonment of notions of history as linear and progressive, a championing of the local and specific, and a commitment to a postmodernist/post-structuralist metaphysics of fluidity and flow *vis-à-vis* former hierarchical modes of dichtomous thought. Within this postmodern/post-structuralist landscape, previously tried and trusted concepts such as class, sex, age and gender, together with the underlying (essentialist) identity assumptions they involve, are rendered problematic. Bodies, too, become dispersed and destabilized as '(inter)textual' effects which are endlessly (re)inscribed through language and the (de/re)territorialized flows of desire. All that is solid, therefore, melts into air, through a deconstructive spirit and relativistic politics of (in)*différance*.

While (French) post-structuralist thought spans a diverse array of writers from Lacan and Derrida to Cixous, Irigaray and Kristeva – two, in particular, have enjoyed considerable prominence in recent years as the post-Foucauldian gurus of the contemporary intellectual scene. In their two-volume *Anti-Oedipus* study of capitalism and schizophrenia (1984, 1988), the French philosopher Gilles Deleuze and his psycho-analytic colleague Félix Guattari challenge Freudian psychoanalysis and its Oedipalizing tendencies, through a Nietzschean celebration of the liberatory potential of desire. Clearly this is not the time or place to go into a detailed exposition of their work, but two issues in particular merit further discussion as a backdrop to our deliberations on pain and the (post)modern condition. First, contra previous formulations as lack, Deleuze and Guattari reconceptualize desire as a productive, actualizing, force involving libidinal intensities, nomadic flows, linkages and 'machinic alliances' which threaten to smother the body politic. *Anti-Oedipus*, in other words, seeks to (re)discover the 'deterritorialized' flows of desire, the flows that have not been reduced to Oedipal codes and neuroticized territorialities, the desiring-machines, modelled on nomadic schizophrenic processes, that escape such codes and lead 'elsewhere'.

Second, in keeping with this reformulation of desire, the body too is reconceptualized, not simply as a (modernist) 'organism', but rather as a political surface of (de)territorialized intensities and flows: a body with-out organs (BwO). As Deleuze and Guattari explain, the BwO is the (non)place where an unlimited and unblocked productivity of desire occurs. As such, it stands firmly opposed to any 'organization' involving blockages and interrupted flows. While opposed to the organism, the BwO is not, however, opposed to the organs. Rather, it merely ensures its own, and their, opposition to the organism. From this we arrive at what is, perhaps, Deleuze and Guattari's most general statement of the BwO:

> The body without organs is the matter that always fills space to given degrees of intensity, and the partial objects are these degrees, these intensive parts that produce the real in space starting from matter as intensity = 0. The body without organs is the immanent substance, in the most Spinozist sense of the word; and the partial objects are like its ultimate attributes, which belong to it precisely insofar as they are really distinct and cannot on this account exclude or oppose one another. The partial objects and the body without organs are the two material elements of the schizophrenic desiring-machine . . . the two together in a relationship of continuity from one end to the other of the molecular chain of desire.
>
> (1984: 327)

These seemingly abstract Deleuzo-Guattarian notions of positive desire as a self-actualizing nomadic force, and the BwO as a political surface of shifting libidinal investments and intensities, have recently been taken up and developed, alongside the work of other writers such as Derrida and Cixous, by Fox (1993) in his critique of a modernist sociology of health and illness. Drawing on the Derridean notion of *différance*, Fox focuses on the undecidability of language and the endless 'deferral' or 'slippage' of meaning. As he explains, Derrida's analysis of difference builds on the discovery in semiotic theory that language constitutes meaning not in terms of the *essence* of a thing, but in terms of its *difference* from other things. Derrida, in other words, forces us to abandon any foundational search for 'real' essences, searching instead for 'the movements of difference which constitute the world' (Fox 1993: 8).

This notion of *différance* in turn keys into a second major problematic centred around the issue of *logocentrism* and the claims to '*presence*' it involves. Logocentrism concerns the claim to authoritatively 'speak the truth' about something, while 'presence', itself a closely allied concept, constitutes this 'unmediated' knowledge of the world: religion and science being prime examples. For Fox, the critique of logocentrism opens up a new problematic for a postmodern social theory, namely, '*how claims to presence are constituted in discourse*' (1993: 9).

This focus on difference and logocentrism enables Fox to organize his postmodern social theory of health (PSTH) – as opposed to a modernist sociology of health and illness – around what he terms the 'politics of health talk'. As he explains:

> The discursive character of health-talk, and in particular the expertise by which 'health' and 'illness' become inscribed on bodies, is available for analysis in deconstruction in terms of how it can make its claims to truth. But we are now faced with the position that the facticity of 'health' and 'illness' must be questioned: rather *they are highly contested, fragmented and fluctuating struggles for the body, constituted in the social, and resisted by desire* . . . the perspective of the PSTH is no longer to try . . . to enhance 'health' or limit 'illness'. *Health and illness turn out to be aspects of power/knowledge inscribed on the Body-without-Organs* and – in the era of ultra-oedipalization . . . – the symbolic familializing of health care.
>
> (1993: 43–4, our emphasis)

Against these various 'healths', Fox develops a form of 'resistance' which he terms 'arche-health' and 'arche-illness'. Arche-health, we are told, 'refuses to be reduced to language or discourse', and is best understood as the '*play of pure difference*, which, as soon as it becomes text, ceases to be "arche-health"' (1993: 45). As such, it is said to possess emancipatory possibilities which, in turn, are grounded in a broader postmodernist commitment to 'otherness' and an endless process of 'becoming'.

For our purposes, however, what is most important in all of this is the postmodern analysis of pain. Although allegedly a 'private' or 'inner' sensation, pain, Fox argues, has been problematically transformed through a modernist model of the 'fabricated' human subject within the sociology of health and illness. Key features of this 'modernist' model include a focus on the *meaning* of pain, one which 'fleshes out' the sociological subject as carrier of identity and biography, located at the nexus of structure/agency debates. In contrast, Fox's postmodernist position seeks to 'challenge' this ontology of the human subject and the character of the physical body as both creator and mediator of the lived experience of pain. For Fox, the anatomical body is not, in fact, the 'carapace of the self'. If the self *does* inhabit such an 'interior' location, then this is as a consequence of discourse, of a territorialization into 'the organism' – a body with organs. In contrast, following Deleuze and Guattari, Fox argues that the organism is an effect, a 'pattern of intensities on the BwO', which in the modern period is exemplified, *par excellence*, by medical discourse (1993: 145). From this 'decentred' perspective on the 'postmodern self', lived experience is simply the:

fabrication of a BwO, a political locus, stratified by discourse, desire and physical sensation (including pain). Pain – as sensation – has no implicit meaning. But a territorialization of the BwO as organism (creature of biomedical and more recently human sciences discourses) provides the possibility for pain to signify. Once it signifies in relation to the organism, it contributes to the self, to subjectivity. In this reading, it is not the self which experiences pain or attributes meaning to it, the self *is* the pain, the self is an effect of the meaning.

(Fox 1993: 145)

To put the matter another way, discourse on health and illness within the medical and human sciences contribute to a particular territorialization of the 'pained' BwO, organized in terms of the 'organism': a biomedical or biopsychosocial body with organs.[2] Similarly, the modernist focus on issues such as biographical disruption and the search for meaning and legitimacy merely serve to 'fabricate' a subject who is effectively 'trapped' within her/his 'pained' body and is required to 'adjust' or 'adapt' to the limitations this engenders. As a consequence, the effects of the disciplines of the body (including sociology) in constituting this kind of subject remain obscured (Fox 1993: 146).

In keeping with his general postmodernist stance, Fox's proposed 'solution' to this modernist dilemma of the (pained) BwO and the 'fabricated' human subject is to 'de-territorialize' the body without organs in order to facilitate 'arche-health' and the endless process of 'becoming'. As he reminds us, 'intertextual practices' make 'resistance possible'; a position which emphasizes the 'undecidability' of meaning, its continual 'deferral' or 'slippage'. Clearly, to the extent that postmodern/poststructuralist critiques are able to deconstruct existing conceptualizations of desire, subjectivity, the body and health, they have an important role to play in helping us move towards a new ethics of trust, intimacy and care: one grounded in a commitment to *différance* and 'otherness'. However, while modernist sociology comes in for considerable criticism, postmodernists and post-structuralists, in their quest for reflexivity and the endless deferral of meaning, appear rather less willing to examine the problems inherent in their own position. In particular, it is possible to raise at least five main objections to this postmodernist/poststructuralist position.

First, for an allegedly non-dualist position, it is notable how poststructuralist writers such as Deleuze and Guattari proceed by means of a series of conceptual oppositions including modernism/postmodernism, production/anti-production, the body with/without organs, schizophrenic/neurotic desire, hierarchical/non-hierarchical, static/ nomadic, smooth space/striated space, and so on.

Second, we must seriously question whether Deleuze and Guattari's BwO, itself a political surface of investment, is really much of an advance on the Foucauldian 'discursive' body. Indeed, despite non-dualist pretensions, postmodernism and post-structuralism still nonetheless prioritize a view of the body as a 'text', a surface without depth, through an emphasis on processes of 'inscription' and the (de)territorialization of desire. As a consequence, the materiality and coherence of the body are lost through a radically reconfigured ontology of fragmentation and flux, fluidity and flow.

Similarly, while the self is clearly social, the post-structuralist emphasis on the fabricated, decentred subject as a 'textual effect' without any (inner) core or essence, appears to neglect important elements of continuity and coherence across the biographically embodied lifecourse; issues which stem from the organic mooring of identity as the material vehicle of personhood. If, as Deleuze and Guattari advocate, we all become 'schizophrenic' in a process of Oedipal resistance, then where on earth would we be and how would anything be possible? Certainly, while both positions have their drawbacks, a 'neurotic on the analyst's couch' seems infinitely preferrable to a 'schizophrenic out for a stroll' (Deleuze and Guattari 1984: 1).

As Grosz (1994) notes, the upshot of this is the 'acidic dissolution' or 'de-massification' of the body alongside the subject (i.e. the process of 'becoming-imperceptible'); a position which, quite simply, loses too much in the 'process'. A similar fate, therefore, befalls the Deleuzo-Guatarrian and Foucauldian body: first it becomes elusive and eventually it 'disappears' altogether. Indeed, the dangers of this position are recognized by Deleuze and Guattari themselves when they acknowledge the need for some degree of 'organization' or 'coherence' to the BwO in order to prevent its complete disintegration or collapse. There must, in other words, be some 'pockets of subjectivity' and 'significance' left in order for the BwO to 'survive' (Grosz 1994). As they state:

> You have to keep enough of the organism for it to reform each dawn, you have to keep small supplies of significance and subjectivity, if only to turn them against your own systems when the circumstances demand it. . . . You don't reach the BwO, and its plane of consistency by wildly destratifying . . . if you blow apart the strata without taking

precautions, then instead of drawing a plane you will be plunged into a black hole, or even dragged toward catastrophe.

(1988: 161–2)

A catastrophic black hole indeed.

Third, following on directly from this last point, the postmodern/ post-structuralist commitment to the local and specific – a commitment which, it should be conceded, is also evident in certain strands of 'modernist' social theory – threatens to undermine other forms of praxis founded on the politics of collective identification. Ultimately, the decentring of subjectivity, identity, agency, translates into an equally problematic schizophrenic position which limits potential sites of collective political action and resistance based on a common identity and shared interests. The championing of difference, therefore, runs the risk of political indifference. 'Scream your own screams', 'Think your own thoughts' seems to be the message; anything goes if desire flows!

Fourth, returning to the above example, we must also confront the very real question of just how helpful, or indeed novel, is a postmodern analysis of pain? In constituting his problematic, Fox claims that he is not in any way concerned to enhance 'health' or limit 'illness'. Rather his aim is to promote a form of 'arche-health' and 'arche-illness' grounded in a process of intertexuality and resistance to control through the (endless) deferral of meaning. This seems fair enough, but would a person in pain, we feel compelled to ask, be reassured to learn that their suffering is really the product of a subtle play of power/knowledge on the BwO: a bio-medical territorialization of nomadic desire involving a fabrication of the subject and an ultra-oedipalization of care? Surely the answer to this is clear enough to all but the most hardened postmodernists. Ultimately, in keeping with Deleuze and Guattari's general advocacy of schizophrenic desire as a mode of resistance, the postmodern message seems to run as follows: don't call the doctor/therapist or run to the medicine cabinet next time you are in pain, opt instead for a de-territorialized form of 'arche-health': *vive la différence!* To this 'playful' deconstructive post-modernism we feel it is time to declare that the 'emperor' has no clothes. In truth, as Charlton (1993) rightly observes, postmodernism is really only an option for the healthy, not the sick. When we are ill, when the taken-for-granted relationship we have to our bodies is rendered problematic, we need the 'certainties', however provisional, which modernist medicine can afford. Seen in these terms, modernism is eminently preferable to postmodernism: an issue to which we shall return in the conclusion to this chapter when considering an ethics of care for people in pain.

Last, but certainly not least, it is equally clear that a concern to 'decon struct' essentialism and to transcend the dualist legacies of the past do not, in fact, necessitate a 'slide' into postmodernism or post-structuralism. Rather, a range of other anti-dualist traditions is available which appear equally viable as critical attacks on the disembodied Cartesian rationalist actor. This, in turn, raises other fundamental questions about just how new the postmodernist project actually is. At the very least it appears to share important elements of continuity with earlier versions of baroque culture in the seventeenth century; a movement which challenged new forms of Protestant asceticism through a revival of traditional patterns of political and social relations (Turner 1996).

In developing these issues further, we hope to show how traditional dualist ontologies, including the division between mind and body and the dismissal or neglect of emotions, can be overcome through an *embodied* approach to pain and culture within the sociology of health and illness. As we shall see, pain serves to highlight the 'discursive limits' of the body through its shattering of the self into a series of lived oppositions and its 'making' and 'unmaking' of the world. In seeking to 'flesh' out this anti-dualist, foundationalist ontology further, we begin therefore with a critical exploration of the lived body as an ongoing, pre-objective structure of lived experience; one in which mind and body, reason and emotion, pleasure and pain are thoroughly interfused.

PAIN, EMOTIONS AND THE 'MINDFUL' BODY (WITH ORGANS)

Pain is never the sole creation of human anatomy or physiology. Rather, it emerges only at the intersection of bodies, minds and culture (Morris 1991). Moreover, pain is never simply a form of physical suffering, but also encompasses emotional and affective dimensions, feelings which, in turn, are crucially linked to 'gendered' modes of bodily being (Bendelow 1993). In ancient Greek, for example, the word used most often for physical pain was *algos*, which derives from roots indicating neglect of love (Procacci and Maresca 1985: 201). Another Greek word is *akos*, meaning 'psychic pain', from which we derive the English word 'ache'.

Implicit in these meanings is a broader definition of pain than the narrowly defined Cartesian proposition which inevitably acts to divorce mental from physical states and tends to attribute single symptoms to single causes. Indeed, the notion of pain having a substantial emotional component, literally the obverse of pleasure, is much older than that of pain being a physiological sensation and can be traced back to Plato's

(429–347 BC) deliberations on extremes and opposites in the World of Forms. Literature, theology and philosophy abound with considerations of the nature and purpose of pain (among many others, see Tillich's *Systematic Theology*, vols 1–3, 1968, or Kierkegaard's *Works of Love* 1962 [1847]). Within these diverse traditions, the pleasure/pain dichotomy is constantly evoked and reinforced.

It is, however, Merleau-Ponty who has done most, perhaps more than any other philosopher, to overcome the dualist mind–body legacy of the past. For Merleau-Ponty, the central phenomenological task is to break with the 'critical attitude' which mistakenly begins with objects, and to 're-establish the roots of the mind in its body, and in its world' (1962: 3). Since the subject–object distinction is already a product of conscious reflection and analysis, Merleau-Ponty instead seeks to reflect upon the unreflected, the aim of which is to 'recover' or bring back to the centre of our attention and awareness that *pre-objective*, primordial relationship we have to our bodies and the world; one which objective thought loses sight of (Crossley 1995).

For Merleau-Ponty, the body can never simply be an object for itself. Rather, it is instead 'a spontaneous synthesis of powers, a bodily spatiality, a bodily unity, a bodily intentionality, which distinguishes it radically from the scientific object posed by traditional schools of thought' (Langer 1989: 56). This, as Vrancken puts it: '. . . is the "lived body", the body as subject, the embodiment which one is: I *am* my body. This body is not a body in itself, but a body through which the subject acts in the world' (1989: 441). Seen in these terms:

> Man [sic] taken as a concrete being is not a psyche joined to an organism, but the *movement to and fro of existence* which at one time allows itself to take corporeal form and at other times moves towards personal acts. . . . It is never a question of the incomprehensible meeting of two causalities, nor a collision between the order of causes and that of ends. But by an *imperceptible twist* an organic process issues into human behaviour, an instinctive act changes direction and becomes a sentiment, or conversely a human act becomes torpid and is continued absent-mindedly in the form of a reflex. Between the psychic and the physiological there may take place *exchanges* which almost always stand in the way of defining a mental disturbance as psychic or somatic. . . . *The union between soul and body* is not an amalgamation between two mutually external terms, subject and object, brought about by arbitrary decree. *It is enacted at every instant in the movement of existence.*
>
> (Merleau-Ponty 1962: 88–9, our emphasis)

As Turner (1992) argues, a phenomenology of the body, or 'embodiment', has particular importance for medical sociology, providing as it does a sensitive and sophisticated appreciation of issues such as pain, disability and death. From this perspective, human beings can be seen to have a dual nature; one succinctly captured in the German language by the terms *Lieb* which refers to the animated, living, experiential body (i.e. the body-for-itself), and *Korper* which refers to the objective, exterior, institutionalized body (i.e the body-in-itself).[3] This distinction between being and having a body expresses the essential ambiguity of human embodiment as both personal and impersonal, objective and subjective, social and natural. Moreover, it also serves to highlight the weakness of the Cartesian legacy for sociology, which has resulted in an almost exclusive treatment of the human body as *Korper* rather than simultaneously *both Korper and Lieb*. Indeed, in our view, it is this phenomenological emphasis upon the 'lived' body, one in which the objective body (*Korper*) is not treated as separate from the inner sensations of the subjective body (*Lieb*), which seems to have particular relevance for the sociology of pain as an 'embodied' emotional and affective experience.

As Leder (1984–5, 1990) argues, the normal taken-for-granted relationship we have to our body (what he terms 'bodily disappearance') tends to be profoundly disrupted in the context of factors such as pain, disease and death. Here the body becomes a central aspect of experience, albeit in an alien and dysfunctional manner. The body in pain, in other words, *dys*-appears (i.e. appears in a *dys*-functional state). Suddenly we may come to feel *dys*-embodied, alienated and betrayed by our bodies:

> (severe) pain . . . produces alienation, an existential vacuum; being cut off from the outer world, thrown back upon the body in itself, is isolation, disintegration, pain. . . . Immediately a dichotomy is brought about . . . through the unpleasantness of pain, the body and 'I' instantly seem to have parted company. For the sake of the integrity of our personality we make an 'it' of the body and an abstraction of pain. . . . Pain makes us believe that we can cut our*self* off from the body. Through rationalizing pain . . . 'I' and my body become two separate entities. Thus *pain can be depicted as the experience of psychophysical dualism.*
>
> (Vrancken 1989: 442)

In this respect, illness, pain and suffering affect what may be termed an *intentional* disruption (i.e. pain's intensity renders unimportant projects which previously seemed crucial) and a *spatiotemporal* constriction (i.e. self-reflection and isolation) of our lives (Leder 1990). Consequently, the body in pain emerges as an estranged, alien, 'thing-like' presence, separate from the self, which exerts a *telic demand* upon us. This telic demand can, in turn, be further subdivided into a *hermeneutical* and a *pragmatic* component. At the hermeneutical level, pain and suffering give rise to the quest for meaning, interpretation and understanding (see pp. 139–41), while at a pragmatic level, the telic demand of pain is to get rid of it or to master one's suffering; instead of just acting *from* the body, I act *toward* it in the hope of finding relief (Leder 1990).

The upshot of these arguments is clear. While at an *analytical* level the study of illness, pain and suffering demand the dissolution of former dualistic modes of thinking in drawing attention to the relatedness of self and world, mind and body, inside and outside, we must also confront and account for the enduring power and qualities of these dichotomies at the *experiential* level of suffering (Leder 1990). The sick body, in other words:

> menaces. It erupts. It is out of control. One damned thing follows another. . . . The fidelity of our bodies is so basic that we never think of it – it is the grounds of our daily experience. Chronic illness is a betrayal of that fundamental trust. We feel under siege: untrusting, resentful of uncertainty, lost. Life becomes a working out of senti- ments that follow closely from this corporeal betrayal: confusion, shock, anger, jealousy, despair.
>
> (Kleinman 1988: 44–5)

As Good's case study shows, rather than simply 'live through his body in the "world of everyday life" ', Brian, a chronic pain sufferer, has instead been 'taken over' by pain. In effect, Brian 'objectifies' his body and his pain as 'thing-like': 'when I think . . . I'm outside myself . . . as if my mind were separated from myself' (1992: 39). Alternatively, people in pain may seek relief by moving toward the opposite pole of increased subjectification of their suffering; one which is less concerned to reduce the power of pain by claiming its non-existence, than with attempting to (re)integrate the pain more closely with the self. In this sense, as Jackson suggests, pain confounds any simple subject–object dichotomy: 'Whilst the subject can be the conscious mind "having" an objective body and an objective pain, it is also true that the subject can combine with pain, becoming the "pain-full me" (perhaps contemplating a past or future "pain-free me")' (1994: 203, 207). *Objectification* and *subjectification*, therefore, stand in a *dialectical* relationship to one another. For the most part, however, people in pain see their problem as one of 'matter over mind' because the intractable nature of their condition makes them feel that their bodies are 'powerfully influencing' their minds. Many such people have found that their lives, their emotions, their spirituality, their personalities, their destinies shattered and dominated by their 'painful bodies' (Jackson 1994: 207).

The fact that body, mind and self are thoroughly interfused in pain, albeit in a problematic way, also points to another fundamental issue raised earlier, namely: that physical experience is inseparable from its cognitive and emotional significance. As we have argued elsewhere (Bendelow and Williams 1995a, 1995b; Williams and Bendelow 1996), the study of emotions requires a conception of the human body as a lived structure of ongoing experience (see also Denzin 1984). Indeed, the meaning and understanding that arises out of the universal human experience of pain can be used to describe not only physical agony but also emotional turmoil and spiritual suffering (Leder 1984-5). As Turner states:

> If we recognise pain as an emotional state, then we immediately begin considering the idea of the person as an embodied agent with strong affective, emotional and social responses to the state of being in pain. . . . [This draws] attention to a neglected aspect of the sociology of health and illness for which a theory of embodiment is an essential prerequisite for understanding pain as an emotion within a social context.
>
> (1992: 169)

Insofar as emotions entail both embodied feelings and cognitive orientations, public morality and cultural ideology, they provide an important ' "missing link" capable of bridging mind and body, individual, society and body politic'. In this respect, explorations of sickness, madness, pain, disability and death are human events literally 'seething with emotion' (Scheper-Hughes and Lock 1987: 28-9). Grief, for instance, is an example of emotional pain which is inseparable from its 'gut churning, nauseating experience', while physical pain bears within it a 'component of displeasure, and often of anxiety, sadness, anger that are fully emotional' (Leder 1984–5: 261). The study of pain, therefore, requires a conception of the 'mindful' emotionally 'expressive' body (Scheper-Hughes and Lock 1987; Freund 1990); one which oscillates precariously between unity and dissolution (Williams 1996c).

Gender, of course, alongside other factors such as class, age and ethnicity, is crucial here. Bendelow (1992, 1993), for example, in an in-depth qualitative investigation into these issues, found that both men and women attributed females with a 'natural' ability to cope with pain

lacking in men, and explained this in terms of their biological and reproductive functioning. For example, a woman stated:

> Women are made to suffer pain because we have periods and child-
> birth. Whatever social climate, women end up child-rearing, there-
> fore, they don't have the 'privilege' of giving in to pain and sickness.

Similarly, a man succinctly remarked:

> Women have more physical awareness – a more intimate and
> responsible instinct to their biology – all we do is shave!

While all Bendelow's respondents acknowledged or made reference to
the existence of emotional pain as a concept, men were more likely to
operate with mind/body splits in conceptualizing pain. Women, in contrast, tended to operate with a more holistic or integrated approach to
pain, one which acknowledged a sense of 'emotional vulnerability'. For
example, a woman stated:

> Emotions are definitely crucial to physical sensations of pain – when I
> can step back from what's going on and detach myself – when I can
> recognise that I'm more than this body that's going through its pro-
> cess in its own way. The body has a strong self-righting mechanism
> that when I can detach from it, I can let it work itself out, it can
> balance itself. I don't need pain-killers, but then also if you are in
> extreme pain and you don't have a strong enough sense of your own
> being as apart from your body, then it can just compound it. I have
> become interested in consciousness through this and I practise medi-
> tation – I think that an awareness is essential, not only for the health
> of the body but of the mind and emotions.

In contrast, a man commented:

> Of course there is mental pain as well, but in its true sense pain is
> physical – I mean they're not the same thing. I mean the pain that I've
> known has been purely physical sort of thing. I mean the other sort of
> pain comes through problems, but it's not related to the physical
> part. I suppose the few times I've been in jail I would say it's painful
> but not physically so.

Whilst emotions provide one way of 'healing' mind/body, self/society
splits, narrative and culture provide another: offering us a far richer,
more detailed and complete picture of the *dialectical* relationship between a foundationalist ontology and a social constructionist epistemology of the 'mindful' body (in pain). Hence it is to this key issue of the
'mediatory' role of narrative and culture that we now turn.

PAIN, NARRATIVE AND CULTURE: FROM FOUNDATIONALISM TO SOCIAL CONSTRUCTIONISM

As we have argued elsewhere, pain needs to be reclaimed from exclusive bio-medical jurisdiction (Bendelow and Williams 1995a, 1995b; see also Morris, 1991, 1994). People in pain need to find a *meaning* for their suffering, even if it is 'dysfunctional' from an orthodox (scientific) viewpoint. As Hilbert (1984) suggests, we need to find a 'natural home for chronic pain in culture'. Without such a meaning feelings of loneliness, isolation and despair may develop (Priel *et al.* 1991). Pain poignantly thrusts upon us questions such as 'Why me?', 'What purpose does it serve?' which demand answers. In this respect, pain is open to a variety of interpretations and meanings which go far beyond the sheer hurt of its physical presence. On the one hand, we may experience pain as a constriction of our essential possibilities and come face-to-face with our 'vulnerability, finitude and the untimely nature of our death'. As the very sensation of something wrong, or bad, pain may be identified with 'moral evil, the result of an external malignant force, or as punishment for our sins' (Leder 1984–5). Here, as Turner (1992: 252) comments, the concept of theodicy in Weber's analysis of religion (i.e. the classical problem of explaining a 'just' God in an 'unjust' world) addresses fundamental questions of meaning which, at the ontological level, are inevitably associated with shared aspects of our embodiment such as pain and suffering, sex and death.

On a darker note, it is also possible that the very meaning of pain may be the negation of all meaning. As Scarry suggests, pain may serve to 'deconstruct' or 'unmake' our habitual world, the sheer severity of pain may negate all interpretation: coming 'unsharably' into our midsts as 'at once that which cannot be denied and that which cannot be confirmed' (1985: 4). In this sense, pain may be seen as a pre-linguistic, unpleasant sensation which resists all meaning; something which is compounded by its invisibility (Jackson 1994: 213). Indeed, perhaps the main problem for those with chronic pain is that they are bereft of adequate cultural resources for organizing their experience, a situation which recalls Durkheim's classic concept of 'anomie' (Baszanger 1989). Pain, in other words, exists as a 'soundless scream', a 'solipsistic inwardness', involving 'psychic splintering' and 'disintegration', devoid of content, entirely cut off from the surrounding sociocultural world (Morris 1994: 13). Here, in this world of 'meaningless torment', sufferers frequently report that it is only fellow sufferers who can really understand their pre-object, pre-abstract experiences of pain (i.e. audit it empathically). This understanding, however, as Jackson (1994) argues is not achieved through the normal medium of communication (i.e. everyday language), but rather through intuitive, pre-linguistic modes of communication involving a *communitas* of mutual recognition and understanding The language of pain, in other words, becomes a kind of 'anti-language'; antithetical to ordinary everyday language, but a code nonetheless, which communicates something meaningful on a deeper primordial level (Jackson 1994: 213–14). This primordial, pre-linguistic level of pain, in turn, highlights the 'discursive limits' of postmodernist/post-structuralist accounts of the body, illness and disease discussed earlier. Pain as a malevolent, pre-social, primitive and primordial force, not only exists beyond but defies language, rendering all modes of discursive organization problematic: the 'limits' of the 'social', the 'return of the repressed'?

On a more optimistic note, pain may also signal something positive. It may, for example, bring us to an 'authentic recognition' of our own limitations and possibilities. It may also be 'creative', not only in the sense of childbirth but also in terms of physical, emotional, spiritual and artistic achievements, or it may serve as a 'catalyst' for much needed changes in our lives (Leder 1984–5). In this respect, pain may be actively used, instead of our falling passive victim to it:

> Constructive use of pain can only be achieved if we can see the pain as an ally – if we confront it. The natural response is to express; the social response is to suppress. Fearing it, distancing it, protecting ourselves from it, makes it stronger. The more you push it away the more it pushes its hooks into you . . . you need to confront it, enter into a dialogue with it, asking it what it is saying to you . . . anger can provide a substitute for pain, but may be used destructively rather than constructively . . . permanent anger is a stuck form of pain. What is useless is denial or avoidance of pain; we need, as Camus advised in *The Plague*, to root ourselves in our distress.
>
> (Carmichael 1988: 9)

Through a process of social 'narrativization', the individual is encouraged to turn the alien 'it' of pain and illness which imposes itself in such an unwelcome way upon our lives into a meaningful story which she or he tells. In this sense narratives are fundamentally embodied and are essential to the coherence of our lives and our selves. The objective of narrative is to render the 'contingency' and 'lack' in illness meaningful: 'When illness is told, its lack becomes producing, and as desire becomes producing, contingency becomes possibility' (Frank 1991: 88). The recurrent effect of narrative on physiology and of pathology on narrative combines feelings, thoughts and bodily processes into a single vital structure underlying continuity and change in illness (Kleinman 1988: 55). Bodies impose themselves on social categories just as social categories shape bodies: materiality and culture are therefore dialectically intertwined. Here we begin to glimpse the fact, contra Descartes, that reason, meaning and imagination are all fundamentally embodied (Johnson 1987) and that discourse itself exists in and through bodies and their techniques as a recursive communicative medium of exchange. By focusing on narratives one is able to shift the dominant cultural conception of illness away from passivity (i.e. the sick person as a helpless 'victim of disease') to activity, thus transforming 'fate' into 'experience', and joining bodies together in a 'shared sense of vulnerablity' (Frank 1995: xi). Stories, in short, like physicians, 'can heal', and it is through narrative that, in the absence of overarching metaphysical systems of 'containment', bodies are joined and transformed in their search for meaning, legitimacy and a lost ethics of existence (Frank 1995).

Additionally, of course, any investigation into the nature of pain must also include philosophical consideration of the capacity of humans to inflict pain on their own, and other, species. The need to understand how it is possible for one human being to stand beside another and to disregard that the fact that s/he may be inflicting agonizing pain is evoked as a central issue in Scarry's (1985) powerful linguistic analysis of *The Body in Pain*. For Scarry, torture is an extreme event parallel to war. The object of war is to kill people, whereas torture mimes the killing of people by inflicting pain; 'substituting prolonged mock execution for execution', which is made all the more frightening by its 'acting out' properties (1985: 27). By inflicting bodily suffering in this manner, pain destroys and replaces personal language with the objectification and 'deconstruction' of the body and the person. Arguing polemically, both torture and war may be regarded as essentially '*masculine*' phenomena (cf. Frank's [1991] 'dominating' body), counterposed to '*feminine*' ways of thinking, knowing, feeling and acting (cf. Frank's [1991] 'communicative' body, Theweleit's [1987, 1989] *Male Fantasies*. See also Belenky *et al.* 1986; Ruddick 1990.) Again, this highlights the importance of an approach to pain which is sensitive to the social construction and influence of gender (Bendelow 1993).

CONCLUSIONS

A central problematic of this chapter has been the modernist/ postmodernist debate over the body, pain and suffering. As we have argued, while postmodernist and post-structuralist perspectives do indeed have merit in challenging previous dualist approaches and pointing to the linguistic construction of the body and self as '(inter)textual effects', they also suffer from a number of limitations as a consequence of the prioritization of the social over the material, and of *representation* over *experience*. Given these difficulties, we have chosen instead to address the problems of essentialism, mind–body dualism, and the self, through an approach which seeks to combine a foundationalist (i.e. realist) ontology with a social constructionist (i.e. relativist) epistemology of the emotionally 'expressive', 'mindful' body. In doing so, our aim has been to explore the relationship between the lived experience of pain as a mode of bodily *dys*-appearance and the 'symbolic bridge' which narrative and culture provide between the immediate embodiment of disease as a physiological process and its meaning-laden nature as human experience (Kleinman 1988). As we have argued, bodies, healthy and sick, are real, material, recalcitrant entitities, which impose themselves on sociocultural categories, just as sociocultural categories shape bodies. Never simply a 'fabrication', human embodiment, including the structures of selfhood to which it gives rise, lies ambiguously across the nature – culture divide.

Doubtless, in advancing these arguments, postmodernists would claim that we have fallen into a variety of 'modernist traps'. Our account, for example, is simply another logocentric discourse on 'the social'; one which, in seeking to challenge postmodernism, claims an ontologically privileged presence by virtue of its association with 'the real'. This may, indeed, be so but, in the light of the critique developed above, some forms of knowledge, we would argue, are more useful than others. In taking this pragmatic epistemological line, our approach, we believe, offers a more satisfactory foundational account of pain as embodied human experience; one in which the shifting sands and incorporeal forms of postmodernism are rendered problematic. As suggested earlier, the playful deconstructions of postmodernism are really only an option for the healthy, not the sick, and while we too endorse the need to 'move beyond' the bio-medical model – thus helping 'reclaim' pain from exclusive medical jurisdiction – this does not mean throwing it out altogether, or losing sight of the practical role which modernist 'territorializations' of the BwO (as an 'organism') can play in the alleviation of human pain and suffering. To do so would clearly be premature and naive, not to mention inhumane.

Seen in these terms, while the (endless) pursuit of arche-health, the deferral of meaning and the commitment to (new?) forms of care based on the 'gift' (i.e. 'feminine' generosity and trust) as opposed to the 'proper' (i.e. 'masculine' control and possession) form an important intellectual basis for a reworked postmodern ethics of existence, any position which treats pain and the suffering self as modernist 'fabrications'/'intertextual effects' surely amounts, in the last instance, to an evasion of our responsibilities in the 'real' world, however constituted. Indeed, if social theorists themselves have difficulty getting to grips with the finer points of postmodernist/post-structuralist arguments, then what real hope does arche-health offer for people in pain? This, it should be emphasized, is not to concede that the sociology of health and illness should be uncritical of bio-medicine (i.e. return to a sociology *in* medicine), but it is to say that the perspectives it seeks to fashion, critical or otherwise, should at least resonate in some way with the everyday practical problems and experiential concerns of those it seeks to study.

These debates look set to continue for some time to come, as postmodernists fight a rearguard action against the reassertion of realist perspectives in contemporary sociological theory (Layder 1996). In this respect, perhaps a pertinent, if somewhat rhetorical, note to end on is to ask, in the spirit if not the 'essence' of Bradbury's (1989) fictitious anti-hero Henri Mensonge, who is a postmodernist these days anyway?

NOTES

1 For useful debates in medical sociology on the nature and status of biomedical knowledge, the body and disease see: Bury (1986, 1995), Kelly and Field (1994, 1996) and Williams (1996a,b,c).
2 In discussing pain and its territorialization of the BwO, Deleuze and Guattari use the example of masochism. As they state: 'What is certain is that the masochist has made [*sic*] himself a BwO under such conditions that the BwO can no longer be populated by anything but the intensities of pain, *pain waves* . . . that he engenders and augments.' The same, they claim, goes for the 'drugged body' and its intensities on the BwO of 'cold, *refrigerator waves*' (1988: 151).
3 Berger and Luckman (1967), and Plessner (1970), make similar distinctions, namely, that each of us *is* and *has* (i.e. experiences) a body.

REFERENCES

Baszanger, I. (1989) 'Pain: its experience and treatment', *Social Science & Medicine*, 29(3): 425–34.

Belenky, M., Clinchy, B., Goldberger, N. and Tarule, J. (1986) *Women's Ways of Knowing*, New York: Basic Books.

Bendelow, G.A. (1992) 'Gender differences in perceptions of pain', unpublished PhD thesis, University of London.

—— (1993) 'Pain perceptions, gender and emotion', *Sociology of Health and Illness* 15(3): 273–94

Bendelow, G. and Williams, S.J. (1995a) 'Transcending the dualisms: towards a sociology of pain', *Sociology of Health and Illness* 17(2): 139–65.

—— (1995b) 'Pain and the mind–body dualism: a sociological approach', *Body & Society* 1(2): 83–103.

Berger, P. and Luckmann, T. (1967) *The Social Construction of Reality*, London: Allen Lane.

Bradbury, M. (1989) *Mensonge*, London: Arena.

Bury, M.R. (1986) 'Social constructionism and the development of medical sociology', *Sociology of Health and Illness* 8(2): 137–69.

—— (1995) 'The body in question', *Medical Sociology News* 21(1): 36–48.

Carmichael, K. (1988) 'The creative use of pain in society', in R. Terrington (ed.) *Towards a Whole Society*, London: Richmond Fellowship Press.

Charlton, B. (1993) 'Medicine and postmodernity', *Journal of the Royal Society of Medicine* 86: 497–9.

Crossley, N. (1995) 'Merleau-Ponty, the elusive body and carnal society', *Body & Society* 1(1): 43–66.

Deleuze, G. and Guattari, F. (1984) *Anti-Oedipus: Capitalism and Schizophrenia, vol. I*, trans. by R. Hurley, M. Seem and H.R. Lane, Preface by M. Foucault, London: Athlone Press.

—— (1988) *A Thousand Plateaus: Capitalism and Schizophrenia, vol. II*, trans. by B. Massumi. London: Athlone Press.

Denzin, N.K. (1984) *On Understanding Emotion*, San Francisco: Jossey Bass.

Fox, N. (1993) *Postmodernism, Sociology and Health*, Milton Keynes: Open University Press.

Frank, A.W. (1991) 'For a sociology of the body: an analytical review', in M. Featherstone, M. Hepworth and B.S. Turner (eds) *The Body: Social Process and Cultural Theory*, London: Sage.

—— (1995) *The Wounded Storyteller: Body, Illness and Ethics*, Chicago/London: University of Chicago Press.

Freund, P.E.S. (1990) 'The expressive body: a common ground for the sociology of emotions and health', *Sociology of Health and Illness* 12(4): 452–77.

Good, B. (1992) 'A body in pain – the making of a world of chronic pain', in M.-J.D. Good, P.E. Brodwin, B.J. Good, and A. Kleinman, (eds) *Pain as Human Experience: An Anthropological Perspective*, Berkeley, CA and Oxford: University of California Press.

Grosz, F. (1994) *Volatile Bodies: Toward a Corporeal Feminism*, Bloomington and Indianapolis: Indiana University Press.

Hilbert, R. (1984) 'The acculturation dimension of chronic pain: flawed reality construction and the problem of meaning', *Social Problems* 31: 365–78.

Jackson, J. (1994) 'Chronic pain and the tension between the body as subject and object', in T.J. Csordas (ed.) *Embodiment and Experience: The Existential Ground of Culture and Self*, Cambridge: Cambridge University Press.

Johnson, M. (1987) *The Body in the Mind: The Bodily Basis of Meaning, Imagination and Reason*, Chicago: University of Chicago Press.

Kelly, M. and Field, D. (1994) 'Comments on the rejection of the biomedical model in sociological discourse', *Medical Sociology News* 19(2): 34–7.

—— (1996) 'Medical sociology, chronic illness and the body', *Sociology of Health & Illness* 18: 241–57.

Kierkegaard, S. (1962 [1847]) *Works of Love: Some Christian Reflections in the Form of Discourses*, London: Collins.

Kleinman, A. (1988) *The Illness Narratives: Suffering, Healing and the Human Condition*, New York: Basic Books.

Langer, M.M. (1989) *Merleau-Ponty's Phenomenology of Perception: A Guide and Commentary*, London: Macmillan.

Layder, D. (1996) 'Review essay on contemporary sociological theory', *Sociology* 30(3): 601–8.

Leder, D. (1984–5) 'Toward a phenomenology of pain', *Review of Existential Psychiatry* 19: 255–66.

—— (1990) *The Absent Body*, Chicago: University of Chicago Press.

Merleau-Ponty, M. (1962) *The Phenomenology of Perception*, trans. by C. Smith, London: Routledge & Kegan Paul.

Morris, D. (1991) *The Culture of Pain*, Berkeley, CA: University of California Press.

—— (1994) 'Pain's dominion', *Wilson Quarterly* Autumn: 8–26.

Plato (1978) *A Collection of Critical Essays, 1: Metaphysics and Epistemology*, edited by G. Vlastos, Notre Dame: University of Notre Dame Press.

Plessner, H. (1970) *Laughing and Crying: A Study of the Limits of Human Behaviour*, Evanston, IL: Northwestern University Press.

Priel, B., Rabinowitz, B. and Pels, R. (1991) 'A semiotic perspective on chronic pain: implications for the interaction between patient and physician', *British Journal of Medical Psychology* 64: 65–71.

Procacci, P. and Maresca, M. (1985) 'A philological study on some words concerning pain', *Pain* 22: 201–3.

Ruddick, S. (1990) *Maternal Thinking*, London: Women's Press.

Scarry, E. (1985) *The Body in Pain: The Making and Unmaking of the World*, Oxford: Oxford University Press.

Scheper-Hughes, N. and Lock, M. (1987) 'The mindful body: a prolegomenon to future work in medical anthropology', *Medical Anthropology Quarterly* 1(1): 6–41.

Theweleit, K. (1989 [1977]) *Male Fantasies*, vol. 1, Cambridge: Polity Press.

—— (1987 [1978]) *Male Fantasies*, vol. 2, Cambridge: Polity Press.

Tillich, P. (1968) *Systematic Theology*, Welwyn, Herts: Nisbet.

Turner, B.S. (1992) *Regulating Bodies: Essays in Medical Sociology*, London: Routledge.

—— (1996) *The Body and Society*, 2nd edn, London: Sage.

Vrancken, M. (1989) 'Schools of thought on pain', *Social Science & Medicine* 29(3): 435–44.

Williams, S.J. (1996a) 'The body in question: a rejoinder to Mike Bury', *Medical Sociology News* 21(2): 17–24.

—— (1996b) 'Medical sociology, chronic illness and the body: a rejoinder to Kelly and Field', *Sociology of Health and Illness* 18(5): 699–709.

—— (1996c) 'The vicissitudes of embodiment across the chronic illness trajectory', *Body & Society* 2(2): 23–47.

Williams, S.J. and Bendelow, G. (1996) 'Emotions and health: the "missing link" in medical sociology?', in V. James and J. Gabe (eds) *Emotions and Health*, Sociology of Health and Illness Monograph Series No. 2, Oxford: Blackwell.

Chapter 8

Ageing, the lifecourse and the sociology of embodiment

Mike Featherstone and Mike Hepworth

AGEING AND THE LIFECOURSE

In Western culture human ageing is seen as a process in which the body and the lifecourse are closely related in two significant ways. First, there is the issue of the biological finitude of the human body: increase in life expectancy means that more human beings than ever before grow old and death in old age is increasingly regarded as the norm. 'Dying on time' in hospital is in Western societies, and increasingly on a global level, regarded as the predictable terminus of a lifecourse of 70–90 years – the 'image of death alone in a modern hospital' (Seale 1995: 192). Second, this means that the biblical 'three score years and ten' are increasingly a reality rather than a pious ideal. The traditional imagery of the human lifespan as a series of ages or stages which decorated the walls of churches and the margins of sacred and secular books, for example in the Middle Ages (Dove 1986; Sears 1986), is no longer a sign of pious hope but a demographic reality.

The traditional Western conception of the lifecourse as a linear trajectory, and time as a finite resource, results in a conception of ageing as a one-way process:

> Western notions of an ageing process are based on several funda-
> mental assumptions about chronology. We organise our temporal
> perceptions by connecting the past to the present, and this to the
> future in linear terms. References like 'stream of experience', 'the
> march of time', 'time flies', and so on, convey the progression. . . .
> The linear, progressive lifecourse is an artefact of this chronology.
>
> (Gubrium *et al.* 1994: 35)

But because the 'artefact' of the lifecourse as linear and progressive is grounded in the biological limitations of the lifespan, it inevitably raises important questions about the nature of human embodiment and the boundaries between culture and biology. For some analysts of the social construction of ageing the 'body in decline' (Marks 1986: 181) is the final biologically determined limitation to human potential. Kathleen Woodward in her influential work on attitudes towards ageing and old age in Western culture returns frequently to the final encounter with 'the tension between the social construction of the body and the lived experience of the body, the facticity of the *materiality* of the body, the phenomenology of the body in advanced old age' (1991: 193–194). 'My guess is', she writes, 'that as we move towards the limits of old age – and that limit is death – we move towards the limits of representation' (1991: 194). In other words, when we survive into 'deep old age' the body becomes the bottom line: socially constructed differences such as race and gender blur and blend into the final triumph of the natural over the social: 'The difference of age is the one difference which we will ultimately all have in common, if we live long enough. The subject of ageing is one that belongs to us all' (1991: 23).

The finitude of the human body is also crucial to the sociological analysis of human ageing of Norbert Elias. For Elias the lives of human beings are subject, certainly in the present state of development of scientific knowledge, to biological limitations. There is only one realm of experience: the social world as a living experience albeit shaped by centuries of the 'civilizing process'. There is the 'simple reality of a finite life' (1985: 66): the body inevitably deteriorates with age and death 'hides no secret', 'opens no door' (1985: 67). When he wrote these words Elias was himself, as he movingly acknowledges, an old man. One of the tasks facing humanity is the age-old struggle to 'come to terms with the finiteness of life' (1985:1). A task that is both human and sociological.

The work of Elias is valuable in its acceptance of the human body as a limited biological resource. Although, in the model of the civilizing process, the body is historically determined and inseparable from the social, it never loses its materiality and therefore biological finitude. On the occasion of an interview given in 1984 when he was aged 87 he was asked: 'Is there a place where you would most like to die?'

> NE: No, the place does not matter; I should only like a painless death. When I become decrepit and of no use to anyone any more, I should like to disappear. But where that happens does not interest me.
>
> Q: And where would you like most to be buried?
>
> NE: That would no longer be 'I'.

Q: But sometimes people have very exact wishes on that point.

NE: Not I – I have not even thought about it. I am concerned with problems of the living, and I did actually write in one place: 'Dead people have no problems.'

(Elias 1994: 80)

Individual humanity is a collective historical construct persisting after death in the living memories of those who have been left behind.

Coming to terms with 'the body in decline' is therefore a central issue in contemporary society but this must not be taken to imply that in preceding historical periods, when life expectancy was in general much shorter and religious thought more socially dominant, people were necessarily more predisposed to embrace death and did not strive to prolong their lives. The history of prolongevity, as Gruman (1966) has shown, is evidence enough of the fear of death and the desire to prolong the pleasures of the material world. In his study of attitudes toward death in eighteenth-century France John McManners (1985) has shown how the comparative brevity of life did not necessarily diminish the fear of death, the intensity of grief over a bereavement, or make death somehow more acceptable than it is today. The difference was that an everyday familiarity with death fostered a much more fatalistic outlook. 'Compared to us', he writes, 'these folk faced heavy odds: they had none of our complacent expectation of a standard life span.' They could hope with the poets for time to suspend its flight and this 'permissible hope, so far as duration is concerned, was much the same as ours, except that theirs was barely permissible and ours is a confident assumption' (1985: 650). Even so, there is also evidence of changing attitudes towards the later part of life during the course of the eighteenth century:

When his wife died, and with his daughter safely married, one of the abbé Prevost's heroes retires, at the age of fifty, to a monastery, as a lay guest of the Community, withdrawn from society and mourning his lost companion. Yet after three years he comes out of seclusion to accompany the son of a great nobleman on an educational tour, and once back in the world, falls in love again. The story is a parable of the psychological change which was fulfilled in the second half of the century. Before they knew for sure that the pattern of mortality was improving, some of the affluent minority were abandoning fatalism about growing old and dying. Against logic, they were wanting to live longer, and they were discovering the logic to insist on enjoying life and being useful at a greater age.

(1985: 84)

In any discussion of the interconnections between ageing, the life-course and embodiment it is important to try to discover what is new about the fear of old age and the wish to prolong life in late twentieth-century society. Among the tangled web of historical continuities and discontinuities in the history of ageing and old age one issue stands out: the issue of the positive evaluation of youth and a revulsion towards or fear of physical decline. 'Preference for youth and antipathy toward old age are immemorial and almost universal sentiments', proclaims David Lowenthal in his authoritative survey of Western attitudes towards the concepts of age and history (1986: 129). And Margaret Morganroth Gullette (1988) returns a similar verdict in her careful cultural analysis of the emergence of the 'mid-life progress novel' in twentieth-century fiction. Until recently, personal progress in fictional literature (and in other forms of cultural expression) was equated with youth and youthful struggles to come to terms with the vicissitudes of life. The literature of subsequent years in the lifecourse tended to be one of psychological decline: an essentially pessimistic record of the psychological storms and stresses provoked by an increasing awareness of physical decrements. According to Gullette this pessimistic element in Western attitudes to ageing into old age is highly significant. It represents, she argues, espe-cially in high culture, an essential belief that reality is bad news: 'The consensus since ancient times has stacked the cultural cards in favour of grim assessments and prognostications' (1988: 147) and the majority of influential writers and thinkers have come to the conclusion that life is worthless:

> Although essentialism has been widely discredited . . . forms of liter-ary pessimism that rely on it have not thereby lost ground. For narra-tion, which needs the illusion of change, pessimism invented the plot of decline – simple, formulaic, an exercise in subtraction. Its prolifer-ation has been astounding – in novels, film noir, the detective story, and slice-of-life and minimalist fiction. . . . All of them rely on an alleged 'truth': that passing of time always, and inevitably, involves irreversible decay. Where personal time is concerned, ageing is the enemy.
>
> (1988: 150)

It is precisely in the struggle to reconstruct this cultural inheritance of pessimism that the element of difference between past and present atti-tudes towards ageing through the later period of the lifecourse may be found (Hepworth and Featherstone 1982; Featherstone and Hepworth 1989). It is in the struggle to move away from conceptualizations of ageing into old age as a melancholy process of decline towards a vision of life from middle age to the end of the lifecourse as a period enriched with distinctive creative possibilities. As a struggle against pessimism it inevitably engages the emotions for, as Joe Bailey has indicated, pessimism 'is the name we give to our gloomy expectations, to our self-conscious engagement in our own fears and dreads about what might occur . . . our trepidations and our social evaluations' (1988: 5). An optimistic, or to borrow Margaret Gullette's term, 'meliorist' alternative (1988: 150), is required if the structure of feelings and attitudes towards the ageing body is to be socially reconstructed.

In what is essentially a social constructionist analysis of the emergence of mid-life as a distinctive stage in the lifecourse, Gullette detects in the closing years of the nineteenth century and throughout the twentieth century a significant cultural process at work. For the first time, she argues, a concerted effort is made to challenge the dominant model of middle age as the beginning of an inevitable process of decline and to replace it with 'a new ideology of ageing' (1988: xi). Such an act of 'cultural prestidigation' (1988: xii) literally involves, as we have noted above, the invention of the mid-life progress novel where the potential for adult development and growth replaces the traditional ideology of the primacy and relatively fixed influence of child socialization. In the typical mid-life progress novel the ageing character is no longer trapped in the experiences of the past but faces the possibility of actively engaging with the processes of biological ageing in a struggle to sustain self-identity and discover new sources of personal power and strength. In proclaiming the 'idea of adult growth' is not 'an illusion' (1988: xxi) Gullette is implicitly pursuing the concept of adult socialization and personal change in adult life (Becker 1970; Glaser and Strauss 1971), and the broader and more nuanced interpretation of the concept of the life 'career' of the self (Goffman 1968) which emerged during the later 1950s and 1960s in the work of sociologists associated with symbolic interactionism:

The new consensus in serious psychodynamic theory is that development is probably a life-long process. This version of ageing is trying to displace a persistent older myth: that some essence (sometimes called 'human nature' or 'character ') gets *fixed* in human beings at a very early age. The progress fictions I describe and these theories have thus been developing along parallel lines. Indirectly at least, they must animate each other.

(1988: xxi)

Thus the 'safe' in being 'safe in the middle years' refers in Gullette's work to 'a state of mind, comprising skills and powers and certain attitudes towards time.' There is no completely guaranteed and permanent state of safety, because it is an 'attitude towards time, safety is always comparative' (1988: 24). In later work (1993) Gullette describes the processes of mutual animation which constitutes the 'new middle age' (Hepworth and Featherstone 1982) as a series of cultural 'intersections':

> Different voices – female and male, feminist and antifeminist, of various ages, speaking out of medical and sexual, economic and sociological context, publishing in diverse media – were at work making meanings out of *age*, *gender*, and *creativity*, at the multiple places where they were said to intersect.

(1993: 20)

The process of ageing from mid-life onwards envisaged by Gullett and others requires an acceptance of the body in biological decline but at the same time a rejection of socially constructed conceptions of concomitant social and psychological impairment. This does not mean the body ceases to age or to grow sick unto death but that an older person may be biologically reduced yet socially and psychologically secure. Ageing is not therefore a unitary process. Whilst the basis is regarded as biologically determined, biology is continually modified by culture and always open to reinterpretation and reconstruction. These arguments help to show how tricky the subject of the materiality of the human body is for sociologists. Whereas, for example, Elias sees the biological grounding of old age and the inevitability of death as natural (1985), although always mediated through the civilizing process, there are those who would detach the body entirely from biology and place it completely within the realm of culture. In his analysis of the social formation of gerontological knowledge, inspired by the work of Michel Foucault, for example, Stephen Katz (1996) sees the association between ageing and death as a form of discourse. Although human beings are subject to certain undeniable biological limitations the body is not so much a physical terminus as a kind of terminus in the circulation of power. Our knowledge of old age is essentially a social construct shaped by the desire of interest groups such as practitioners of geriatric medicine to make claims for a specialized form of knowledge and to legitimate the imposition of controls over ageing members of the population. Ageing and old age, as the subjects of knowledge, are known through the disciplines specifically created to separate them out from other bodily states such as pathology and disease. Knowledge is literally power. Gerontology, he writes, 'did not gradually and scientifically discover the secrets of age in the body but inherited a new vision of the aged body as a totality burdened with secrets requiring scientific discovery' (1996: 29). As a follower of Foucault, Katz does not explicitly deny the biological reality of old age or its ending in death but he does argue for a sociological interpretation of the body as open to conflicting and ever-changing interpretations. What is involved is an ongoing series of power struggles. And it is because human beings have the potential to resist the efforts of others to impose their will upon them that the ageing and aged body is a site of multiple meanings endlessly open to question and to reinterpretation. The modern notion of the ageing body as dying is therefore yet another discourse imposed by medical science.

While Katz has no alternative but to agree that the concept of a life-span limited to 80 to 90 years 'is obviously more realistic than one of 200 years' (1996: 45), he does argue that the intervention of medical science during the nineteenth century imposed a more restricted concept of the lifecourse on concepts of the ageing body than had existed during the pre-modern period. In effect doctors imposed scientifically legitimated interpretations of the ageing body as senescent in order to further the interests of their emergent profession. Old age came to be seen as a form of pathology and the body in decline became a medicalized reality:

> medicine decontextualised the body and situated it biologically in terms of time and space. In time the body was given a relatively fixed lifespan, one that was indifferent to a person's moral, social, or environmental contexts. In space the body became a fixed network integrating the cells, tissues, organs, and systems of circulation, respiration, and digestion. . . . On a second plane, medicine invested the body with the meanings of old age through a set of perceptual techniques that equated pathological disease, decline, and incapacity with the normality of the aged body. The attributes of old age and the aged body became entrenched indicators of each other's supposedly normal/pathological states.'
>
> (1996: 47)

The finitide of human life is not so much in dispute here as the social meanings given to the body and the pressures from the medical profession to claim a monopoly over definitions of the nature of human ageing. This struggle is essentially a struggle over narratives: the kinds of stories that can be legitimately be told about the experience of human ageing and, in particular, the relationship between the ageing body and the self.

What is most important from the point of view of the sociological analysis of ageing is that the power struggle envisaged by Katz helps to
legitimate and thus reinforce the traditional concept of life as structured
in terms of a number of predetermined stages. The triumph of modern
medicine over the pre-modern 'polysemic body' does not reject a structured conception of human life ordered in terms of a time-honoured
number ages or stages. It simply converts mythological and other forms
of imagery into medical or scientific knowledge. In this sense Katz's
Foucauldian analysis can be read alongside the work of Gullette and
other literary gerontologists who find in fictions of mid-life and old age a
challenge to the medically legitimated wisdom of ageing as inevitable
decline.

In this critical interpretation the traditional concept of the lifecourse is
transformed into a powerful resource for a multiplicity of everyday
efforts to make sense of ageing and old age. Subjected to biological
limitations, the lifecourse is transformed into a socio-psychological arena
of potentially positive creative energy. In certain respects the institutionalized framework of the lifecourse resembles the ticking clock in
Gubrium's review of the 'ordinary features of everyday life [which] provide the substance of meaning from which individual selves are constructed' (1995: 8). Referring to a wife's agonized deliberations over the
point at which she will have to put her increasingly frail husband in to a
nursing home, Gubrium records her references to the constant ticking
of the clock as a means of articulating her essentially subjective and
emotionally conflicting experiences of the exhausting wear and tear of
endless care:

> 'Winding down', we soon learn, refers to the gradual decline and
> eventual ill health of the care-giving wife who does not keep an eye on
> the proverbial clock, needlessly wasting herself away being the martyr
> for someone who has become the 'mere shell' of a former self. . . .
> The clock is a visible representation of a self that otherwise might not
> be readily communicated. Indeed, for some, the inner experience of
> no longer being recognised as a husband or wife by one's lifelong and
> now demented spouse cannot be put into words, shareable only in
> what 'plain words' cannot communicate, except in such modes as
> poetry, song, or story.

(1995: 14)

Like the ticking of the clock, the ages and stages model of the lifecourse
is a 'cultural cliché' (Gubrium 1995: 15). As such it is a shareable
cultural resource that can be reflexively drawn upon to give socially

meaningful expression to possibly complex and conflicting subjective experiences and emotions. Mundane and collective resources (including the literary resources in Gullette's analysis) are creatively utilized to communicate diverse individual selves in later life. The 'ordinary' is thereby reappropriated for self-reconstruction in the face of biological and temporal adversities.

THE SOCIOLOGY OF EMBODIMENT

It should be clear from our preceding discussion of key issues in the sociology of later life that ageing into old age raises important questions concerning the social construction of the human body. In particular, as we have previously noted, there is the thorny problem of the limits of the social. This is inevitably implicated in the persistent element of dualism in Western thinking about the body and the self. The dualistic belief in the separation of body from soul, reinterpreted through the thought of Descartes as a separation of mind from body, and more recently as an ontological difference between body and self, continues to exercise a strong influence over conceptualizations of human ageing and the struggle to replace negative images of decline with more positive conceptions of 'progress' in mid- and later life. Recent gerontological concerns over the tension between positive and negative forms of ageing can be approached through the sociological concept of embodiment.

In his book *Physical Being,* Rom Harré argues that bodies are more than biological entities with empirically observable properties but differ significantly from other material 'things' because of the part they play in the embodiment of personal and social identity: 'human bodies are the bodies of persons' (1991: 15). Rejecting a dualistic interpretation he regards the body and self as essentially interdependent although this seamless process of interaction is masked by an extensive range of 'separation practices' by means of which the separation of the person from the body is 'routinely accomplished' (1991: 15). Such practices include anaesthetization for surgery, ritually and drug-induced states of ecstatic disembodiment, and murder. Harré describes death as a 'terminal consequence of embodiment' (1991: 29), the 'biological fact of organic death, bodily decay and personal senescence can hardly be totally ignored by human beings'. Yet at the same time death in common with 'every other aspect of our embodiment . . . enters life through an interpretation' (1991: 31). Cultural interpretations of the meaning of life, death and the nature of what it is to be human are inextricably intertwined with the material facts of existence. Although the death of the body takes place within the temporal sequence of a determinate lifespan the biological lifecourse is only one strand of three. The life-course in its complexity also includes a 'social lifecourse and a personal lifecourse for every human being, each with its own beginning and end' (1991: 35). A complete understanding of the ageing process therefore requires a fully integrated knowledge of the composite strands of the lifecourse. Bodily and biological conditions enter human life through the interpretations that are made of them in different cultures and during varying periods of human history:

> A person's social identity may well begin before their bodily identity has taken shape in the parental definition of the child to come. And it may persist long after bodily identity has perished by the dissolution of death and decay of the body in funereal celebrations and, in some cases, enduring monuments. . . . Paradoxically, though conception and death are absolutes in the human time frame, they are external to our sense of ourselves and stand outside both social and personal being.
>
> (1991: 35)

For Harré, culturally prescribed 'separation practices' enable human beings to establish a distance between body, self, and society and to artificially disentangle what is in reality a seamless interactive web. Thanks to culture, the body can assume a different ontology from the self and those essential biological bench marks of the lifecourse, birth and death, can appear to be 'imposed, even cruelly imposed, from out-side on an essentially timeless consciousness' (1991: 35). Individuals can thus deceive themselves that they will live for ever.

But if the historical development of human beings is essentially a gradual process of symbolic emancipation from instinctual drives – an increasing dependence on the social rather than the biological (Elias 1991) – then the task of coming to terms with death inevitably becomes much more than an exercise in self-deception. It becomes, as Margaret Gullette (1988, 1993) and other constructionists have observed, not a denial of biological decline but an exercise in the *social construction* of the denial of the inevitability of decline. It becomes a denial of the valid-ity of an ideological preoccupation with youthfulness and the dissoci-ation of later life from the potential for positive change. The struggle is not therefore with biology but with specific cultural configurations of a process of psychosocial decline which it is presumed begins during middle age. And if the body is coextensive with culture, inseparable from it as Harré and others argue, then an opportunity would seem to exist, especially in modern/postmodern society, for the radical reconstruction of ageing through the lifecourse.

The debate over the limits of the social in the ageing process has been critically extended in recent feminist analyses of the social construction of gender as applied to the menopause. In the traditional imagery of ageing as a series of transitions from one biologically determined period to another the menopause or cessation of the capacity to conceive a child has been a particularly convenient peg on which to hang biologically determined theories of mid-life change (Featherstone and Hepworth 1985a, 1985b). Yet the precise effects of the gradual cessation of the capacity to conceive have proved impossible to isolate from their socio-psychological context and attempts to biologize and medicalize the menopause, though not without some success as the publicity over Hormone Replacement Therapy (HRT) indicates, have attracted considerable well-argued criticism from advocates of various branches of social constructionist thought. One of the most prominent of these is Germaine Greer whose book *The Change* (1991) provides an eloquent summary of the arguments against the belief that the loss of fertility signifies the end of an actively creative feminine engagement with the world. But the book is more than a cogent feminist critique of attempts by doctors to impose a masculine conception of gender where fertility is closely linked with femininity, sexual attractiveness and social worth. In pursuing this critique it also offers an alternative construction of the role of mid-life in the gendered ageing process. In other words, it is yet another example of the increasing movement to restructure the lifecourse and offer an alternative model of change to that of biological and socio-psychological decline.

In Greer's work the biological menopause provides an opportunity for women to reject the patriarchally imposed equation between fertility, sexual attractiveness, social worth and self-respect. It is regarded as an opportunity to create a positive rite of passage in the social space where there was nothing except a depressing invitation to the prospect of disengagement and decline. Such a transformation requires a new model of 'the ages of woman':

My definition of the seven ages of woman does not . . . correspond to Shakespeare's ages of man in all respects. Women's seven ages begin with the first critical phase or climacteric, which is birth and infancy; the second stormy passage is adolescence, the third defloration, the

fourth childbirth, and the fifth, menopause. . . . The fifth is exceeded
in significance only be the grand climacteric of dying.

(1991: 56)

The cessation of ovulation does not signal the end of being a woman, she
argues, but an opportunity to realize the full promise of the fifth age: of
femininity before it was curtailed in response to sexist beliefs and practices: 'the change back into the self you were before you became a tool of
your sexual and reproductive destiny' (1991: 62).

For Greer biological changes to the body of the ageing woman provide the stimulus for psychological and social liberation from male constructions of the ideal feminine body. Her ultimate vision of liberation
from biology is the sexless 'crone', an ideal type of post-menopausal
woman: 'the lucky ones . . . [who] lose interest in sex after menopause'
(1991: 337). The feminist interpretation of the word 'crone' celebrates a
reversion to the pre-Judeo-Christian conceptualization of the menopause as an affirmation of woman's harmony with the essentially cyclical
processes of nature (Walker 1985). The natural processes of ageing, a
biological truth, were to be embraced as a source of spiritual truth in the
shape of female wisdom. In her original form, before patriarchal religion
became dominant, the crone (subsequently transformed into the
'witch') was an embodiment of positive ageing. According to this natur-
alistic and matriarchal interpretation of the history of the lifecourse, the
wrinkles of older women are badges of honour; the outward physical
signs of a life which has realized its full potential. In Walker's reading of
history, to live out the entire lifespan of the pre-Judeo-Christian lifecourse is for woman to participate in a cosmic cyclical process: 'Ancient
cyclical images of the cosmos necessarily recognised a recessive period
in every cycle, since a continuously affirmative system (such as the
Christian notion of heaven) would cease to be cyclical at all' (1985: 12).

In Walker's influential analysis the cosmic harmony of body and self –
a form of holistic embodiment – is repressed with considerable force
when the patriarchal Judeo-Christian religion becomes dominant in
Western culture. The result is that the dualistic conceptualization of
body and soul/body and self replaces the earlier vision of integrity and
the process of human ageing is transformed into a series of ritualized
social practices producing the separation of self from body. This change
is epitomized in the proliferation of gendered images of the 'ages of
man' and the 'ages of woman' in both religious and secular culture
which have, as we noted above, become the predominant framework for
making sense of ageing into old age (Kammen 1980; Covey 1989). And,

according to the feminist analysis of the gendering of these processes, it is women who have most acutely experienced old age in the form of a biological mask repressing the self within (Featherstone and Hepworth 1993).

The emergence in recent years of a critical feminist sociology of the body has had a profound influence over the sociology of ageing. The specific attack on dualism and more generally on its origins within a patriarchal conceptualization of ages of man and ages of woman, has, as we have previously noted, been sharply focused on the issue of the menopause. In sociological analyses of the menopause two models, as Kwok Wei Leng has noted, 'stand opposed: the biomedical and the feminist' (1996: 33). The basic question is one of the nature of the relationship between the ageing body, the social and the subjective self. As such it is inevitably an issue of embodiment and brings us back to the point at which this chapter began: the nature of the boundary between the biological and the social. The difference is simply one of degree: the controversy surrounding the 'death of the ovaries' prefigures the final problem of the death of the body and the fate of the self.

In the literature of the menopause there is abundant evidence that the symptoms associated with the gradual cessation of ovulation are variable both within Western cultures and between Western and other cultures (Hepworth 1982). There can no longer be any doubt that the fact of biological change does not in itself cause the socio-psychological symptoms, positive or negative, which have at least since the latter part of the eighteenth century been associated with 'the change' (Wilbush 1988). Furthermore, sociological analyses of the increasing publicity given over recent years to the 'male menopause' have tended to reinforce the argument that it is the meanings which are given to biological changes in mid-life which are the crucial factor (Featherstone and Hepworth 1985a, 1985b). A moment has been reached where attempts to separate body from self and self from society no longer seem either analytically plausible or socially rewarding.

If attempts to analytically separate the self from the body and society are no longer intellectually defensible then what is the alternative? Sociologists of the body who combine feminist with postmodern critical theory argue for an approach to the problem of embodiment which takes into account the radical social and technological innovations characteristic of the late twentieth century.

If earlier feminist critiques of the bio-medical model of the menopause – cessation of ovarian oestrogen as the essential biological boundary between youth and middle age – looked to a prior concept of nature

unspoilt by patriarchal interventions as a source of feminine consciousness of the body growing older in harmony with the self, then a counter-
critique has more recently emerged which sets out to replace these two
opposing yet fundamentally essentialist models with a thoroughly sociologically grounded conceptualization of biology *and* nature. In her
summary of this line in sociological thinking Kwok Wei Leng argues for
a totally cultural understanding of the construction of the menopause.
She is dismissive of any social constructionist analysis based upon a
conception of a biological or natural basis:

> The trouble is, when we go to look for nature and its normal body, it
> is somehow never there. For one thing, the menopausal body itself is
> not as fixed as it is hoped. It has been known to wander about, as in
> the case of the woman of times past, who bred more and bled less,
> often moving smoothly from her last pregnancy or state of lactational
> amenorrhoea to menopause. For such a woman, the menopause as
> the last bleed never comes. Second, the menopausal body can inhabit
> the young woman: 'ovarian resistance syndrome', as it is known, can
> occur in women in their twenties.... But third, and most import-
> antly, the message ... is that there is no innocent natural bedrock
> that observation or theory can 'discover'. There is no natural body
> and by extension no natural menopause. 'Nature' is as constructed as
> anything else of human thought, such that nature is quite possibly a
> groundedness that we add *after* the event to ensure nothing less than
> the constructedness of culture.
>
> (1996: 45)

We began this chapter with a discussion of the recurring issue of the
human body as a finite resource. We noted the strong presence of a tragic
subtext in social gerontology where the central thesis is the problem for
both society and the individual of coming to terms with 'the body in
decline'. And we touched on the question of how the fact of the ageing
body (or more precisely bod*ies*) seemingly becomes even more urgent
with the ageing of the population and the mass increase in life expectancy. We also discussed evidence in literary gerontology of the will to
challenge the assumption that the ageing of the body is necessarily
accompanied by the ageing of the self and an inevitable disengagement
from active life. But we also noted the impact of postmodern feminist
critiques of dualistic conceptualizations of embodiment and, in particular, their potential for challenging the biological determinism of ageing
through a more deeply grounded appreciation of the essential cultural
interdependency of body, self and society. Any divide between nature

and culture has become increasingly difficult to defend in late twentieth-century society where the claims of knowledge disciplines to absolute authority and the boundaries between them can no longer be maintained. Advances in cosmetic and body-part replacement surgery, artificial intelligence, the Internet, and above all the cyborg, have led to a situation where 'the "leakiest" distinctions or boundaries are those between the human and the animal, the human and the machine, and the physical and the non-physical' (Wei Leng 1996: 46).

The implications for the sociology of ageing are clear: it is no longer possible to make adequate generalizations about the ageing process that are grounded on biological assumptions about the ages of life. Nor is it particularly useful to adopt schemata of the lifecourse based upon loosely conceptualized models of unspecified processes of interaction *between* the ontologically distinctive entities, body, self and society. As a consequence contemporary models of ageing into old age must be increasingly postmodern, by which we mean they must anticipate even more advanced forms of bio-cultural destabilization.

TECHNOLOGICAL FUTURES

What, then, are the implications of these changes for ageing, the lifecourse and the sociology of embodiment? First, the changes we have outlined imply an even greater diversity in experiences of ageing than has so far been postulated or empirically recorded. It is commonplace for sociologists to define ageing as a complex multidimensional process and the globally ageing population as diverse and heterogeneous. In their overview of 'ageing into the twenty-first century', John Bond and Peter Coleman refer to the impact of accelerating social change on the question 'What will social life be like when I'm older?' Part of their answer is especially suggestive: 'Perhaps it is the science fiction writers of today who would make the better attempt at predicting the future for elderly people' (1993: 340).

Yet if we look into the realm of science fiction a comforting vision of the future of ageing is by no means assured. One of the most obvious sources in this context is the influential 'cyberpunk' novelist William Gibson. The term 'cyberspace' was invented by Gibson (1986) to refer to an advanced combination of the Internet and virtual reality, which provides a three-dimensional space, a computer-generated world which permits a high level of sensory realism. Cyberspace, is not, however, a more advanced form of television; like the telephone it permits two-way interaction, but in this case it is not just voice interaction, it is full face-to-face interaction within a three-dimensional virtual space via a puppet-like simulational construct of one's body. The virtual world is a digital space in which bits of information are constructed into architectural forms: in effect financial, technological, military or archive data are given three-dimensional forms and assembled into 'data cities'. Cyberspace is the locus of corporate struggles to gain and protect information. Those who inhabit this realm, who can move with speed and ease amongst the data architecture, often develop according to Gibson a 'contempt for the meat', a profound sense of the limitations of the human body they are constantly seeking to escape.

In the world outside cyberspace there is a whole range of cyborg and post-human forms of life. The range includes humans who have undergone cosmetic surgery (youth culture groups with identical 'Sony Mao face'); cosmetic animal transplants (canine toothbud transplants again used by youth groups as identity styles or weapons), prosthetic device implants (the 'razorgirl' Molly Millions, who has cat-like retractable surgical steel scalpel blades grafted into her nails as well as custom-made wraparound dark glasses fixed to her eyesocket bone-structure which combine infra-red night and telephoto zoom-lens vision, with a computer screen data read-out/video link/playback function); memory chip implants (Johnny Mnemonic, whose brain is used as a data store for computer data); cloning (the Tessier-Ashpool family, which runs one of the major multinational corporations has cloned some of its members – e.g. CJane3); cryonic suspension (the head of Tessier-Ashpool is frozen and revived numerous times, as is the Ninja, the Japanese martial arts expert in Johnny Mnemonic, who is thawed out only to complete a specific task); artificial intelligences (which run multinational corporations and which can take on the disguise of human form in cyberspace). This is a world in which the rich are able to repair or replace any body part which under-performs as well as upgrade the human senses with prosthetic devices (the central character Case, in Gibson's first cyberpunk novel *Neuromancer*, is saving up for a new liver in order to cope with the toxins which are poisoning his body). The poor, on the other hand, face a life with a very different sense of embodiment, the vulnerable biological body constantly open to the dangers of violation, destruction and disease without recourse to the power resources to hold these forces at bay.

William Gibson's (1986, 1987, 1988) cyberpunk trilogy offers a dystopian perspective on technological changes. A fascination with technology coexists alongside a loss of the belief that technology will be able to offer a solution to all our personal and social problems. This contrasts with the predominant Western view of technology, which, since the onset of modernity, has granted technology a redemptive power. In effect the faith of modern societies in scientific and technological process, the idea of an upward curve of development inevitably transporting us in the direction of a better world, has a religious quality to it. This is the argument made by Vattimo (1988) that modernity's notion of progress leading to the perfectibility of human beings and society is merely the secularization of Judeo-Christian notions of redemption and salvation. In the United States in particular, technoscience, it is argued, is a millenarian discourse about beginnings and ends, about suffering and progress (Haraway 1997: 10). It contains powerful images of how nature, the human body and the social world can be re-made and reconstructed. The term 'technicity' captures this Western concern for construction and reconstruction: it amounts to a reduction of all essential qualitative differences to codes (molecular, genetic or digital) so that the basic building blocks of life and culture can be discovered.

When, therefore, we consider the relationship between technology and the ageing body, we discover a strongly divided reaction. On the one hand there are those who see technology as capable of solving all the problems of the ageing process, coupled with the belief that human beings will eventually possess the capacity to reconstruct the human body in a range of post-human forms. The alleged fixities and limits of the body, the lifespan, cellular decline and death itself, can be reconstructed. On the other hand there are those who advocate the acceptance of the limits of the body and the ageing process as producing its own positive gains. To accept and redefine the loss of fertility, sexuality and physical attractiveness as an opportunity (as for example in the writings of Germaine Greer [1991] on the menopause), is to promote a particular image of the natural lifecourse as a healthier and more appropriate way to live. The natural truths of biological ageing should not be resisted and the cessation of the menses should be welcomed as opening up the possibility of a post-sexualized later life and the life-enhancing benefits of spiritual wisdom. But the problem with this approach is that it reifies a particular cultural image of the natural body. It adopts a negative attitude towards technology, in which HRT and other forms of medical intervention are viewed not only as unnatural but also as perpetuating a subservient image of womanhood. The potential of women to integrate technology into their bodies as a source of positive empowerment is not addressed or is pessimistically dismissed. Perhaps this is because those who advocate a return to the natural body operate with too powerful a dichotomy between nature and culture coupled with a chronically suspicious attitude towards technology. Yet it can be argued that this form separation is no longer valid. Technology does not have an existence outside or beyond nature and culture. Increasingly, all forms of cultural production are fed through technology. All culture is in effect technoculture. Our capacity to make sense of the body, to map the limits of the ageing process, is not only conducted through discourses produced increasingly via technological means (using computers to write, access databases, view three-dimensional models or photographic or moving images of bodies), they are also interfused with powerful technological images of the flexibility and mutability of the boundaries and limits of the body.

If we consider the relationship between human beings and nature, it makes sense not to see technology as a detached third external factor. Instead we need to see the relationship as one in which nature and human bodily nature become transformed through technology; as nature, the human body and culture as dynamic processes. Through technology human beings can not only develop modes of theoretical and practical knowledge which enable them to control and dominate nature and their own bodies, the transformative process is also one which involves acts of fabrication. Technology should not be regarded simply as a set of tools or techniques for the efficient domination of nature, rather, technology unlocks the potential of human beings to create new forms of constructed natures. To make nature anew is one of the dreams of technology in the Western tradition. Technology ceases to be merely tools which can be picked up and abandoned when obsolete, technology enables human beings to reconstitute and fabricate new environments, or worlds, which they can then inhabit.

It follows that it makes sense to conceive not of one single nature, but of a series of natures. It is best to imagine natures as part of a process entailing a number of major stages which have acted as time–space environments or worlds, which necessarily act as horizons which delimit and structure the possibilities for social life. The first nature is the original nature, the ecological biosphere which envelops and resists us. Here nature is seen as 'that which cannot be produced'. The second nature is the technosphere, the anthropogenetic domain of the built environment and material urban landscape which human beings have created and inhabit. The third nature is the cybersphere, a second anthropogenetic domain, but in this case the structure is built from 'bits', not atoms, to produce the digitalized information world (the Internet, cyberspace, virtual reality) (Luke forthcoming). The fourth nature is the sphere of artificial life, a post-anthropogenetic domain; a domain in which the genetic structures of life-forms are reduced to an information code which can be replicated, manipulated and engineered to reproduce and make new life. These new life-forms will inhabit and introduce complexities into any of the three previous domains of nature – new plants, new animals and eventually humans.

If we focus on the emergence of the 'cybersphere', the shift in our mode of representation to one produced primarily through computers not only increases the amount of information at our fingertips through access to databases and the Internet, it also changes the form in which the information is presented. We are used to getting information about our bodies and the ageing process from a number of popular culture sources such as newspapers, magazines, television, which tend to develop unified mass audiences. Our previous writings on the role of the body within consumer culture, with its predominance of images of youth, fitness and beauty which encouraged older people to strive to retain the positive youthful images of ageing, was based on this assumption of the extension of mass audiences (Featherstone 1982, 1991; Hepworth and Featherstone 1982). The new information technology, on the other hand, threatens to reverse this process. Not only has it the potential to produce multimedia forms which digitalize and merge together text, sounds, music, images and video images into new forms, it is unlikely that we will use these forms in the old ways. The volume of different types of product available, and the speed with which they can be accessed or downloaded, from the Internet and various databases, means that people will rarely be using the same material at the same time. Selectivity, how to choose what to see and navigate where to go on the Internet, becomes the main problem.

Furthermore, the traditional linear narrative form for reading text, or watching a television programme or movie, is superseded as digitalization means that all forms can be reduced to flows of 'bits' and can easily be broken down into 'chunks', which can be hypertexted and accessed in any order. The experience becomes one of jumping across and out of texts and image-sets, leading to a more fragmented and complex experience of reading/viewing. This is something which currently is experienced through CD-ROM, but, with increasing use of three-dimensional data architecture and moving images on the Internet, it can be made into a feature of the organization of many different types of information. This capacity to select and navigate one's own route through a 'sea of data', means a greater level of interactivity, something which is compounded by the fact that the Internet shares many of the capacities of the telephone as opposed to the television. In effect, the one-way process of the old mass media gives way to two-way interaction: we will be able to speak to, engage in textual exchanges, rewrite and restructure the material we view, or see the other person or set of interactants in near full co-presence in the new multimedia forms. Textual and cultural production will be less 'signatory' or authored and take on a more transitory and impermanent status as the familiar gap between cultural producers and consumers recedes.

If our capacity to produce and consume culture is increasingly mediated by information technology to the extent that we have to speak of a 'technoculture', then how will this affect our perception of the body and the ageing process? In the first place, we will potentially have access to a good deal of previously unavailable information about our own bodies and the human body in general. While questions of access to medical records and databases are controversial issues, the new technologies and the Internet are often seen to represent a democratic potential for deprofessionalization and a greater potential for wider access to information. The capacity for self-monitoring the body, collecting and feeding in information on height, weight, blood pressure, heart rate and projecting this into digitalized image-based systems whereby one can see one's own bodily changes through the ageing process, will increase. Hence there is the potential for greater reflexivity about one's body. A good example is the Visible Human Project (VHP), a digital anatomical atlas created by the National Library of Medicine in Maryland, USA. For the first time an accurate three-dimensional digitalized human body has been created, an exact replica complete in every detail which can be viewed through a computer display screen. The VHP project is a medical technology which has obvious uses in surgery and medical pedagogy, yet its availability on the Internet also has potential to modify lay perceptions of the body, both by taking the viewer away from the sticky, visceral, fleshy body and in the way that the perpetuation of the digital body bypasses the question of physical death (Walby 1997).

This points towards a second development, in which information technology is not used to further individual understanding of the actual body but more to escape from its limitations. A good deal has been written about the capacity of the Internet and cyberspace to offer forms of intimate friendship with distant others. In the absence of the co-present body, it is alleged, there are greater possibilities to 'really get to know a person'. The misleading social markers inscribed on to bodies – the signs of gender, ethnicity, class and age – are no longer visible in the more anonymous interactions of the Internet (Featherstone 1995b; Turkle 1995). For the ageing individual the possibility exists of escaping from some of the stigmata attached to the visible signs of the ageing body: the social distaste for the frailty, wrinkling, the loss of mobility, and impairment of vision, hearing and speech, which are often regarded as distressing consequences of the ageing process. Interactions through multi-user domains (MUDs and MOOs) and e-mail not only hold out the promise of anonymity, but also offer the potential for disguise or what has been referred to as computer cross-dressing.

With the replacement in the next few years of the current hypertext language of the Internet (HTML) by virtual reality modal language (VRML), we are taking the first steps towards turning the Internet into a cyberspace medium. There will be a greater capacity for exchanges which are not textual but involve interactions between simulations of one's body. In effect one individual will be able to interact with highly realistic digitalized constructs of the human body, which permit each party in the interaction to receive an almost complete range of sensory information (body language, tone of voice, posture and other cueing devices) which are unconsciously absorbed and used as auxiliary sets of information to clarify the intentions of the spoken words of another individual. At the same time there need be no guarantee that the simulational construct of the individual one interacts with is an accurate representation of the other's actual living body. It could well be the case that one participant has chosen a younger body, or different gender or ethnicity. Hence the developments of networked computers will, like the telephone, enhance flexible interactivity and feedback. Yet the difference is not simply the addition of a visual dimension, transforming the telephone into a videophone; it represents two qualitative shifts beyond this.

First, one does not watch a screen, but is co-present with a simulation of the other person and oneself in a three-dimensional virtual space which provides a strong sense of realism and immersion. Second, the simulation of oneself will follow all the gestural and body language of one's actual body and translate this into the actions of one's simulational body in the virtual environment. Yet as the virtual body is a digitalized construct, it can easily be modified and reformatted. In short, it is not produced in the analogue manner of a photographic image, it is a three-dimensional digitalized data construct whose base characteristics can be easily restructured. One could therefore adopt a James Dean or Marilyn Monroe body into which one mixes one's own body language, voice and gestures. This capacity to 'morph', which was used in the film *Jurassic Park* to produce realistic simulations of dinosaurs, has also been used in other movies with human beings. A digitalized data construct of the body of Brandon Lee, the star of *The Crow*, who died in shooting, was produced to enable the film to be completed. On an experiential level this not only enhances the capacity to masquerade, to have a repertoire of different representations of one's self to use in virtual interactions with others, it could also result in the capacity to construct and preserve a digitalized image of oneself or one's partner, to be used in 'interactions' after death.

While the new information technology developments will, therefore, offer a range of 'out of body' or 'post-body' experiences and new possibilities for representation and masquerade, it is important to stress that the effects of the computer digitalization of information will be more widespread. If the definition of a cyborg is a human–machine hybrid, then on one level to drive a car or use a computer is to integrate the human body into a machine system (Fuchs 1995; Featherstone and Burrows 1996). One of our most powerful images of the cyborg draws on the successful Hollywood movie *Robocop*, in which the hero's body is completely rebuilt with machine parts. The capacity to introduce machines into bodies to increase the efficiency of internal functioning and motor performance will clearly expand with the development of more sophisticated medical technology. Yet, it has also been argued that we are on the verge of a further breakthrough with the development of nanotechnology. This is based upon molecular engineering, the capacity to build miniature machines, which can rapidly and cheaply assemble molecules from atomic elements. Not only would we be able to recycle all matter, we would also be able to place miniature machines inside the human body, to repair organic functioning, or to roam the blood stream to detect and remove viruses and other threats to the body (Crandall 1996). Here is a further example of the breakdown of the boundary between the organic, the machinic and the human, which points in the direction of the post-human.

A further key feature of the new technology is the fact that all forms of engineering and technology will be developed through information technology. Nanotechnology will work through computer programming and information technology systems. Information technology is becoming the key technology, which will make all other technologies possible. It is therefore possible to conceive of information technology as a meta-technology.

If it is becoming increasingly impossible to conceive of culture and the body as independent from information technology, then we should beware of assuming that this will necessarily result in a linear development with a new unified form of technoculture, or embodied lifecourse being followed by all. Rather, we should be aware that the modes of implementation of technological change are necessarily uneven and currently depend upon the social and economic priorities of governments and corporations. In the current phase of global economic development characterized by marketization, deregulation and fluidity of capital flows, the bio-technological and information sectors have been defined as 'leading edge' and are attracting high levels of investment. Yet this does not mean that governments, non-governmental organizations and agencies, consumer groups and social movements which operate in the public sphere cannot seek to impose the ethical and social cost criteria associated with the 'risk society' (Beck 1992).

The Internet itself has the potential to play an important role in the development of public debate and the posting of alternative information about the uses of technology. In addition, the sense that the Internet, like the telephone, facilitates two-way and multiple interchanges, has a democratizing potential and can open up discussion of a series of issues on ageing and the lifecourse including critiques of the medicalization of ageing and the development of alternative models of normal ageing. The experience of social movements in the United States that successfully fought to change both the definition of AIDS as a terminal condition and the nature of the medical care offered to AIDS patients is a good example. They challenged not only the assumption that patients would be dead within two years, but also the conventions of the medical secrecy and depersonalized patient care. It showed the ways in which bureaucratic and administrative conventions are often incorporated into and hide behind seemingly impartial medical judgements.

As the term 'cyberspace' suggests, the new medium provides a new space which is highly relevant to the conceptualization of the ageing process. In all analysis and discussion of ageing and the lifecourse, the focus is inevitably upon time and diachronic change. Ageing is always conceptualized in terms of images of the temporal changes to which human bodies and selves are subject: all life-forms are perceived as essentially temporal and defined by the running down of the life clock. At the same time, bodies are tangible material entities that necessarily inhabit space and it has recently been argued that in many ways the spatial dimension of social life has been largely taken for granted (Soja 1996). Developments in information technology, however, add a particular twist to the relevance of space for our understanding of the embodied lifecourse. On one level it transports us out of the lived spaces we conventionally inhabit into the new form of virtual spaces within which we can interact with other people. It can therefore compress or collapse the physical space which has hitherto separated us from others in different parts of the world.

Traditional notions of identity and the belief that the lifecourse involves the well-regulated stages of development discussed at the beginning of this paper (childhood, youth, early adulthood, etc.) was implicitly based upon a particular conception of space. In order to develop an identity an individual occupied a social space within which age-related patterns of social relations were enacted, a process which required some sense of shared culture and a common set of sentiments and feelings which became inscribed in bodies through common practices and rituals. Identities developed in relation to shared moments of feelings in the flow of social activity – what Vico called 'commonplaces' (Shotter 1993: 135).

It can be argued that the unfolding dynamic in the movement from modern to postmodern societies, coupled with the greater mixing and fluidity of cultural flows through globalization, has meant that our identities are less grounded in commonplaces – indeed our attitudes towards shared moments have become increasingly ambivalent. Mobility and the possibility of identity change, of gathering new experiences from different places, has become an important additional theme alongside this process. Tourism is about to become the world's major industry. The developments in transportation technologies which rapidly move us around the world, have also been paralleled by developments in information communication technologies which rapidly move images and information. What are the effects of this increased mobility on the process of identity formation across the lifecourse?

On the one hand it has been argued that the use of computer technology involves a move away from stable identities towards more fragmented multiple selves, a transformation which fits in with the notion of postmodern identities (Turkle 1995). The Windows system used on most PCs involves the capacity for 'parallel processing', carrying out a number of discrete tasks at the same time. The hypertext structure of information programmes which are becoming increasingly common on CD-ROMs, in PCs and the Internet also encourage increasing mobility and less rigid ways of handling information and learning. As we have already mentioned, bulletin board discussion groups also encourage the more playful adoption of multiple selves.

In the 1950s psychologists operated with the notion of the need to work towards an integrated and stable identity where multiple selves were regarded as dangerous. The notion of a life cycle involving steady progress through a series of pre-defined stages, with life as a *Bildungs-*

process or educative self-formative process in which the self becomes developed in a more balanced and mature manner, is central to many of the models of lifecourse development from Erikson down to Levinson. It is also found in popular self-help manuals and advice books. The bestseller *Passages: Predictable Crises of Adult Life* by Gail Sheehy (1977) popularized the work of Levinson and others, inviting ordinary people to reflect on their lives and to 'develop' and change. Yet in the 1990s one of the popular advice books to emerge from the United States was Mary Catherine Bateson's *Composing a Life* (1990) which characteristically comprises a mix of biography and autobiography and many of the contemporary literary and social science commonplaces shared by college-educated people. Completely absent from the book were recommendations to follow a continuous idealized life cycle. In their place the process of transition through the lifecourse was presented as 'an improvisatory art' involving a cultivation of the capacity to adjust to discontinuity (Shotter 1993: 188).

In 1950s sociology, too, the problem of being between cultures, what was referred to as 'the marginal man', was seen as potentially dangerous with the possible negative outcomes of anomie (the dreaded 'normlessness') and role confusion. Whereas in the past an individual caught between two cultures was advised to make a commitment to one of the alternatives, in contemporary society the intensified flows of people around the world and the trend towards multicultural societies mean that for some the plural self is seen as a positive bonus as the terminological shift from 'halfies', to 'doubles' indicates (Featherstone 1995a). This is of course nothing new; modern societies have always contained models which advocate the need for stable identity development and the dangers of normlessness alongside more antinomial models of the benefits of the nomadic life found, for example, in many strands of artistic modernism. It can be argued that, with the developments of consumer culture, globalization and the technological changes we have discussed, the latter model has become a more powerful strand of everyday life. Certainly, with travel and tourism becoming more popular, not least among those who are retired and in late life, there is a persistent sense that movement to new places will provide valuable and transformative experiences. The movement away from one's accustomed place, translating one from the commonplace, is no longer a regenerative strategy of the privileged few and is something more widely sought by new middle-class groups and others. One's sense of self, one's sense of the nature and possibilities of both one's self and body, are no longer seen as constants, nor are they regarded as merely the outcome of chronological changes; they are also seen as a function of place.

One example can be found in Glenda Laws's (1995) observations about the Sun City retirement communities in the United States. In this work the author makes significant connections between embodiment and emplacement. The identities of the retired residents, she observes, are inscribed not only on their bodies but also, and equally significantly, created in the 'separate landscapes for older people' known as 'Sun City' (1995: 254). Such landscapes make an important contribution to the social construction of the postmodern lifecourse. As sites of consumer culture, retirement communities like Sun City separate out older members of society and dissolve their traditional ties with other generations. Their ageing bodies are thus located in a specially landscaped space, a social arena which calls for consumerist styles of embodiment and a detachment from traditional roles. The transference of older bodies from their traditional households and collective emplacement in a specially built physical environment initiates a new set of meanings for retirement and offers a new package of expectations in later life:

> it is interesting to ask how this spatial separation of the household has re-presented the respective roles of household members, roles which often depended on particular and emplaced images of the body: the nurturing mother in her suburban home, the sprightly older aunt in her Florida condominium, the doddering grandfather in the nursing home. In her account of the lives of residents of Sun City Centre in Florida, Frances Fitzgerald notes that dependence on children is seen as a weakness, so much so that it is represented in the language of disease: 'a woman going north to be with her children and grandchildren is said to have "gramma-itis"' (1986: 242–243). Such a condition can be fought, just as the debilitating effects of arthritis or osteoporosis can be staved off with the right lifestyle adjustments . . . older 'independent' people with 'frail' bodies who might need assistance with the 'activities of daily living' can purchase such assistance from a range of visiting nurses and home help programmes. The notions of an 'independent body' in an 'independent environment' are thus fluid.
>
> (Laws 1995: 258)

Our increasing capacity to move between and inhabit different geographical spaces, coupled with our increasing use of the capacity of information technology systems to move us in and out of the virtual spaces of cyberspaces, therefore, leads to a sense that the singular bounded spaces of culture and the lifecourse are becoming undone.

REFERENCES

Bailey, J. (1988) *Pessimism*, London and New York: Routledge.

Bateson, M.C. (1990) *Composing a Life*, New York: Penguin Books.

Beck, U. (1992) *Risk Society*, London: Sage.

Becker, H. (1970) 'Personal change in adult life' and 'The self and adult socialisation', in *Sociological Work: Method and Substance*, London: Allen Lane/The Penguin Press.

Bond, J. and Coleman, P. (1993) 'Ageing into the twenty-first century', in *Ageing in Society: An Introduction to Social Gerontology*, 2nd edn, London: Sage.

Covey, H.C. (1989) 'Old age portrayed by the ages-of-life models from the Middle Ages to the 16th century', *The Gerontologist* 29(5): 692–8.

Crandall, B.C. (ed.) (1996) *Nanotechnology: Molecular Speculations in Global Abundance*, Cambridge, MA: MIT Press.

Dove, M. (1986) *The Perfect Age of Man's Life*, Cambridge: Cambridge University Press.

Elias, N. (1985) *The Loneliness of the Dying*, Oxford: Blackwell.

—— (1991) *The Symbol Theory*, London: Sage.

—— (1994) *Reflections on a Life*, Oxford: Polity Press.

Featherstone, M. (1982) 'The body in consumer culture', *Theory, Culture & Society* 1(2): 18–33.

—— (1991) *Consumer Culture and Postmodernism*, London: Sage.

—— (1995a) *Undoing Culture: Globalization, Postmodernism and Identity*, London: Sage.

—— (1995b) 'Post-bodies, ageing and virtual reality', in M. Featherstone and A. Wernick (eds) *Images of Ageing: Cultural Representations of Later Life*, London and New York: Routledge.

Featherstone, M. and Burrows, R. (eds) (1996) *Cyberspace/Cyberbodies/Cyberpunk: Cultures of Technological Embodiment*, London: Sage.

Featherstone, M. and Hepworth, M. (1982) 'Ageing and inequality: consumer culture and the new middle age', in D. Robbins, L. Caldwell, G. Day, K. Jones and H. Rose (eds) *Rethinking Inequality*, Aldershot: Gower.

—— (1985a) 'The male menopause: lifestyle and sexuality', *Maturitas* 7: 235–46.

—— (1985b) 'The history of the male menopause 1848–1936', *Maturitas* 7: 249–57.

—— (1989) 'Ageing and old age: reflections on the postmodern lifecourse', in B. Bytheway, T. Keil, P. Allatt and A. Bryman (eds) *Becoming and Being Old: Sociological Approaches to Later Life*, London: Sage.

—— (1993) 'Images of ageing', in J. Bond, P. Coleman and S. Peace (eds) *Ageing in Society: An Introduction to Social Gerontology*, 2nd edn, London: Sage.

Fitzgerald, F. (1986) *Cities on a Hill: A Journey Through Contemporary American Culture*, New York: Simon & Schuster.

Fuchs, C.J. (1995) 'Death is irrelevant: cyborgs, reproduction and the future of male hysteria', in C.H. Gray (ed.) *The Cyborg Handbook*, London and New York: Routledge.

Gibson, W. (1986) *Neuromancer*, London: Grafton.

—— (1987) *Count Zero*, London: Grafton.

—— (1988) *Mona Lisa Overdrive*, London: Grafton.

Glaser, B.M. and Strauss, A.L. (1971) *Status Passage*, London: Routledge & Kegan Paul.

Goffman, E. (1968) 'The moral career of the mental patient', in *Asylums: Essays on the Social Situation of Mental Patients and Other Inmates*, Harmondsworth: Penguin Books.

Greer, G. (1991) *The Change: Women, Ageing and the Menopause*, London: Hamish Hamilton.

Gruman, G.J. (1966) 'A history of ideas about the prolongation of life: the evolution of the prolongevity hypothesis to 1800', *Transactions of the American Philosophical Society* 56(9).

Gubrium, J.F. (1995) *Individual Agency, the Ordinary and Postmodern Life*, Milton Keynes: Open University, Centre For Ageing and Biographical Studies.

Gubrium, J.F., Holstein, J.A. and Buckholdt, D.R. (1994) *Constructing the Life Course*, Dix Hills, NY: General Hall Inc.

Gullette, M.M. (1988) *Safe at Last in the Middle Years. The Invention of the Midlife Progress Novel: Saul Bellow, Margaret Drabble, Anne Tyler, and John Updike*, Berkeley: University of California Press.

—— (1993) 'Creativity, ageing, gender: a study of their intersections, 1910–1935', in A.M. Wyatt-Brown and J. Rossen (eds) *Ageing and Gender in Literature: Studies in Creativity*, Charlottesville and London: University Press of Virginia.

Haraway, D. (1997) *Modest Witness @ Second Millennium*, London and New York: Routledge.

Harré, R. (1991) *Physical Being*, Oxford: Blackwell.

Hepworth, M. (1982) 'Sociological aspects of mid-life', in P.A. van Keep, W.H. Utian, and A. Vermeulen (eds) *The Controversial Climacteric*, Lancaster/Boston/The Hague: MTP Press.

Hepworth, M. and Featherstone, M. (1982) *Surviving Middle Age*, Oxford: Blackwell.

Kammen, M. (1980) 'Changing perceptions of the life cycle in American thought and culture', *Proceedings of the Massachusetts Historical Society* 91: 35–66.

Katz, S. (1996) *Disciplining Old Age: The Formation of Gerontological Knowledge*, Charlottesville and London: University Press of Virginia.

Laws, G. (1995) 'Embodiment and emplacement: identities, representation and landscape in Sun City retirement communities', *International Journal of Ageing and Human Development* 40(4): 253–80.

Lowenthal, D. (1986) *The Past Is a Foreign Country*, Cambridge: Cambridge University Press.

Luke, T. (forthcoming) 'Simulated sovereignty: telematin territoriality: the political economy of cyberspace', in M. Featherstone and S. Lash (eds) *Spaces of Culture*, London: Sage.

Marks, E. (1986) 'Transgressing the (in)cont(in)ent boundaries: the body in decline', *Yale French Studies* 72: 181–200.

McManners, J. (1985) *Death and the Enlightenment: Changing Attitudes to Death in Eighteenth-Century France*, Oxford/New York: Oxford University Press.

Seale, C. (1995) 'Society and Death', in B. Davey (ed.) *Birth to Old Age: Health in Transition*, Buckingham: Open University Press.

Sears, E. (1986) *The Ages of Man: Medieval Interpretations of the Life Cycle*, Princeton, NJ: Princeton University Press.

Sheehy, G. (1977) *Passages: Predictable Crises of Adult Life*, New York: Bantam Books/Corgi.

Shotter, J. (1993) *Cultural Politics of Everday Life*, Milton Keynes: Open University Press.

Soja, E. (1996) *Thirdspace*, Oxford: Blackwell.

Turkle, S. (1995) *Life on the Screen: Identity in the Age of the Internet*, Cambridge, MA: MIT Press.

Vattimo, G. (1988) *The End of Modernity*, Oxford: Polity Press.

Walby, C. (1977) 'Revenants: the Visible Human Project and the digital uncanny', *Body & Society* 3(1): 1–16.

Walker, B.G. (1985) *The Crone: Women of Age, Wisdom, and Power*, San Francisco: Harper & Row.

Wei Leng, K. (1996) 'On menopause and cyborgs: or, towards a feminist cyborg politics of menopause', *Body & Society* 2(3): 33–52.

Wilbush, J. (1988) 'Climacteric disorders – historical perspectives', in J.W. Studd and M.I. Whitehead (eds) *The Menopause*, Oxford: Blackwell Scientific Publications.

Woodward, K. (1991) *Ageing and its Discontents: Freud and Other Fictions*, Bloomington and Indianapolis: Indiana University Press.

Chapter 9

Risk, governmentality and the reconceptualization of citizenship

Paul Higgs

The concept of 'risk' has had a meteoric rise in sociological importance over the past few years. Used as a shorthand to describe some of the most notable cultural changes of the last two decades of the twentieth century it also helps to provide an agenda for future political action. This has led to a problem because, viewed from the perspective of sociology, the concept focuses on issues of uncertainty and fear. This ignores whole areas of discussion about risk which do not concentrate on 'not knowing' but rather on 'knowing and acting'. In particular, discourses developed in the health, social and educational services of the welfare state have as their intention the possibility of intervention in 'risky' situations to achieve the positive goals that they have set themselves. The importance of linking up these two areas of discourse around risk is not to prove one set of literature correct over another, but rather to point to the organizing role that a third area – social policy – has in relating the two conceptions of risk to the wider project of governing society. In this chapter I will attempt to show how the awareness and surveillance of risk are central features of the reworking of citizenship along communitarian lines – a reworking which puts a heavy emphasis on individual agency and choice, so long as this occurs within increasingly circumscribed limits. This shift seems to reflect social and cultural changes where the construction of self-identity and lifestyle have become paramount influences and where the collectivist vision of a universalist welfare state has become anachronistic. To underpin my argument I will concentrate on the fate of old age in modern society.[1]

RISK SOCIETY

Ulrich Beck's *Risk Society* published in English in 1992, is often cited as the most significant piece of work alerting us to the importance of 'risk' in constructing the parameters of late or high modernity. It has been used by figures as influential as Anthony Giddens as a basis for an analysis of modernity that goes beyond the sterile polarization of modernity/ postmodernity and seeks to clarify what could reasonably be said about society at the turn of the millennium. At the heart of Beck's position on risk, however, is a belief that as a result of reflexivity we now live in a society where the identification and awareness of risks (however defined) overwhelms the project of modernity. The very success of industrialism has brought pollution and ecological disaster onto the developed as well as the developing world. As is well known, the distribution of such risks is not, according to Beck, something that affects only the subaltern classes; it also affects those who have benefited from industrialization. On top of this is the problem of the interpretation of evidence of risk which, because of the speed of dissemination of information, becomes more and more difficult to establish with any certainty. As Beck points out, this gives opportunities for many different groups to pronounce on risks and to be 'experts'. Concerns with risk, then, create the most notable feature of contemporary society; concerns which, as Beck points out, cannot be assuaged by conventional means.

These themes have been taken up by Giddens (1991) in relation to what he calls 'manufactured uncertainty'; where one of the overriding themes of contemporary life is the inability to predict what is going to happen next in society. He points to the paradox that while we are more and more dependent on expert systems about which we have only rudimentary knowledge, those same systems cannot adequately anticipate the future. This has mainly been discussed in relation to issues such as 'global warming' and 'acid rain', but it also has a crucial impact on our ability to organize societies and especially social welfare. In *Beyond Left and Right* (1994) Giddens discusses the collapse of what he calls the cybernetic model of society, when it seemed simple to create the kind of society that was desired. While Marxism was the most obvious example of this approach, the post-war welfare administrations were also formed in this image. Such welfare states would be able to make judgements about the needs of individuals and families and ensure that, with a few modifications, progress was possible. Giddens argues that one of the implications of risk society is that none of this is possible. Welfare states were dependent on the notion of actuarial risk where potential outcomes were pretty much known in advance. Manufactured uncertainty on the other hand throws this whole approach out of the window. Not only is it impossible to calculate risk any longer but such an approach is positively harmful.

Such an assessment obviously has implications for the nature of social policy. Giddens argues that the existing welfare institutions no longer fit with the reality of high modernity. In part they seek to deal with problems which no longer can be successfully dealt with, such as full employment and the creation of equality. Of equal significance is their role in creating and recreating the gendered division of labour which underpins the patriarchal family. Modern social relations do not correspond to these ideals or assumptions, and Giddens argues that we need to reconceptualize our understanding of the focus of social policy around what he terms 'positive welfare'. The ageing of the population, argues Giddens, provides a test case for his ideas. Making many of the points familiar to social gerontologists of the structured dependency school, he points out the negative social status of being a pensioner and argues: '[a]geing is treated as "external", as something that happens to one, not as a phenomenon actively constructed and negotiated' (Giddens 1994: 170). In line with his reworking of the implications of risk society, Giddens sees the future of old age as lying in the removal of this external label by making the older person more involved in creating their own future. In practice this means that older people need to take responsibility for their own individual health and well-being. More controversially it means removing the state pension as an unnecessary form of what he terms 'precautionary aftercare'. This is to be done with the intention of creating an "autotelic self" with self-respect and ontological security, but it also challenges risk as a way of achieving self-actualization. As he writes:

> Schemes of positive welfare, orientated to manufactured rather than external risk, would be directed to fostering the autotelic self. The autotelic self is one with an inner confidence which comes from self-respect, and one where a sense of ontological security originating in basic trust, allows for the positive appreciation of social difference. It refers to a person able to translate potential threats into rewarding challenges, someone who is able to turn entropy into a consistent flow of experience. The autotelic self does not seek to neutralise risk or to suppose that 'someone else will take care of the problem'; risk is confronted as the active challenge which generates self-actualisation.
>
> (Giddens 1994: 192)

In Giddens's shift from risk as a cultural category to positive welfare we are made aware of one of the central themes of both Beck and Giddens's idea of reflexive modernization, namely the idea of the project of the self and the way in which the categories of risk influence it. Beck claims that risk society leads to the demise of class society through the processes of individualization; but the 'reflexive conduct of life, the planning of one own's biography and social relations, gives rise to a new inequality, the *inequality of dealing with insecurity and reflexivity*' (Beck 1992: 98). Giddens also places considerable weight on the project of the self and the processes involved in reflexivity. In *The Transformation of Intimacy* (1992) he discusses at length the expert knowledges available to individuals to enable them to experience the pure relationships of mutual self-actualization. He also points to the fact that such expert systems exist in an environment where they may contribute to the break-up of relationships that do not meet these high standards by suggesting that perfection is possible. Both Giddens and Beck are ultimately positive about the benefits that can accrue to the individual as a result of accepting the challenges offered by risk and reflexive modernization but to do so also means abandoning some of the securities of the past.

Zygmunt Bauman (1992) also believes that the latest stage of modernity is one where the ability to understand, know and change society has been radically undermined by the scepticism engendered by modernity itself. He also believes that social processes have come to focus on the construction of individual identity, albeit in a fragmented form. Again, this is enabled by discourses of individual perfection and of consumption. Crucially, he also points to the significance of the body and of surveillance. The combination of the first two in the context of the latter two puts a totally different spin on our understanding of risk.

In *Life in Fragments* (1995), Bauman focuses on two important characteristics of modernity: the enhancement of health and the elimination of disease. He describes how good health has become everybody's concern and, more importantly, everybody's task, if not duty. He writes:

> The fulfilment of the duty took the form of a strictly observed bodily regime – of regular exercise, a balanced diet, a carefully structured daily and annual rhythm of activities, a consistently growing list of avoidances and self denials. The body itself turned into an object for technology; the owner of the body was now a manager, a supervisor and an operator rolled into one, and the medical profession supplied him or her with ever more complex technological products to perform these functions.
>
> (Bauman 1995: 169–70)

These processes connected to the unfolding of modernity become dispersed in a world characterized as postmodern or late modern. Instead of the state administering health and seeking out disease the concerns have become 'privatized'. He argues that the gap left by the transcending state leaves individuals to construct and reconstruct their identities. Again to quote Bauman:

> The huge State-wide garden has been split into innumerable small allotments. What used to be done in a condensed and concentrated fashion, through universal laws instilled thanks to the state's normative fervour and guarded by the state police, is now done in an uncoordinated way by commercial companies, quasi-tribal groups, or the individuals themselves.
>
> (Bauman 1995: 173–4)

Bauman does not see this 'colonization of private life' as the end of the matter; he goes on to argue that much of contemporary politics is an extension of 'bodily obsession':

> If individuals scared of the innumerable threats to life and health unite forces for common action, it is more often than not in order to chase away or trample down a danger which they see as threatening them individually, but too resilient or too powerful to be defeated by individual efforts. Joint action is, then, a struggle against 'health hazards consolidated'.
>
> (Bauman 1995: 177)

In this way we return to the issue of risk but in a significantly different way. Risk can now be an environmental hazard but it can also be a group of people or practices who, once defined, can be separated off and banished. Bauman has in mind the way in which such separation can be used as the basis for a resurgence of tribalism.

Taking this theme further Bauman (1996) has addressed the negative side of the renewed interest in forms of communitarianism as solutions to the fragmenting processes of modernity. He identifies a hankering in communitarian discourses for a closure on the choices that individuals are allowed to make because it is in these choices that community values are undermined. To overcome this problem lip service is paid to the exercise of freedom, but the 'good choice is the choice of what is already given' (Bauman 1996: 81). This, however, of necessity means the privileging of one choice over the others and establishes the importance of making the right choice. In this way the construction of identities which is one of the features of consumer society is problematized and a hierarchy imposed. While much of this can be related to the evolution and failures of the nation-state over the past century it is also reintroduces Beck's idea of the risk society and the uncertainties that it fosters.

Bauman points out that the relationship between consumer society and communitarianism is paradoxical:

> individuals, torn between intoxicating freedom and horrifying uncertainty, desire the impossible; they want no less than to eat a cake and have it – relishing and practising their freedom of choice while having the 'happy ending' guaranteed and the results insured. Whatever name they select to call their worry, what individuals truly resent is the risk innate in freedom; whatever they call their dreams, what they desire is a *risk-free freedom*. The trouble is, however, that freedom and risk grow and diminish only together. Thus the ultimate solution to the plight of the modern individual is not on the cards.
>
> (Bauman 1996: 85)

Notwithstanding the above, communitarianism is an attempt to create a 'natural community' that can resolve the inherent contradictions of modern life, but which is constructed in the private sphere rather than through the state and based on the dictum 'choose, but choose wisely'. The dangers inherent in such a position are clear. Again, to quote Bauman: 'It is the individual *responsibility* for choice that is equally distributed, not the individually owned *means* to act on that responsibility' (Bauman 1996: 88). Who decides what are the right choices and who acts as guardian of the community are only two of the disturbing questions related to this shift in political desire.

RISK ASSESSMENT AND SOCIAL POLICY

One of the central ideas featuring in Beck's conception of 'risk society' is the growth of technologies for identifying risk. For him they have the effect of producing panic and insecurity in the public as more and more aspects of social life are shown to involve risk. Paradoxically, it is also the case that those who construct such measures see such knowledge as creating the basis for a better world. As Gabe (1995) points out, from this perspective risk is viewed as a technical matter relying on the development and quantification of accurate scientific information. Within this approach there is also the assumption that all risks are discoverable, measurable and, with the right expertise, controllable. While much of the work has been concerned with problems in engineering, toxicology and road transport (see Adams 1995), risk assessment has also come to play a major role in the area of medicine and health care. Skolbekken (1995) points out that since 1987 more than 80,000 articles on risk have been published in medical journals. Drawing attention to this torrent of work he concludes that we face a 'risk epidemic' of studies which lack any underlying coherence regarding what constitutes risk. Consequently, while risk has a 'taken-for-granted' status there are many different notions of the concept 'to which various ideological meanings have been attached' (Skolbekken 1995: 297). Through what Petersen and Lupton (1996) describe as the 'web of causality', risk is constructed out of multi-causal models which turn statistical relationships into causal ones and in turn allow risks and risk factors to become realities in their own right.

Consequently, the utilization of risk and risk assessment can play different roles in different parts of social and health policy. Sometimes the stress is on environmental factors, sometimes on genetic ones. As these are difficult to modify, however, of particular significance has been a shift in the notion of locus of control and the importance of recognizing this change:

> Throughout human history the major threats to our health have come from risk factors outside of our control, from nature itself or what we have seen as supernatural powers.
>
> Correspondingly, our attitudes towards these risks were mainly fatalistic, our perceptions dominated by religious beliefs, superstition and destiny, and the means of handling risks were mainly restricted to prayers, sacrifices and other ritualistic behaviours.
>
> Substantial changes in the beliefs regarding risks and the handling of them have come about in the past three centuries, due to scientific and technological developments within medicine and other disciplines. Most present risks can be seen as created by humans, being side effects of developments that are mainly viewed as benefits to humans. These recent advances have contributed to a change in the basic attitudes where matters of life and death are concerned. The risk acceptance that is internalised in a fatalistic attitude to these matters is being replaced by an ideology whose primary goal is to gain control over life and death, where identification of and the struggle to reduce/eliminate risk factors have become activities of considerable importance and prestige within the health professions.
>
> (Skolbekken 1995: 297)

The identification of risk and its assessment leads logically to treatment, and here we can concur with Lupton's emphasis (1993) on the construction of risk as a result of lifestyle choices made by individuals and the way in which this results in health promotion strategies focused on changing behaviours. While she is particularly concerned with the issues surrounding AIDS, it is possible to extend this approach to many other areas. Colella (1997) has written about how the Salience of Lifestyle Index developed by Pill and Stott (1987) has come to be used as a diagnostic measure in the targeting of health promotion towards those most vulnerable to strokes. Colella points out that using the SLI, respondents would be categorized as either lifestylist or fatalist depending on their responses. Fatalists are seen to be less amenable to health promotion and therefore more at risk of stroke. Even though more systematic interviewing of subjects produced a more complicated picture than the one produced by the SLI, what is significant is the way in which this approach has been adopted as a public health measure. Tesh (1988) argues that the popularity of lifestyle accounts of health is based on a number of factors. In the USA practising health promoting behaviours is seen to represent individualism and upward mobility. More significantly, it also means that the pursuit of public health can be achieved by individual action, thereby avoiding the need to change government policies or to accept social responsibility for the distribution of morbidity and mortality.

Moving away from behaviours, we can see that at the level of reproduction the techniques created by the new genetics and the new reproductive technologies also operate within a discourse of risk assessment. These forms of knowledge and techniques open up new dilemmas of both a practical and ethical nature. Genetic screening can indicate the possibility of conditions that might not be immediately apparent, such as Muscular Dystrophy, and can have different effects at different points in the life course (Parsons and Atkinson 1993). Concerns about amniocentesis and chorionic villus sampling, both procedures for detecting abnormalities in foetuses, not only relate to the information produced but may also be a source of further risk (Doyal 1995). The medicalization of childbirth has also been widely documented (Doyal 1995) and childbirth is seen as a site of considerable risk best dealt with in a hospital.

Risk is also utilized in more formalized areas of social policy. Within the arena covered by community care policy in Britain a massive transformation has occurred with the vaguely organized idea of 'need' becoming reified as 'risk'. The criticisms of previously existing social care policies operated by local authorities were that they were badly organized, unresponsive to their clients and did not address the real needs of users (Griffiths 1988). After the implementation of the 1990 NHS and Community Care Act in 1993, local authorities were expected to assess the needs of individual clients and to provide appropriate packages of care for them. All of this was designed to ensure that the various parts of the welfare state did not try to 'load shed' their responsibilities onto other agencies or have perverse incentives to use residential care inappropriately. From its roots in the Kent Community Care scheme, however (Davis and Challis 1980), the implementation of community care was based upon its financial effectiveness and, in consequence, it was not long before 'needs assessment' became reduced to risk assessment as cash-limited managers tried to get the best set of outcomes from the lowest input. Assessment forms would distinguish between needs that were not important enough to warrant intervention and those that could result in harm if no action was taken (Lewis *et al.* 1995). The distortion of community care that this promotes, whereby cost not need dictates what services are offered, has led to the policy of community care failing in its objectives to provide a comprehensive system of social care (Walker 1997).

In fact Salter (1992) argues that avoidance of risk is the real purpose of a lot of services offered to older people. She cites the case of Day Centres where some older clients are placed because they are thought to be at risk. This allows them to be surveyed and kept safe even though there is little practical treatment going on. Shildrick (1997) extends this notion of surveillance in her deconstruction of the 'Disability Living Allowance' scheme. She argues that the self-assessment form used to ascertain eligibility not only demands great detail but also obliges the applicants to 'turn a critical gaze upon their own bodies' (Shildrick 1997: 51). This produces a 'personal accounting' of the dimensions of the individual's disability as she distinguishes between the activities that she can and cannot perform. This not only promotes individual failing above environmental or social concerns but also internalizes the risk faced through the failure to be able to undertake certain tasks.

Another significant area where the concept of risk is widely used is in mental health where the Supervision Register for mentally ill people was introduced in 1994 in order to identify and provide information 'on patients who are, or are liable to be, at risk of committing serious violence or suicide or serious self-neglect' (NHS Management Executive 1994: 1). Such individuals were to be placed on the register not only to ensure that they received a full programme of care but also to reassure the public that apparent failings in the community care of discharged psychiatric patients were going to be dealt with. While according to one researcher (Isherwood 1996) there is considerable variation in the organization of such registers and who should be included on them, the emergence of such documents represents the legalization of the status of risk.

What this section has attempted to demonstrate is that the utilization of a risk discourse in social policy has flowed from a modernist belief in the control of nature and social phenomena. While it is also true that risk and risk assessment are in themselves socially conditioned, this has not stopped the process of seeking better and more effective ways of preventing risk. In the next section I will show how this is linked up with processes reshaping the modern state and especially its relationship with the citizen.

GOVERNMENTALITY

If risk has come to dominate much sociological thinking then the concept of governmentality (Foucault 1991) has had an equal rise to prominence. An idea first used by Foucault in the period between *Discipline and Punish* and the *History of Sexuality* the concept lies uneasily between his better known notions of 'disciplinary power' and 'the care of the self' (Miller 1995). Relating to the 'conduct of conduct', governmentality focuses on the deployment of 'technologies of the self' in the conduct of social policies (Nettleton 1997). Lupton (1995) argues that governmentality incorporates an analysis of the coercive and non-coercive strategies which the state and other institutions urge on individuals for their own benefit. It is crucially reliant upon systems of expert knowledge which constitute and define the objects of their knowledge, mediate between individuals and authority, measure progress and set up the markers of compliance. This is not to argue that governmentality is essentially a form of domination, rather it is a way of directing 'free will'. Dean (1994) makes this point when he writes that it 'concerns strategies for the direction of conduct of free individuals' (Dean 1994: 174).

By emphasizing the aspect of free will, the concept has been used to underpin the view that social policies conducted by the liberal state are benign rather than essentially coercive – in this way connecting with Foucault's view of power as enabling (Barry *et al.* 1996). This is in part a reflection of the de-radicalization of the Foucaldian problematic as it encountered postmodernism but could also be said to be a response to the growing importance of lifestyle in modern societies (Bocock 1993) and the cultivation of the self that formed the backdrop for Foucault's last works (Foucault 1979, 1990).

It is possible to link governmentality to the 'disembedding' tendency of late modern societies identified by Giddens (1991). Such processes have a negative effect on the ontological security of the modern individual and lead Giddens to acknowledge the importance of personal 'narratives of the self' as solutions to this problem. This leads us back once more to the importance of lifestyle. The problem still arises, however, as to which narrative is to be chosen and against what criteria.

While there has been a considerable literature written about the individual as actively involved in the creation of lifestyle, it is only when we relate this to the idea of governmentality that we can properly understand it. As indicated earlier, not all choices are regarded as wise or to be encouraged, and here we can see how shifts in the organization of modern welfare systems have come to operate on a notion of governmentality, where primary responsibility is located with the individual who is expected to adopt certain lifestyle choices and is rewarded or punished accordingly (Petersen and Lupton 1996; Petersen 1997).

CITIZENSHIP

If governmentality represents a way of organizing social policy around 'technologies of the self', does the more conventional idea of citizenship become redundant? Or has it been radically transformed to connect with a social world where the ideas of consumerism and individualism are dominant? As is well known, T.H. Marshall's model of citizenship (Marshall 1992) placed an emphasis on the importance for the individual of collective social rights relating to social security, health and education. The principles of universalism and, to some degree, equality were to serve as protection from the negative consequences of a market society.

While it is important to recognize that a range of criticisms has been directed at Marshall's account of citizenship centring on issues such as its historical accuracy (Rees 1996); its Anglo-centrism (Mann 1987); its failure to acknowledge the importance of conflict (Giddens 1982); its gender blindness (Lister 1990); and its conflation of nationality with citizenship (Rees 1996), it has, nevertheless, constituted a powerful account of what the relationship between the citizen and the state should be about.

What might have been true for a considerable part of the post-war period has been radically changed since the 1980s with the ideas of universalism and collectivism coming under serious attack and the assumptions of the 'new right' taken as common sense. The negative impact of public spending is taken for granted (Kymlicka and Norman 1994) and welfare rights and collective provision are seen to be inefficient and promoting dependency (Taylor-Gooby 1991). There has been considerable agreement that the need for 'socialized consumption' has declined as real incomes have risen (Saunders 1993). This affluence, as well as the increased cost of welfare, has resulted in an emphasis on 'privatized consumption' where being a purchaser of services is as important as the issues of quality and choice. Within this shift of focus from the collective to the individual comes a profound alteration to the assumptions lying behind social policy. Le Grand (1997) talks about the notion of the population as 'knights' being replaced by one of the population as 'knaves', a transition from being essentially good to one of being essentially self-serving. It is not surprising, then, that the whole notion of public welfare is seen as undesirable, the space occupied by the potentially undeserving. Fraser (1997) identifies the way in which 'welfare dependency' has become what she terms a 'postindustrial pathology'. Patricia Hill Collins (1997) argues that in the USA the public sphere is now seen as the site of danger because it indicates the failure of the individuals reliant on it. Freedom, on the other hand, is associated with the private domestic sphere of consumption where true liberty resides.

Such differentiation obviously has its effects on those left behind, who are not only seen in terms of their 'cost' and their 'motivation', but also suggest or provoke comparisons with those able to privatize their consumption. This point is also made by Zymunt Bauman (1988), when he highlights the undesirability of being a recipient of state welfare. As mentioned earlier, in an era characterized by consumption and choice, people use commodities to establish their self-identities. Those who do not have the resources to participate in the market become "repressed" welfare clients, subject to the controlling disciplinary mechanisms of the state.

It is not just the undesirability of being a recipient of state welfare that matters in this reworking of social and welfare policies, it is also the context in which the new citizen is expected to operate. Miller and Rose (1990) argue that citizenship is no longer construed in terms of solidarity and welfare, rather it is to be re-cast in terms of the free exercise of personal choice:

> Programmes of government are to be evaluated in terms of the extent to which they enhance that choice. And the language of individual freedom, personal choice and self-fulfilment has come to underpin programmes of government articulated across the political spectrum, from politicians and professionals, pressure groups and civil libertarians alike.
>
> (Miller and Rose 1990: 24)

Accordingly, the concept of citizenship has been progressively tailored to a number of procedural rights for individuals. The *Citizen's Charter* of the 1990s Conservative government provides a model of the new relationship between the state and the individual. The citizen can expect to be treated in certain ways and can reasonably expect specified levels of service. Treatment that does not meet with these standards can be complained about and compensation secured.

Central to this model is the idea of contract which is not only applied positively to members of the public dealing with large public and private sector organizations, but also negatively to those receiving welfare benefits. Unemployed people seeking the 'jobseeker's allowance' now make a formal contract to undertake certain jobseeking activities, such as regularly going to a jobcentre or applying for a specified number of jobs every week, in order to be eligible for benefit. The idea of entitlement, as conceived by Marshall, has been replaced by a 'bourgeois' concept of contract. The use of the Social Fund exemplifies this approach where ability to pay back a 'loan' is an equal criterion for entitlement with need.

Bryan Turner (1988) argues that these developments are not just political changes but are intrinsically bound up with the nature of modern society.[2] As traditional occupational structures become less important, a multitude of lifestyle choices come to replace them. Status politics conflicts based around such group identities are played out in the realm of the welfare state or in the grey area of the state-assisted voluntary organization. To extend Turner's argument, the collapse of the dominance of class in society is reflected in the rejection of mass provision of welfare. This changes the way that the welfare state operates because status groups primarily want their particular needs met and may be unconcerned as to how. Special interest perspectives and budgetary control over resources might go a long way in weakening the hold of a universalistic, public-sector dominated, mass welfare system.

As can be seen, individuation and consumerism are the starting points of this new reworking of the idea of citizenship. As such it reflects aspects that have always been present in civil society: the importance of contract, equality of treatment, freedom of choice, etc. (Green 1993). It would be a mistake, however, to view these changes simply as a return to the *laissez-faire* social policies of the Victorian era. Rather than being a retreat from the welfare state it represents a change in the organizing principle of state welfare and, in particular, in how the citizen is expected to act.

GOVERNMENTALITY, CITIZENSHIP AND RISK

We now return to the ideas of governmentality and risk discussed earlier because, as Turner (1997) points out, these two concepts locate the real tensions of modern society between the deregulation of the macro-level and the micro-level requirement for a continuing micro-politics of surveillance and control. As he writes:

> To some extent we might argue that financial deregulation in the 1980s produced a global environment of political and economic uncertainty between nation-states but within each industrial society the need for micro-surveillance and discipline continued with greater intensity; indeed the importance for a carceral society has increased with the growth of externalised macro-risk. As the global economy develops into a culture of risk, the nation-state is forced to invest more and more in internal systems of governmentality. . . . Finally, the notion of generalised risk in the environment may lead to greater surveillance and control through the promotion of preventive medicine. The AIDS 'epidemic' creates a political climate within which intervention and control are seen to be both necessary and benign. Individuals need, especially in the area of sexual etiquette, to become self-regulating and self-forming.
>
> (Turner 1997: xviii–xix)

Consequently the notion of governmentality locates itself within the idea of citizenship where the abstract individual that exists in civil society becomes more than just the 'docile body' of disciplinary power. The technologies of the self are ordered by techniques from which the model citizen can be created out of a composite of norms, values and statistics and against which real ones can be measured and assessed (Rose 1996). Deviations from this frame of reference are then the appropriate subject of social policy, which is fundamentally concerned with how to get individuals back to conforming to this model or, if this fails or is impossible, with how to exclude and control the particular deviant individual or group. Armstrong (1995) has talked of the emergence of what he terms 'surveillance medicine' where the whole of the individual's life is subject to scrutiny for risky behaviours that might give rise to future health problems. This process does not just exist at a medical level or indeed just for adults, it also relates to education, social services and disability (Hewitt 1992) In each of these areas expert-derived concepts of normality or appropriateness are utilized and those individuals causing concern by not meeting them given special attention (Rose 1996). Poster argues that such forms of surveillance constitute: 'a Superpanopticon, a system of surveillance without walls, windows or towers or guards. The qualitative advances in the technologies of surveillance result in a qualitative change in the microphysics of power' (1995: 87). All parts of social life are encoded into data, not only to be used for the purposes of establishing normality and risk, but also to 'create' the individual who is constituted therein.

While the idea of governmentality is fundamentally concerned with the ordering of individuals around particular ideas or discourses, it is important to realize that this is a double-edged process concerned also with identifying potential risk at a population level. Castel (1991) points out that populations are monitored in terms of risk but adds:

> A risk does not arise from the presence of a particular precise danger embodied in a concrete individual or group. It is the effect of a combination of abstract 'factors' which render more or less probable the occurrence of undesirable modes of behaviour.
>
> (Castel 1991: 287)

The implications of governmentality for the state are immense. If the organization of welfare can be understood as a technical problem of risk avoidance then the nature of state welfare can be radically re-arranged. Assessment and administration become the main, if not the sole functions of the welfare state. As Castel points out, in an era of state welfare contraction: 'the interventionist technologies which make it possible to "guide" and "assign" individuals without having to assume their custody could well prove to be a decisive resource' (Castel 1991: 295).

The utilization of the technologies of risk also performs another crucial function, namely the identification of 'risky' groups or individuals who refuse or are incapable of adequately undertaking technologies of the self; a distinction Dean (1995) describes as between the 'civilized' and the 'marginalized'. Here we are able to bring in a crucial fourth dimension to the idea of governmentality – the idea of social integration based on a moral consensus. As Douglas (1966) has pointed out the notions of risk have traditionally been used to underpin normative values and this is nowhere more obvious than in the response to those identified as at risk or posing a risk. The systematic social crises of which postmodernism is merely a cultural response have demonstrated the classic Durkheimian problem of social integration (Turner 1994: 171), highlighting a situation where the problems of an unfettered market economy have resulted in a decline in social consensus. Obviously, whether or not such a consensus was real or imposed can be debated. What is more important, however, is the desire to recreate consensus. The 1997 general election in Britain was noticeable for the emphasis placed on morally rearming the nation. This moved from sleaze through 'fat cat' salaries to the appropriate strategies to get welfare recipients back to work. The themes of governmentality and surveillance became pronounced as attempts were made to pull back from the individualism of neo-liberalism. Certain of the concerns associated with welfare citizenship were addressed, such as education, health care and employment, but the relationship was now very different. Collective rights were to be replaced by individual obligations. Failure to comply with the selected 'technology of the self' would invite sanctions. To quote from Tony Blair's mission statement for his 'welfare to work' policy:

> This new alliance of interests to build a 'one nation Britain' can only be done on a basis of a new bargain between us all as members of society. The basis of this modern civic society is an ethic of mutual responsibility or duty. It is something for something. A society where we play by the rules. You only take out if you put in. That's the bargain.
>
> (*Guardian* 3 June 1997)

As Simon Hoggart helpfully pointed out in an accompanying piece, what this amounted to was the offer of help to the unemployed 'provided they agree a) not to lie in bed all day and b) not to nick our stuff'. It is interesting to note that much of the inspiration for this strategy originates in Australia, where the 'Working Nation' policy was implemented by the Labor government in 1994 (Finn 1997). The idea was to get the long-term unemployed or those at risk of long-term unemployment back into work. In order to make participants 'job ready' they were allocated case managers who had responsibility for policing the behaviour of their clients. Again, as in Britain, the emphasis was on developing appropriate skills and encouraging flexibility towards the job market. Whether or not the policy was successful in providing permanent jobs is not the issue, rather it is the notion that unemployment is an issue of individual behaviour which, if appropriately modified, will overcome the problems of the general labour market. Commenting on the same policy Dean (1995) argued that those practices 'become involved not simply in governmental practices but in ethical practices, and what emerges is a kind of governmental sponsorship and resourcing of certain kinds of ethical or ascetic practice' (Dean 1995: 567). This approach fits in well with the modern communitarian approach advocated by Etzioni

(1995) where the obligation to work is a moral requirement of citizenship (Bowring 1997) and seen in practice in societies such as Singapore (Tremewan 1996; Chua 1997)

Governmentality, then, can provide some of the solutions to the problems of modern welfare states by reordering the relationship between the citizen and the state and providing a moral component to social life. There are those who rise to the challenge of modern life and those who fail. The rewriting of the compact with old age is an example of the transformation of collective welfare benefits into individual ones. The acknowledged connection between the state pension and poverty (Evandrou and Falkingham 1993) which has been caused in part by breaking the link between the state pension and average earnings, is not to be dealt with by increasing the rate at which the pension is to be paid. Instead, compulsory secondary private pensions are proposed which would be dependent on the amounts paid into the fund, leaving the ultimate pension to vary considerably.

This policy builds upon processes that have already occurred in the restructuring of the welfare state where many different tiers of pensioner have come into existence. Already we have evidence, because of the growth of occupational and private pensions, of a separating out of a group of older people as primarily welfare benefit recipients among a population of self-supporting, self-reliant older people (Higgs 1997). The first group becomes a 'problem' needing a solution if the nation is not to be 'ruined'. This same dichotomy is played out in relation to health care. Here older people are presented with two images: one is the physically frail and dependent 'fourth ager' while the other is the active and healthy 'third ager'. The first is a drain on resources, especially if he or she needs high levels of care, while the other is the acme of agency and is the target of lifestyle advertising. It is therefore not at all surprising that services for older frailer people (such as long-stay hospital beds) are being reduced or made the individual's liability (payments for nursing homes) at the same time that there is a concentration on positive images of ageing.

These conundrums illustrate the contradictory nature of this new mode of citizenship. Old age seems to present particular problems in a society ordered around governmentality and risk. Citizens are encouraged to take greater personal responsibility for their health and for extending the period of a fit and healthy third age; however, old age is ultimately a physiological process that cannot be overcome by any technologies of the self. This moves the old into the category of risk. They become transformed from consumers into objects of consumption as various packages of care are assembled around them. Surveillance becomes almost statutory at the age of 75 and turns the old person's body into little more than an object of health care discourse (Gilleard and Higgs 1996). This reality maybe acts as a limit on the possibilities for institutional reform. The vicissitudes of old age cannot be turned into an agentic engagement with risk and this may provide an explanation why some advocates of setting limits to care for older people do so on the basis of accepting 'natural' limits to life (Moody 1995). Rationing becomes a way to avoid disappointment.

CONCLUSION

This chapter has been concerned to describe the importance of risk for the understanding of contemporary social and health policy. Most writing on the subject has been concerned to locate risk within a cultural critique of modern society, a critique seriously challenging the modernist conflation of knowledge with control. Taking such a position underplays the significance of the continuity in risk discourse regarding the opportunities for control within structures of the welfare state. Examining key areas such as health promotion and community care we can see how risk plays an important role in locating appropriate sites of activity. Community care has become the repository of the identification of risk because it deals with a dependent group whose needs can only be understood in terms of the cost that they place on the public purse. Risk in this context provides the triggers for the activities of the minimal state.

Within the health care sector the search for potential risk factors means that the imagery of risk is incorporated into the practicalities of everyday practice as more and more knowledge is disseminated and more and more risk is identified. Health promotion steps into the public domain as a virtuous activity not only promoting health but also the person. While this seems to accord with the modern conception of the agentic individual who can mould himself or herself, it also provides the basis for the new relationship between state and citizen – one concerned with demonstrating the appropriate 'technologies of the self'. The new citizen learns to engage with risks constructively because if he or she doesn't there is no collective security net waiting to make good the damage. Here risk takes on the form of 'dangerousness' and the surveying processes that have become the core of the modern state have a need to identify such potential trouble. The nature of such potential 'risks' range from the failing school to the delinquent child, from the welfare mother to the unmotivated jobless teenager, and from the discharged psychiatric patient to the frail house-bound older person. Each of these categories is a failure in social policy terms and it is the role of the state to provide methods of reasserting the proper order of things. Even with the physically frail and potentially mentally confused older person, the lesson to be learned is to make provision earlier in life so that recourse to the limited resources of the state is not necessary.

This account of the relationship between risk and citizenship has been, of necessity, schematic. It has ignored a number of the other things that have being going on in the welfare state and has underplayed some of the positive aspects of the attempt to reconstruct welfare along lines more appropriate to this stage in history. In trying to demonstrate the links between risk, governmentality and the state, however, we may be able to get a clearer idea of how modernity operates and how it is still possible to influence its direction.

NOTES

1 This chapter develops ideas first published in an article in *Ageing and Society* (Higgs 1995). I would also like to thank the following for their help in discussing the issues in this chapter: Mark Pang, Chris Gilleard, Graham Scambler and Ian Jones. They, of course, bear no responsibility for my conclusions.

2 Turner's more recent work (1993) also tries to relocate citizenship by pointing to the significance of the more culturally fragmented environment of globalization where the nation-state has lost a considerable amount of its power. With the growth of such bodies as the European Union, the repository of social rights has increasingly moved to such pan-national entities. Because such post-national citizenship will have to be based on the idea of European identity, no specific culture can articulate the multiplicity of cultural identities, consequently what Turner posits as 'cultural citizenship' emerges. Situated within a fragmentary postmodern culture, citizenship exists as a basis for mutually acceptable difference from which lifestyle projects can be launched. As Roche (1995) has pointed out, there is a deep acknowledged ambivalence in Turner's work about how the nation-state-based concept of citizenship meshes with postmodern cultural fragmentation and whether the latter will make the former redundant. Roche himself feels that such transnational citizenship is unlikely to be achieved, partly because such bodies as the EU do not have the capacity to grant citizenship themselves but must establish it through one of the member states first and is therefore subordinate to them. Nevertheless, and accepting that these changes may be emergent rather than complete, the effect is to emphasize the fragmentation of modern social relations.

REFERENCES

Adams, J. (1995) *Risk*, London: UCL Press.
Armstrong, D. (1995) 'The rise of surveillance medicine', *Sociology of Health and Illness* 17(3): 393–404.
Barry, A., Osbourne, T. and Rose, N. (eds) (1996) 'Introduction', in *Foucault and Political Reason*, London: UCL Press.
Bauman, Z. (1988) *Freedom*, Milton Keynes: Open University Press.
—— (1992) *Intimations of Postmodernity*, London: Routledge.
—— (1995) *Life in Fragments*, Cambridge: Polity Press.
—— (1996) 'On communitarians and human freedom: or, how to square the circle', *Theory, Culture & Society* 13(2): 79–90.
Beck, U. (1992) *Risk Society: Towards a New Modernity*, London: Sage.
Bocock, R. (1993) *Consumption*, London: Routledge.
Bowring, F. (1997) 'Communitarianism and morality: in search of the subject', *New Left Review* 222: 93–114.
Castel, R. (1991) 'From dangerousness to risk', in R. Burchell (ed.) *The Foucault Effect*, Hemel Hempstead: Harvester Wheatsheaf.
Chua, B. (1997) *Communitarian Ideology and Democracy in Singapore*, London: Routledge.
Colella, T. (1997) 'Perceptions of self-risk in a South London population: domination and control', unpublished MSc Dissertation, University College London.
Davis, B. and Challis, D. (1980) 'Experimenting with new roles in domiciliary service: the Kent Community Care Project', *Gerontologist* 20: 288–99.
Dean, M. (1994) *Critical and Effective Histories: Foucault's Methods and Historical Sociology*, London: Routledge.
—— (1995) 'Governing the unemployed self in an active society', *Economy and Society* 24: 559–83.
Douglas, M. (1966) *Purity and Danger: An Analysis of the Concepts of Pollution and Taboo*, London: Routledge & Kegan Paul.
Doyal, L. (1995) *What Makes Women Sick*, New Brunswick: Rutgers University Press.
Etzioni, A. (1995) *The Spirit of Community*, London: Fontana.
Evandrou, M. and Falkingham, J. (1993) 'Social security and the life course: developing sensitive policy alternatives', in S. Arber and M. Evandrou (eds) *Ageing, Independence and the Lifecourse*, London: Jessica Kingsley.
Finn, D. (1997) *Working Nation: Welfare Reform and the Australian Job Compact for the Long Term Unemployed*, London: Unemployment Unit.
Foucault, M. (1979) *The History of Sexuality*, vol. 1, Harmondsworth: Penguin.
—— (1990) *The History of Sexuality, vol. 3: The Care of the Self*, Harmondsworth: Pengiun.
—— (1991) 'Governmentality', in R. Burchell (ed.) *The Foucault Effect*, Hemel Hempstead: Harvester Wheatsheaf.
—— (1992) *The History of Sexuality, vol. 2: The Use of Pleasure*, Harmondsworth: Penguin.
Fraser, N. (1997) *Justice Interruptus: Critical Reflections on the 'Postsocialist' Condition*, London: Routledge.
Gabe, J. (1995) 'Health, risk and medicine: the need for a sociological approach',

in J. Gabe (ed.) *Medicine, Health and Risk*, Sociology of Health and Illness Monograph Series, Oxford: Blackwell.

Giddens, A. (1982) *Central Problems in Social Theory* London: Macmillan.

—— (1991) *The Consequences of Modernity*, Cambridge: Polity Press.

—— (1992) *The Transformation of Intimacy*, Cambridge: Polity Press.

—— (1994) *Beyond Left and Right*, Cambridge: Polity Press.

Gilleard, C. and Higgs, P. (1996) 'Cultures of ageing: self, citizen and the body', in V. Minichiello, N. Chappell, H. Kendig and A. Walker (eds) *Sociology of Aging*, Melbourne: International Sociological Association.

Green, D. (1993) *Reinventing Civil Society*, London: IEA Health and Welfare Unit.

Griffiths, R. (1988) *Community Care: Agenda for Action*, London: HMSO.

Hewitt, B. (1992) *Welfare, Needs and Ideology*, Hemel Hempstead: Harvester Wheatsheaf.

Higgs, P. (1995) 'Citizenship and old age: the end of the road', *Ageing and Society* 15: 535–50.

—— (1997) 'Older people, health care and society', in G. Scambler (ed.) *Sociology as Applied to Medicine*, London: W.B. Saunders.

Hill Collins, P. (1997) 'The more things change, the more they stay the same: African-American women and the politics of containment', paper presented to the British Sociological Association Conference.

Isherwood, J. (1996) 'Supervision registers and medium secure units', *Psychiatric Bulletin* 20:198–200.

Kymlicka, W. and Norman, W. (1994) 'Return of the citizen: a survey of recent work on citizenship theory', *Ethics* 104: 352–81.

Le Grand, J. (1997) 'Knights, knaves or pawns? Human behaviour and social policy', *Journal of Social Policy* 26:149–70.

Lewis, J., Bernstock, P. and Bovell, V. (1995) 'The community care changes: unresolved tensions in policy and issues in implementation', *Journal of Social Policy* 24: 73–94.

Lister, R. (1990) 'Women, economic dependency and citizenship', *Journal of Social Policy* 19: 445–68.

Lupton, D. (1993) 'Risk as moral danger: the social and political functions of risk discourse in public health', *International Journal of Health Services* 23: 425–35.

—— (1995) *The Imperative of Health: Public Health and the Regulated Body*, London: Sage.

Mann, M. (1987) 'Ruling class strategies and citizenship', *Sociology* 21: 339–54.

Marshall, T.H. (1992) *Citizenship and Social Class*, London: Pluto.

Miller, J. (1995) *The Passion of Michel Foucault*, London: Flamingo.

Miller, P. and Rose, N. (1990) 'Governing economic life', *Economy and Society* 19: 1–31.

Moody, H. (1995) 'Ageing, meaning and the allocation of resources', *Ageing and Society* 15: 163–84.

NHS Management Executive (1994) 'Introduction of Supervision Registers for Mentally Ill People', HSG (94) 5.

Nettleton, S. (1997) 'Governing the risky self: how to become healthy, wealthy and wise', in A. Petersen, and R. Bunton. (eds) *Foucault, Health and Medicine*, London: Routledge.

Parsons, E. and Atkinson, P. (1993) 'Genetic risk and reproduction', *Sociological Review* 41: 679–706.

Petersen, A.(1997) 'Risk, governance and the new public health', in A. Petersen and R. Bunton (eds) *Foucault, Health and Medicine*, London: Routledge.

Petersen, A. and Lupton, D. (1996) *The New Public Health*, London: Sage.

Pill, R. and Stott, N. (1987) 'Development of a measure of potential health behaviour: a salience of lifestyle measure', *Social Science & Medicine* 24: 125–34.

Poster, M. (1995) 'Foucault and databases: participatory surveillance', in B. Smart (ed.)(1995) *Michel Foucault 2: Critical Assessments*, vol. 7, London: Routledge. (Orig. 1990.)

Rees, A. (1996) 'T.H. Marshall and the progress of citizenship', in M. Bulmer and A. Rees (eds) *Citizenship Today: The Contemporary Relevance of T.H. Marshall*, London: UCL Press.

Roche, M. (1995) 'Citizenship and modernity', *British Journal of Sociology* 46: 715–33.

Rose, N. (1996) 'Governing "advanced" liberal societies', in A. Barry, T. Osbourne and N. Rose (eds) *Foucault and Political Reason*, London: UCL Press.

Salter, C. (1992) 'The day centre: a way of avoiding society's risk', *Critical Public Health* 3(2): 17–22.

Saunders, P. (1993) 'Citizenship in a liberal society', in B. Turner (ed.) *Citizenship and Social Theory*, London: Sage.

Shildrick, M. (1997) *Leaky Bodies and Boundaries*, London: Routledge.

Skolbekken, J. (1995) 'The risk epidemic in medical journals', *Social Science & Medicine* 40: 291–305.

Taylor-Gooby, P. (1991) *Social Change, Social Welfare and Social Science*, Hemel Hempstead: Harvester Wheatsheaf.

Tesh, S. (1988) *Hidden Arguments: Political Ideology and Disease Prevention*, New Brunswick: Rutgers University Press.

Tremewan, C. (1996) *The Political Economy of Social Control in Singapore*, Oxford: St Antony's.

Turner, B. (1988) *Status*, Milton Keynes: Open University Press.

—— (1993) 'Postmodern culture/modern citizens', in B. van Steenbergen (ed.) *The Condition of Citizenship*, London: Sage.

—— (1994) *Orientalism, Postmodernism and Globalism*, London: Routledge.

—— (1997) 'From governmentality to risk: some reflections on Foucault's contribution to medical sociology', in A. Petersen and R. Bunton (eds) *Foucault, Health and Medicine*, London: Routledge.

Walker, A. (1997) 'Community care: past present and future', in S. Iliffe and J. Munro (eds) *Healthy Choices: Future Options for the NHS*, London: Lawrence Wishart.

Chapter 10

Medicine and complementary medicine
Challenge and change

Mike Saks

From an author's viewpoint, this chapter is appropriately entitled as being concerned with challenge and change since very little has been written by social scientists specifically on the relationship between medicine and complementary medicine in the context of debates about postmodernity, on which this chapter focuses. Having said that, as will be seen as the discussion unfolds, the interface between orthodox medicine and the popularly labelled 'complementary' therapies that have increasingly emerged in Britain and other Western societies since the 1960s has also been an arena of challenge and change. This applies not just to the health domain itself, but also to the realm of social theory – as contributors to this area have striven to interpret its meaning and significance. As this chapter indicates, the concept of postmodernism potentially has much to offer in understanding the shifting relationship between orthodox and complementary medicine, even if it is not without its limitations. Some basic mapping of the terrain, however, is initially required to set the scene for the discussion.

Orthodox medicine is taken at present to be centred on the bio-medical approach to health care that views the body as a fragmented entity in which treatment is mainly involved in repairing parts through drugs and surgery as and when they malfunction. Despite growing claims by doctors to be adopting a more holistic frame of reference, the mind and spirit in this conceptualization are still typically regarded as relatively peripheral to health care. This contrasts with many so-called 'complementary' approaches, which – while exhibiting considerable diversity – tend to place greater emphasis at the ideological level on dealing with the unity of mind, body and spirit. This distinction has been underlined by their widespread exclusion from such fields as the orthodox medical school curriculum and medical research funding that has for long made their standing appear more 'alternative' than 'complementary'. Such approaches include a range of practitioner-based therapies spanning from acupuncture and aromatherapy to osteopathy and chiropractic. These have been paralleled by a myriad of related self-help activities aimed at promoting health, which the public are increasingly taking up in Britain and elsewhere (Saks 1992).

As will be seen in this chapter, the growth of interest in the West in this wide spectrum of complementary approaches has been viewed as symptomatic of the development of a new age of postmodernity. The concept of 'postmodernity', however, is by no means straightforward, not least because even its advocates differ significantly in their views on the elements defining such a condition and the extent to which change in this direction has occurred (Thompson 1992). What is clear though, as Cahoone (1996) has pointed out, is that any discussion of this concept assumes knowledge about the nature of 'modernism' itself. The notion of 'modernity' will therefore first need to be critically considered in the health context if the exploration of the interface between orthodox medicine and complementary medicine in an apparently postmodern setting is to be appropriately situated.

MODERNITY AND BIOMEDICINE: THE COUNTER-CULTURAL CRITIQUE

At a generic level, modernity is usually regarded as being increasingly characteristic of Western societies over the past two centuries. In this sense, it is seen as being related to the rise of industrialism and the ensuing socioeconomic and cultural changes that have progressively spread throughout the world in the process of globalization. It is associated with, among other things, large-scale bureaucratic forms, growing regulation and surveillance and the ascendance of secular, materialist and rationalist values (Hall *et al.* 1992). In this frame of reference, the role of the complex knowledge employed by experts, much of which may be regarded as scientific, is central (Giddens 1991). Thus, modernism can be viewed as being based on metanarratives derived from the Enlightenment which build upon the notion of rational progress occurring through the establishment of grand theories (Thompson 1992).

This provides a helpful backdrop for understanding the development of biomedicine in the West from the eighteenth century onwards. Before the widespread ascendance of an expert medical profession, a range of approaches to health care was available in countries like Britain, including astrology, herbalism and healing on both a self-help and practitioner delivery basis (Larner 1992). This pluralistic situation in the fast-evolving health care marketplace, however, was gradually super-seded as such practices came to be defined as irrational superstition and marginalized with the development of modern biomedicine. This was based on a modernist scientific worldview and championed by doctors, who gained a position of professional privilege. In Britain, the pivotal legislation in this respect was the Medical Registration Act in the mid-nineteenth century which gave the medical profession the right to self-regulation, as well as a monopoly of title based on an official register of practitioners policed by the General Medical Council (Stacey 1992).

The corollary of the development of biomedicine within a profes-sional frame of reference in the modern world was the objectification and depersonalization of the patient in a positivistic framework – as medicine moved from more of a whole-person approach in which the client was engaged in a dialogue about diagnosis and treatment towards first the classificatory thrust of hospital medicine and then the concept of the patient as a cluster of cells within laboratory medicine (Jewson 1976). Fox (1993) sees modernism in this respect as associated with rational scientific thought – in a biomedical universe in which members of the medical profession have increasingly become wedded to the ideology of seeking to maximize validity and excluding bias in evaluating their interventions. As Hodgkin (1996) notes, this commitment to value-neutral evaluations continued into the latter half of the twentieth century, pivoted on the notion that there is a single objective truth which holds for all times and places as far as medicine is concerned. This has been underpinned by a belief in the scientific method in general and randomized controlled trials in particular.

This is not to say, however, that biomedicine completely dominated health care in the West, even in the period when it gained increasing strength from the mid-nineteenth century to the mid-twentieth century within the medical profession. There is evidence in Britain, for example, that homoeopathy continued to attract considerable popular support in the years up to the turn of the century – and was practised by some doctors themselves, despite opposition from the leaders of the newly forged medical profession (Nicholls 1988). Similarly, the use of a variety of unorthodox self-help remedies continued into the first part of the twentieth century for many common conditions (Stacey 1988). And, while the number of non-medical practitioners of alternative medicine had undoubtedly diminished by this time (see, for example, *Report as to the Practice of Medicine and Surgery by Unqualified Persons in the United Kingdom* 1910), subcultural focal points still existed in fields like herbalism and Christian Science (Inglis 1980) – as in countries like the United States (Gevitz 1988).

Such pockets of deviance from the medical mainstream, however, while challenging, were relatively small in scale compared to the counter-cultural onslaught against modernist conceptions of technocratic rationality that was to be launched in the 1960s on both sides of the Atlantic. Central to this movement were the widespread criticisms that were made of materialistic, secular notions of progress under the guise of technical rationality and the search for alternative lifestyles, at a time when meditation and mysticism came to the fore and social conventions were re-examined (Roszak 1970). The development of this counter-culture provided the watershed in the critique of modernity that is often felt to have signalled the shift to postmodernity in Western societies, leaving behind the mass production, macro-politics and progressive ideologies of modernism and embracing a scepticism about the notion of an overarching rationality based on a single meta-language (Harvey 1989).

In the rhetoric of postmodernism, modernity can loosely be seen to have been deconstructed. The deconstruction is particularly felt to have been reflected in the attack on the monolithic belief in science that is central to modernity. This has involved the demystification of the notion encompassed in the functionalist theory of science set out by Merton (1968) that Western scientific knowledge is based on objective truth – centred on the principles of universalism, communism, disinterestedness and organized scepticism. This theory has been increasingly discredited as being an inappropriate depiction of orthodox Western science (Webster 1991), sustained by the classic critique of the inductive method and verificationism by Popper (1963) and the well-known perspective of Kuhn (1970) that science typically takes place within paradigms consisting of a framework of untestable assumptions that define key concepts, questions that may be asked and methods to be employed in any investigation. Kuhn's contribution in particular counters the idea that there are universal rules of evidence for making scientific judgements and that science is a neutral activity, as it has been commonly depicted in the modernist period.

This construction of science is very important in considering the relationship between biomedicine and complementary medicine, insofar as the former has used its self-proclaimed scientific basis to distinguish itself from the less orthodox approaches of the latter. Despite the widely lauded benefits of the pharmacological revolution and high technology medicine, however, the critique of the modernist view of science has not just been echoed theoretically as far as bio-medicine is concerned. It has also taken a number of populist forms in the contemporary counter-culture, not least being the public outcry about the deleterious consequences of the use of drugs such as thalidomide and the negative effects of unnecessary surgery – as well as the growing awareness that the greatest advances in Western health since the nineteenth century have come from improvements in diet and sanitation, rather than the direct effects of medical intervention (Pietroni 1991). Add to this claims about the limited effectiveness of biomedicine in dealing with the growing amount of chronic illness in an ageing population (Saks 1994) and it can be readily understood why the notion of rational progress in this area has been so heavily questioned within a modernist frame of reference.

These tensions have also been reflected in the shifting academic interpretation of the role of professional experts in this field. With the development of counter-culture, there was a move away from the deference given to professions by functionalist writers like Goode (1960) and Barber (1963) – in which the application of their rational scientific knowledge was seen to justify their elevated position in the division of labour – towards the less reverential neo-Weberian contribution of critics such as Johnson (1972) and Freidson (1994) who give greater credence to the self-serving role of professional interests in decision-making and do not systematically equate occupational privilege and expertise. In the health field specifically, it is interesting now to contrast the classic work of Parsons (1951), who analysed the medical profession through the modernist lens of rationality, with the recent work of Foucauldian contributors who take a critical view of the caring professions, based on more jaundiced accounts of both their historical development and the concept of progress in psychiatry and other medicalized areas (see Jones and Porter 1994). Such work, as Fox (1993) notes, highlights that professional interests can be obscured by scientific pretensions within modernism.

This point is borne out by Larkin (1983) who charts the manner in which the medical profession has established and maintained a position of dominance in relation to groups like physiotherapists and radiographers as well as the professions supplementary to medicine more generally in twentieth-century Britain. A similar interpretation can be made of the historical relationship between orthodox medicine and complementary medicine in this country. This can be seen as a fluid battleground in which the medical elite has successfully employed a variety of mechanisms including ideological invective and promotion/disciplinary levers both internally and externally to preserve and, where possible, enhance its position against the threat of non-medically qualified practitioners of alternative medicine (Saks 1996). The period from the 1960s onwards, though, represents a critical watershed in which this strategy has needed to be rethought – given rapidly expanding consumer interest in a range of complementary approaches to health care in the wake of the development of a stronger counter-culture. This conveniently brings the reader to the concept of postmodernity, on which this chapter will now focus.

POSTMODERNITY AND THE RISE OF COMPLEMENTARY MEDICINE

Having sketched in the background to modernity, the pivotal notion of postmodernity and its link to the recent rise of complementary medicine can be explored, recognizing that there are many differing interpretations of its meaning (Cahoone 1996). Here postmodernity is seen, as Thompson (1992) outlines, primarily as a condition based on diversity, indeterminacy, multiplicity, fragmentation and flexible specialization, in contrast to the totalizing themes of modernity. Thus, the postmodern world is normally conceived as being characterized by a plurality of cultures and social groups, with a tolerance of minorities and a willingness to combine multiple discourses. This mixing of styles and codes is particularly resonant with the expansion of counter-culture in the Western world over the past three decades. This pattern is underlined by the emphasis on popular culture and consumerism sustaining different subcultural identities based on minority social movements in postmodern societies.

A theme also linked to the notion of postmodernity is that in these subcultures there is a focus on immediacy and a loss of a sense of time and geographical place, with the emphasis on pastiche – which is associated with the plundering of history, through the assembly of an eclectic collection of elements from the past. This is felt to lead inexorably to the decline of social coherence and the unified personality of modernism, with understandings being derived mainly from localities as opposed to wider theoretical frameworks (Harvey 1989). This strand of postmodernism is more concerned with style than with substance and utility in consumption. In this respect, as Bertens (1995) observes, postmodernity can be seen as positively restoring the indeterminacy of the world and the choice, freedom and responsibility of the consumer in face of previous patterns of ideological dominance and cultural hegemony. The essence of the postmodern world, therefore, is that it is self-constituted by a range of heterogeneous agents.

A further facet of postmodernity which is worth highlighting in this context is its association with the abandonment of the search for absolute truths based on rational scientific knowledge (Nettleton 1995). As far as science is concerned, there is the denial of a common discourse and metalanguage, with a loss of faith in monolithic accounts of progress. This is replaced by the acceptance of multiple realities and coexisting narratives, with an emphasis on discontinuity and difference as the grand narratives of science, reason and enlightenment are left behind. As Turner (1990) notes, this necessarily has implications for the expert as the impact of consumerism obscures the distinction between intellectual and popular culture. In consequence, hierarchies of knowledge break down, diminishing the standing of the professions as more probabilistic and contingent truth claims prevail.

Given these aspects of postmodernity, it is easy to understand why the development of complementary medicine in Britain and elsewhere could be seen as being symptomatic of a shift towards the postmodern. As Bakx (1991) argues, the decline in the monolithic cultural authority of biomedicine as a result of counter-cultural disillusionment with the modernist project has prepared the way for the coexistence of a diverse range of perspectives, including both the current orthodoxy and unorthodoxy in health care. This has been prompted largely by sharply rising consumer interest in the wide range of complementary approaches on offer, as they have become part of popular culture. In Britain, for example, it is estimated that between one-fifth and one-third of the population have used complementary medicine (Fulder 1996) – roughly the same proportion as in the United States and much of the rest of Europe (Eisenberg *et al.* 1993; Fisher and Ward 1994). The influence of consumers in this sphere, moreover, is underlined in Britain by a series of relatively recent reforms including the introduction of local Community Health Councils and the Patients' Charter (Levitt *et al.* 1995). Such trends, which support claims about the move towards a postmodern condition, have been reinforced by growing efforts to limit escalating health care expenditure and to protect individual rights through litigation in the health field in the international context.

In this respect, Britain has one of the most liberal policies in the West in relation to complementary medicine. Although there are legal constraints on undertaking certain forms of treatment and the therapeutic claims that can be made by lay practitioners, non-medically qualified complementary therapists have generally retained the right to practise under the Common Law (Huggon and Trench 1992). This means that, although complementary medicine does not yet form a mainstream part of the National Health Service and still tends to be primarily concentrated in the private sector (Saks 1994), consumers can in principle select their favoured type of health care. Despite the issue of equality of access that this raises, an increasing variety of health provision has emerged since the 1960s in which individual choice has become more central. Discourses are also often combined, as accentuated by Thomas *et al.* (1991), who found that most consumers of complementary medicine tend to be users of orthodox biomedicine too. The diversity, though, is most starkly reflected in the spiralling numbers of practitioners of many types of complementary medicine – now estimated to total around 50,000 in the United Kingdom, 60 per cent more than the number of general practitioners (Fulder 1996).

The fragmented nature of complementary medicine in Britain has been mirrored by the growing organization of complementary therapists in this country, as they strive to professionalize. In some instances such therapists have become quite strongly coordinated, as in the case of the Society of Homeopaths which maintains a register and a code of ethics covering most non-medical practitioners in homeopathy. In other fields, such as reflexology, practice is more individually based, with as many as eleven associations and over one hundred schools offering training nationally (Cant and Sharma 1995). This highlights the extent to which the contemporary development of complementary medicine has given rise to a plurality of discourses in the health arena. Such diversity has been enhanced further by the wide span of philosophies underpinning them, ranging from all-encompassing systems of thought to more specific and pragmatic frames of reference (Vincent and Furnham 1997), as well as the internal divisions which have prevented complementary therapists from uniting under one umbrella in Britain (Sharma 1995). While orthodox biomedicine has greater ideological coherence, it should not be forgotten that it too has spawned an increasingly complex division of labour ranging from nursing and midwifery to occupational therapy and pharmacy, accompanied by an ever expanding number of specialisms within medicine itself (Levitt *et al.* 1995)

As Fox (1993) observes, postmodernism delights in this kind of difference, in which even modernist professional knowledge can be seen to be fragmented. This point is amplified by the increasing numbers of doctors and other health professionals who are also now beginning to practise complementary therapies (Saks 1994). From a postmodern perspective, moreover, at least some of the diversity involved in complementary medicine is centred on distinct minority subcultural identities – as in the case of Ayurvedic medicine serving Asian populations living in

Britain and other Western countries (Fulder 1996) and the growing range of New Age religions which aims to promote health through self-development and self-actualization (Thompson 1992). Popular therapies like acupuncture and herbalism, deriving from traditional Chinese historical roots, also illustrate the prevalent postmodern theme of the removal of the significance of time and place in the eclectic spectrum of complementary approaches available (Hicks 1996). Indeed, Busby (1996) notes that exponents of Qigong in this country interweave different meanings and interpretations in the spirit of the postmodern, combining an emphasis on relaxed openness with the discipline of regular practice within a Taoist philosophy – while at the same time viewing the knowledge of both traditional Chinese medicine and biomedicine as relative, denying claims to absolute knowledge.

There can also be a greater concern with style than substance in the use of complementary medicine, as indicated by some of the reasons given by Bakx (1991) for the recent growth of public interest in such approaches, alongside the previously highlighted failings of bio-medicine. These include the desire for a culture of self-determination and engagement in health care as an active subject, as opposed to a passive object. Nettleton (1995) also compellingly illustrates the preference for style over substance in relation to self-help, where the employment of exercise bikes and rowing machines – which can be viewed as a postmodern simulation of reality – is paradoxically held to represent a consumption practice that frequently entails mixing body maintenance with high levels of indulgence in eating and drinking. This example accentuates that in a postmodern world there seems to be a shift from bodies as producers of things to bodies as consumers of things – ranging from videos on step aerobics to ginseng and other complementary health products. This is seen to take place in the context of a move from mass universal needs being met by monolithic professionally based bureaucratic organizations to pluralistic health care provided in quasi-markets shaped by the consumer.

Postmodern theorists also often associate such a shift with the abandonment of the search for a single scientific truth as consumers endeavour to find their own truth in exploring the diverse span of complementary therapies now being delivered in the West alongside medical orthodoxy. This goes hand in hand with the development of a more eclectic approach to health care. As Hodgkin (1996: 1568) says: 'In a postmodern world . . . [there] are no overarching frameworks to steer by. Instead, everything is relative, fashion and ironic detachment flourish, and yesterday's dogma becomes tomorrow's quaint curiosity.' The main issue in a world of evidence-based practice, therefore, is whose evidence is to count given the social constructions involved. This point is accentuated by the current debate over the value of the randomized controlled trials so extolled by the biomedical establishment. These are seen by many complementary practitioners not to be readily applicable to their own therapies as they involve dealing with individual cases on a whole-person basis rather than the use of standardized treatment for a given condition (Saks 1994).

From the viewpoint of advocates of the postmodern, therefore, the rise of complementary therapies could be seen to challenge orthodox medicine's epistemological authority, in the wake of the growing plurality of knowledge claims – as biomedicine becomes relativized into yet another discourse in a web of indeterminacy. This is part of a more general move, in the words of Lyotard (1986), to replace the metanarrative of science – based on a single language game to the exclusion of all others – by various discourses which are capable of generating their own authority without having a privileged standing. In the health field, the corollary of the decline of legitimacy of the grand narrative of biomedicine in face of the challenge from complementary therapies, as Turner (1990) notes, is that the hierarchical division between scientific medicine and alternative medicine collapses. This in turn leads to the deregulation of health care in which licences to practise become increasingly irrelevant in the marketplace of hyper-consumption, as society is transformed from the modern to the postmodern.

Cant and Sharma (1996) claim that this helps to explain why the British Medical Association has recently replaced its tendency to discredit alternative medicine as unscientific (see, for example, British Medical Association 1986) with a less prescriptive guide to patients in choosing their therapies from the broad range of orthodox and unorthodox approaches on offer, based on considerations of good practice (British Medical Association 1993). Cant and Sharma (1995) have also argued that the less openly monopolistic new-style professionalization of complementary medicine, involving a more intimate relationship between the therapist and the consumer, is a postmodern phenomenon which has developed as the general stock of the medical profession has been reduced as the contingencies of scientific knowledge become ever more evident. Such postmodern interpretations of the interface between biomedicine and complementary medicine, however, while seductive, are not themselves without challenge.

THE CRITIQUE OF POSTMODERNITY IN THE HEALTH CONTEXT

In terms of the critique of the postmodern perspective on this area, the concept of postmodernity itself has generally been much criticized. Most fundamentally, there are major debates about whether there has been a transition from modernity to postmodernity, not least because there are contradictory signs and the conclusions reached depend on which aspect is being examined (Hall *et al.* 1992). This raises the question of how far there has been a radical break with modernism, as opposed to simply a revolt within modernism (Harvey 1989). In this regard, Giddens (1991) claims that the current period is more like late modernism than post-modernism, without denying that changes are occurring. Bertens (1995: 247) echoes this view, noting that many theorists who claim that a new postmodern order has already been entered, 'overrate the importance of the cultural changes of the recent past'. There are also those who argue that the changes concerned can be wholly accounted for within the framework of capitalism – and a few others who believe that the concepts of capitalism and postmodernism can and must be reconciled (Thompson 1992).

But if postmodern thought has been subject to political challenge, it has also been criticized because its opposition to universal truths means that all that is left is the play of words and meaning. Most significantly here, it has been claimed that the abandonment of the metanarratives of truth and progress have led to its proponents 'courting the "black hole of relativism"' (Fox 1993: 121). This has resulted in some philosophers ruling out postmodernism as a concept because of the self-contradictions involved – in that, by denying the possibility of truth, the work of postmodern theorists themselves could be seen to be undermined (Cahoone 1996). While it would be harsh to dismiss the postmodern interpretation of the world on these grounds, it should also be stressed, as Bauman (1997) indicates, that its underlying ethos is not always as liberating as portrayed. More specifically, the removal of constraints that proponents of the postmodern tend so effusively to depict can just as well be interpreted as representing disintegration and dissolution as re-enchantment and increased choice – even if they do manage to circumvent the authoritarian politics of modernity.

In the health care arena in particular, some of these criticisms carry significant weight, not least in relation to complementary approaches. Caution is certainly needed as regards, for example, how far the current fragmentation associated with the development of complementary medicine supports the notion that there has been a transition to postmodernity. This is because, despite attempts to link a plural structure of choice in health care to postmodernity, such plurality is not historically unique. As Cant and Sharma (1996: 20) affirm, it 'is probably characteristic of any society above a minimal level of scale and complexity that healing practices are diverse and may rest on fairly diverse sets of assumptions about the body and the way it can be healed, even if these are not well articulated or legitimated in the public or official spheres'. One difference, however, as they note, is that, while self-healing and complementary health practices are not completely novel, 'they had, until recently, escaped the control of legitimating authorities linked to the state or powerful elites and had not come to the attention of the funding authorities because of their very locality, their invisibility, the camouflage of implicit knowledge' (1996: 20). As has been seen, this was certainly true in Britain in the period up to the mid-nineteenth century – even if this was to change thereafter, notwithstanding the provisions of the Common Law.

The main distinguishing factor in the contemporary Western world, however, has not so much been the diversity of health care now on offer as the upsurge of interest in complementary approaches by consumers, which has strong postmodern overtones. Even here the position is by no means clear cut. In assessing the extent to which the current challenge from complementary therapists in Britain has symbolized the transformation to postmodernity, fuelled by the fragmenting demand for health care, it should be emphasized that the increased interest in complementary medicine by consumers seems to have been largely as an adjunct, rather than an alternative, to orthodox biomedicine (Thomas et al. 1991). Given, amongst other things, its predominant use in a limited range of conditions – especially musculoskeletal disorders – questions must therefore be asked as to whether the growing demand for unorthodox approaches to health care represents the fundamental shift in consciousness towards New Age thinking that is implicit in the concept of the developing plurality of the postmodern order (Coward 1989).

Indeed, in terms of the services provided to consumers, although non-medical practitioners of complementary medicine have been less tied to the biomedical model, not all of its exponents have substantially challenged orthodox medicine with counterposed philosophies. Complementary therapists in Britain and elsewhere in the West are not always as holistic as their ideologies suggest, as is highlighted by the mechanistic practice of some osteopaths and chiropractors in their narrow focus on the treatment of back complaints (Saks 1992). The recent search for political acceptance through professionalization has also taken such practitioners further in this direction, as well as increasingly focusing debates at a national as opposed to a local level in relation to specific therapies. The limited degree of differentiation of complementary therapists from medically qualified doctors in this respect, moreover, is underlined by the large number of such practitioners who have striven to legitimate their endeavours with reference to orthodox science, whether in terms of the curriculum, research base or simply the symbolism of conventional medicine. And even in the relatively rare cases where complementary therapists have completely cast off the mantle of biomedicine, they have typically sought to work within parallel totalizing metanarratives of their own (Cant and Sharma 1996).

None of this sits comfortably with the concept of a pluralistic postmodern world that has jettisoned the concept of universal truth. This is accentuated by the fact that self-help group activity in Britain has developed in a manner that does not so much signal a consumer revolt against biomedicine, as a reinforcement of its dominance insofar as much of it has been shaped, and supported, by biomedical agendas (Vincent 1992). In this light, questions must be asked as to how far there is a contemporary counter-culture in relation to complementary medicine. This is underlined by the fact that most doctors and allied health professionals who have taken up such therapies – for all their claims to have effected a holistic revolution in linking mind, body and spirit (Gordon 1988) – have tended to employ them in a highly restricted manner. This is well illustrated by the classic case of acupuncture, which has been used primarily as an analgesic, underpinned by orthodox neurophysiological theorizing, abstracted from its traditional Chinese roots (Saks 1995). This is congruent with the positivistic biopsychosocial model of Engel (1980) that has heavily underpinned the efforts of doctors to move in a holistic direction, which is plainly modernist in conception given its bio-medical moorings – despite placing individuals more squarely in their family, community and national setting (Lyng 1990).

In this vein, the apparently more favourable medical stance on complementary therapies at the macro-level in recent times in Britain may not be all that it seems. Nettleton (1995) argues that the changed position from the scathing report of the British Medical Association (1986) on alternative therapies to the more supportive recent report of the British Medical Association (1993) on this subject is indicative of a shift related to late modernism, rather than postmodernism – not least because it can be seen to represent an attempt by leading figures in the medical profession to maintain its hegemony. Crucially, while the latter report argues that doctors need to improve their knowledge of both complementary therapies and their non-medical practitioners, it does so only on the basis that there is increased professional regulation, persisting medical responsibility for the patient, more medicalized input to courses on complementary medicine and no additional research funding identified for applying medically extolled randomized controlled trials to unconventional therapies (Saks 1996). Thus, it can be argued that there is not yet a postmodern profusion of heterogeneity so much as a new way of legitimating the continuing dominance of medical authority through a strategy based on incorporation and subordination, in face of the growing challenge from complementary approaches.

The extent to which this situation prevails in Britain – despite common Marxist claims about the deprofessionalization and proletarianization of medicine in Western capitalist societies (see Elston 1991) – is testimony to the strengths of applying a neo-Weberian analysis of professions in the marketplace, based on their monopolistic power and group interests. This is not to say, though, that the continued marginalization of complementary therapies in the manner described is universally generalizable and rigidly circumscribed in the future, nor that it is the only critique that can be made against postmodern theorists at the macro-level. It is also damaging to the notion of the postmodern that such marginality may in part be sustained through marketing and other channels by the financial influence of privatized multinational corporations – not least in the pharmaceutical and surgical sectors – because of the potential threat to their profits (Saks 1994). Although there are complexities involved, this case highlights the potential difficulties of abstracting the consideration of the relationship between orthodox and unorthodox medicine from the enveloping context of capitalism, the relevance of which is typically denied by postmodern writers.

Finally, in terms of the critique of the applicability of the concept of the postmodern to complementary medicine, issues also need to be raised about the relativism that this engenders. Aside from the philosophical self-contradictions that this generates for its proponents, there are queries about how helpful a postmodern stance is in formulating public policy for health care in general and complementary medicine in particular. As Cant and Sharma (1996: 19) indicate, it is difficult to argue that health policy 'simply descends to the level of practice and the wholesale acceptance of local knowledges. Knowledge may have become more plural but still has to justify its credibility and validity.' This point can be highlighted more generally by the hazards of fashionable but unfounded complementary therapies diverting the customer away from more effective methods of treatment in a market where there is less than perfect information. It is also reinforced by the dangers associated with particular complementary therapies – as illustrated by acupuncture which, in untutored hands, has resulted in a number of potentially life-threatening cases of hepatitis B and collapsed lungs in recent years (Saks 1995). It may therefore be important for the protection of the consumer that governments in Britain and elsewhere retain a consistent metanarrative, setting out the criteria against which orthodox and unorthodox health care can be evaluated.

CONCLUSION

Broad-ranging as such evaluative criteria may be, this strategy, of course, is predicated upon judging postmodern concerns from a modernist perspective. It nonetheless serves to highlight that the implications of a postmodern universe may not be as unremittingly positive as its advocates suggest. This fits in with the theme of challenge and change which has been the hallmark of the discussion to date of the relationship between medicine and complementary medicine. This chapter has explored this shifting relationship primarily from the viewpoint of debates in social theory about modernity and postmodernity. As the specific case of consumer protection illustrates, the concept of postmodernism faces a number of difficulties – many of which are mirrored in its specific application to the study of the links between orthodox and unorthodox medicine. However, as Thompson (1992: 240) rightly observes, whatever the shortcomings of postmodern analyses, its advocates 'have succeeded in opening up fresh and stimulating debates'.

This latter comment, as has been seen, has certainly been endorsed in the consideration in this chapter of the relevance of the conceptual framework of postmodernity to developments in the health field in general and complementary medicine in particular. Indeed, it is sharpened by the fact that, although Britain and the West still cannot uncontentiously be deemed to have entered the postmodern world, it may yet be apposite to argue for such a transition in the future – with all the implications that this carries for studying the interface between medicine and complementary medicine. However, even if – as seems more likely in terms of the established power structures involved – the concept of postmodernity is ultimately relegated to the status of an historical curiosity, significant changes have occurred. In this context, the process of theoretical engagement undertaken here at least begins to enable the social scientific enquirer to gain a firmer grasp of the relationship between orthodox and unorthodox medicine in a fluid and challenging terrain.

REFERENCES

Bakx, K. (1991) 'The "eclipse" of folk medicine in Western society', *Sociology of Health and Illness* 13: 20–38.

Barber, B. (1963) 'Some problems in the sociology of professions', *Daedalus* 92(4): 669–88.

Bauman, Z. (1997) *Postmodernity and its Discontents*, Cambridge: Polity Press.

Bertens, H. (1995) *The Idea of the Postmodern: A History*, London: Routledge.

British Medical Assocation (1986) *Report of the Board of Science and Education on Alternative Therapy*, London: BMA.

—— (1993) *Complementary Medicine: New Approaches to Good Practice*, London: BMA.

Busby, H. (1996) 'Alternative medicines/alternative knowledge: putting flesh on the bones using traditional Chinese approaches to healing', in S. Cant and U. Sharma (eds) *Complementary and Alternative Medicines: Knowledge in Practice*, London: Free Association Books.

Cahoone, L. (ed.) (1996) *From Modernism to Postmodernism: An Anthology*, Oxford: Blackwell.

Cant, S. and Sharma, U. (1995) *Professionalisation in Complementary Medicine*, Economic and Social Research Council Report.

—— (1996) 'Introduction', in S. Cant and U. Sharma (eds) *Complementary and Alternative Medicines: Knowledge in Practice*, London: Free Association Books.

Coward, R. (1989) *The Whole Truth: The Myth of Alternative Medicine*, London: Faber & Faber.

Eisenberg, D., Kessler, R., Foster, C., Norlock, F., Calkins, D. and Delbanco, T. (1993) 'Unconventional medicine in the United States: prevalence, costs, and patterns of use', *New England Journal of Medicine* 328: 246–52.

Elston, M. (1991) 'The politics of professional power: medicine in a changing health service', in J. Gabe, M. Calnan and M. Bury (eds) *The Sociology of the Health Service*, London: Routledge.

Engel, G. (1980) 'The clinical application of the biopsychosocial model', *American Journal of Psychiatry* 137: 535–44.

Fisher, P. and Ward, A. (1994) 'Complementary medicine in Europe', *British Medical Journal* 309: 107–11.

Fox, N. (1993) *Postmodernism, Sociology and Health*, Buckingham: Open University Press.

Freidson, E. (1994) *Professionalism Reborn: Theory, Prophecy and Policy*, Chicago: University of Chicago Press.

Fulder, S. (1996) *The Handbook of Alternative and Complementary Medicine*, 3rd edn, Oxford: Oxford University Press.

Gevitz, N. (ed.) (1988) *Other Healers: Unorthodox Medicine in America*, Baltimore: Johns Hopkins University Press.

Giddens, A. (1991) *The Consequences of Modernity*, Cambridge: Polity Press.

Goode, W. (1960) 'Encroachment, charlatanism and the emerging profession: psychology, sociology and medicine', *American Sociological Review* 25: 902–14.

Gordon, J.S. (1988) *Holistic Medicine*, New York: Chelsea House Publishers.

Hall, S., Held, D. and McLennan, G. (1992) 'Introduction', in S. Hall, D. Held and T. McGrew (eds) *Modernity and its Futures*, Cambridge: Polity Press.

Harvey, D. (1989) *The Condition of Post-Modernity*, Oxford: Blackwell.

Hicks, A. (1996) *Principles of Chinese Medicine*, London: Thorsons.

Hodgkin, P. (1996) 'Medicine, postmodernism and the end of certainty', *British Medical Journal* 313: 1568–9.

Huggon, T. and Trench, A. (1992) 'Brussels post-1992: protector or persecutor?', in M. Saks (ed.) *Alternative Medicine in Britain*, Oxford: Clarendon Press.

Inglis, B. (1980) *Natural Medicine*, London: Fontana.

Jewson, N. (1976) 'The disappearance of the sick-man from medical cosmology 1770–1870', *Sociology* 10: 225–44.

Johnson, T. (1972) *Professions and Power*, London: Macmillan.

Jones, C. and Porter, R. (eds) (1994) *Reassessing Foucault: Power, Medicine and the Body*, London: Routledge.

Kuhn, T. (1970) *The Structure of Scientific Revolutions*, 2nd edn, Chicago: University of Chicago Press.

Larkin, G. (1983) *Occupational Monopoly and Modern Medicine*, London: Tavistock.

Larner, C. (1992) 'Healing in pre-industrial Britain', in M. Saks (ed.) *Alternative Medicine in Britain*, Oxford: Clarendon Press.

Levitt, R., Wall, A. and Appleby, J. (1995) *The Reorganized National Health Service*, 5th edn, London: Chapman & Hall.

Lyng, S. (1990) *Holistic Health and Biomedical Medicine: A Countersystem Analysis*, New York: SUNY Press.

Lyotard, J. (1986) *The Postmodern Condition: A Report on Knowledge*, Manchester: Manchester University Press.

Merton, R. (1968) *Social Theory and Social Structure*, New York: Free Press.

Nettleton, S. (1995) *The Sociology of Health and Illness*, Cambridge: Polity Press.

Nicholls, P. (1988) *Homoeopathy and the Medical Profession*, London: Croom Helm.

Parsons, T. (1951) *The Social System*, New York: Free Press.

Pietroni, P. (1991) *The Greening of Medicine*, London: Victor Gollancz.

Popper, K. (1963) *Conjectures and Refutations*, London: Routledge & Kegan Paul.

Report as to the Practice of Medicine and Surgery by Unqualified Persons in the United Kingdom (1910), London: HMSO.

Roszak, T. (1970) *The Making of a Counter Culture*, London: Faber & Faber.

Saks, M. (1992) 'Introduction', in M. Saks (ed.) *Alternative Medicine in Britain*, Oxford: Clarendon Press.

—— (1994) 'The alternatives to medicine', in J. Gabe, D. Kelleher and G. Williams (eds) *Challenging Medicine*, London: Routledge.

—— (1995) *Professions and the Public Interest: Medical Power, Altruism and Alternative Medicine*, London: Routledge.

—— (1996) 'From quackery to complementary medicine: the shifting boundaries between orthodox and unorthodox medical knowledge', in S. Cant and U. Sharma (eds) *Complementary and Alternative Medicines: Knowledge in Practice*, London: Free Association Books.

Sharma, U. (1995) *Complementary Medicine Today: Practitioners and Patients*, revised edn, London: Routledge.

Stacey, M. (1988) *The Sociology of Health and Healing*, London: Unwin Hyman.

—— (1992) *Regulating British Medicine: The General Medical Council*, Chichester: John Wiley & Sons.

Thomas, K.J., Carr, J., Westlake, L. and Williams, B.T. (1991) 'Use of non-orthodox and conventional health care in Great Britain', *British Medical Journal* 302: 207–10.

Thompson, K. (1992) 'Social pluralism and post-modernity', in S. Hall, D. Held and T. McGrew (eds) *Modernity and its Futures*, Cambridge: Polity Press.

Turner, B. (1990) 'The interdisciplinary curriculum: from social medicine to postmodernity', *Sociology of Health and Illness* 12: 1–23.

Vincent, C. and Furnham, A. (1997) *Complementary Medicine: A Research Perspective*, Chichester: John Wiley & Sons.

Vincent, J. (1992) 'Self-help groups and health care in contemporary Britain', in M. Saks (ed.) *Alternative Medicine in Britain*, Oxford: Clarendon Press.

Webster, A. (1991) *Science, Technology and Society*, London: Macmillan.

Chapter 11

Postmodern adventures of life and death

Zygmunt Bauman

'A free man thinks of nothing less than of death, and his wisdom is a meditation not of death, but of life', so noted Baruch Spinoza. No wonder was he universally acclaimed as a forefather of modern philosophy, of modern life strategy, of modernity itself; he expressed, no doubt, very *modern* opinions of death and life and of life's wisdom, and did it at a time when voicing such opinions was far from common. His almost exact contemporary (born in 1627, just five years before Spinoza), Jacques Bénigne Bossuet, was of a sharply different view. He noted: 'To care about death and rebel against it only when it comes is unbecoming of man', and called his readers to think of death 'in the full sunshine and with full might of reason'. No wonder that Bossuet went down in history as the great codifier of Christian/medieval/scholastic, in other words pre-modern, worldview. He no doubt expressed a very pre-modern view of life and death and of life's wisdom.

According to Spinoza, though, a special *social* condition is needed to stop worrying about death. 'Thinking of nothing less than of death' is not a normal condition of the human being and not just a precept of universal reason, as it was according to Prodicos and Epicurus, the ancient sages, for whom thinking of death was just contrary to nature and logic: 'How can I fear death? When I am, death is not; when death is, I am not.' Spinoza limits his rule to 'a free man'. But who is that free man, who thinks of nothing less than of death? Freedom (as I argued at length in Bauman 1988) is a historically loaded concept, and whenever it is spoken it derives its meaning from the resentment of a particular (and particularly vexing and obtrusive at the time) form of unfreedom, constraint, incapacitation, enslavement. Spinoza's own peculiar personal freedom was his non-belongingness to any of the churches at the time when membership of *a church* was not just a norm, but the preliminary condition of being human. Having left the synagogue, Spinoza joined neither Rome nor her sworn Protestant enemies. What he meant, presumably, was that in order to obtain that kind of freedom – one that entails the capacity not to think of death – one needed to emancipate oneself from the established religion.

As it were, through the two millennia of Christian Europe, the ruling religion built its rule precisely on the universal fear of death. In a sharp opposition to the verdict of Prodicos/Epicurus reason, the Church had its stake in people thinking about death daily and thinking about it more than they think about life. The Kingdom of God which the Church represented was 'not of this world', but it had the sole and uncontested dominion over that other and much more awesome and formidable world, which every human being is bound to enter after death and in which he or she is bound to stay forever and ever after the laughably brief stay inside this mundane, earthly and corporeal world. To secure the Church's rule over the earthly world, the eternal soul had to be made more important than the mortal flesh – and so death more important than life. The meaning of life derived from whatever would happen after it ended. Thinking and worrying about death – such worrying as rendered all mundane troubles small and insignificant by comparison – was to be the natural human condition, since it was the all-too-obvious command of reason imbued with anxiety about heaven, hell and purgatory.

And so it was. Thought of death became human nature for almost two millennia. Throughout that long stretch of history, the temporal, mortal body was experienced as a prison of the spirit, to be treated as prisons are and should be: with disgust, hatred and contempt. Never more, than in Middle Ages, was human life a 'life toward death'; death was the sole significant, sense-giving moment of life – the moment of true liberation and entry into the world that truly counted.

As the Middle Ages progressed, the fear of death saturated every human activity, filled life to the brim and reached a point where proper conduct of earthly affairs became well-nigh impossible. Tending to the needs of the flesh was the road to perdition, while all bodily joy was suspect and, indeed, threatening; all sensuous reward, all corporeal signal of propriety was condemned as the trap set by the Evil One, the temptation to stray from the path of righteousness and the portent of impending condemnation. 'No other era propagated the thought of death with such power, as the fifteenth century', noted Johan Huizinga (1961: 176). The centuries-old Christian message – *memento mori* – sounded then loud as never before and reached further and deeper than ever, penetrating every nook and cranny of Christian Europe. If previously it was aimed at and heeded by only a few saintly artists of piety, who had opted out from active life and already chosen mortification of the body as a lifelong rehearsal of death and preparation for spiritual existence – now, thanks to the swarms of mendicant monks and travelling preachers, it was directed to peasants, craftsmen, traders and other simple folk occupied with mundane chores and busy with the everyday task of survival. It was those simple folk who were now exhorted to fear death rather than enjoy life, to calculate everything they did in terms of its salvation value, to repent sins inherited, committed and yet hidden in many mundane ambushes, to redeem themselves through an abstemious life and neglect of the flesh.

When addressed to the ordinary folk, the *memento mori* message needed new, more weighty and telling, and indeed more frightening, arguments; pointing to the punishments for bodily pleasures rather than rewards for the loftiness and generosity of soul. The vision of purgatory was introduced relatively late in the medieval history; Ray Anderson (1986: 104) rather understates its importance when observing that:

> the concept of purgatory, as a place where purification of the soul from unremitted sins had to occur, burdened the living with emotional and financial stress. Not only did one have to earn enough to live, but also to pay off the 'spiritual mortgage' for the dead as well![1]

Purgatory was more than that; it made of the totality of earthly life one reckless, uncircumspect or just mindless act of mortgaging the heavenly future; it raised the price of mundane delights to the level at which the lasting guilt and fear outweighed the momentary satisfaction they offered. The mortal body was not a value to cherish and preserve, but a barrelful of base temptations which one had to strangle and extinguish. The suffering of the body was thus the common currency with which to repay the mortgage loan in good time – that is, before the time of retribution. In Max Scheler's empathic and insightful interpretation, the late-medieval man was called to 'embrace suffering as a friend'; the Christian man was instructed to refrain from all attempts to escape or alleviate pain and suffering through hedonistic compensation or stoic indifference; he was called instead to accept that his suffering 'is the way of purification, arriving as a gift of merciful love' and 'bringing happiness and safety' (1994 [1916]: 60).

The notion of a life in which death was the event of supreme and superior significance did not augur well for the human body, which one knew from the start was to be no more when the death, that one event-in-life which truly counts, finally arrives, and therefore – reversing the Prodicos/Epicurus antique formula – was not worthy of care and attention. Jean Delumeau, author of the most comprehensive study of the 'culture of sin and guilt' (1990), cultivated by Christianity with particular ardour in the late stage of the Middle Ages, insists on 'homogeneity, constant occurrence, and long posterity' of the doctrine of *fuga mundi* and *contemptus mundi* purveyed by St Augustine, the desert fathers and the increasingly radical religious orders of the tenth to thirteenth centuries, and also on the consistent widening of its intended audience from the original 'small, heroic and ascetic elite' to the Christian Church as a whole, to the high and the lowly alike. 'The Christian concept of death', concludes Delumeau, 'is inseparable from the idea of the ultimate goals of life'; death, and the eternal life that follows, *is* the ultimate goal of life, or rather the beginning of the genuine existence, the moment of passage to such ex-temporal time in which the goal of life (described by the desert fathers in the triple formula 'death, judgment, Hell (Paradise)') is confronted. The advice given by St Pachomius to his fellow monks – 'above all, let us always keep our last day before our eyes and let us always fear everlasting torment' – was destined to become the core motif of the Christian message.

Growing more and more shrill, and reaching its highest pitch from the thirteenth century on, that message called the faithful and the pious to 'disdain worldly goods', reminded them that 'true delight comes after death', and:

> urged penitence and detachment from wordly things such as honours, wealth, beauty, and carnal desire. This seems to be the dominant meaning of the texts and images that, for more than two centuries, stressed the brevity of life and the decay of the body in the tomb.

A fourteenth-century disciple of Meister Eckhart, the Dominican Heinrich Suso, offered a life strategy appropriate to that vision of the world:

> Lift your heart above the ooze and slime of carnal pleasures. . . . You live in a wretched vale of tears where pleasure is mixed with suffering, smiles with tears, joy with sadness, where no heart has ever found total joy, for the world deceives and lies.
>
> (Delumeau 1990: 61, 113–14)

In other words, life had no instrinsic worth, while the sensual, carnal delights it offered were too brief and saturated with pain to be worth the effort, carrying besides far too heavy a price in the shape of eternal condemnation. The only sensible way to spend life was to prepare for death, shunning carnal desires and diligently collecting merit credit points to be redeemed in the afterlife. Today's suffering was the bond to be repayed in eternal bliss. The more the time-bound body suffers now, the more complete will be the spiritual happiness in eternity.

For better or worse, the message has lost its appeal and persuasive force in the disenchanted world of modernity. Contrary to a widespread stereotyped opinion, that era did not proclaim human omnipotence; it only declared out of order all 'metaphysical', non-empirical ruminations about *illusory* problems – that is, things which by no stretch of imagination can become objects of human practice, things 'one can do nothing about'. Only such things are worthy of the modern mind's thought and the modern man's effort as are within human power and may, in principle at least, be subjected to human design and subordinated to the tasks which the humans, collectively or singly, may realistically set. Death, most certainly, does not belong among them. For this reason, it needs to be banished from human life and exorcized from human consciousness – together with prejudice, superstition and idle fantasy.

Since death as such resists the practical measures which human reason is capable of conceiving, all concern with death needs to be *suppressed*. Life needs to be structured in such a way as to make the intractable inevitability of death *irrelevant* to the conduct of daily life: Spinoza's free man is to be liberated from the incapacitating worry fed by the thought of inescapable mortality. According to Max Scheler, modern man found the effective formula for such a liberation in the elevation of work and acquisition to the rank of the most worthy of life's pursuits. 'The new type of man no longer fears death', writes Scheler, as 'his boundless preoccupation with work and appropriation puts him outside all contemplation . . . and in a peculiar way drugs him against the thought of death.' Immortality has been elbowed out of human life-concerns by its substitute, the idea of *progress*, which is 'devoid of sense and objective', the 'moving forward being its only sense'. Modern man 'lives one day at a time, until one of the days proves to be the last'. In the result of all this, 'the non-existence of death is a sort of negative illusion ingrained in the consciousness of the modern type of man'; 'death descends as a catastrophe'; death is always a 'phenomenon caused by something ultimately external' – 'the mechanistic concept of life must construe each case of death after the pattern of the death brought by a pistol shot' (Scheler 1994: 95–7).

We may comment: the corollary of the 'disenchantment of death', the resolute modern refusal to 'think through death', the decision to exile it to the margins of awareness together with everything else which has been proclaimed unknown and unknowable, and the related *suppression* of death-fright – is the dispersion of the issue of mortality in the plethora of single, always individual and unique, cases of death. This means, on one hand, dismantling (and in the end denying) the philosophical-existential significance of the irreparable mortality of human beings, and its removal from the range of legitimate concerns of human reason. On the other hand, however, this means *deconstructing* the intractable issue of human mortality into the set of 'pistol shots', the 'ultimately external' causes which human wit, know-how and dexterity can tackle. Only such 'causes' which one can avert, divert, 'detoxify', 'neutralize' and otherwise 'do something about' have the right to remain inside the realm of rational thought and practice.

The struggle against death as such is banned from human concerns and all but poetic imagination. Instead, fighting every single, named or nameable cause of death is a *duty* (according to the supreme principle of modern attitude, which assumes that the possibility of doing something is a sufficient reason for doing it, and requires that whatever human practical ability and knowledge can do should be done). The modern price for liberation from death-fright is a daily preoccupation with innumerable, ubiquitous 'specific causes' of dying. If a cause has been discovered and located, its way of working must be revealed, and dismantling it then becomes the joint obligation of the medical profession and the population whose mode of living it now scripts, monitors and supervises; failing to do this is a case of inexcusable negligence – reneging on one s duty. As Maurice Maeterlinck observed as early as 1913, 'the doctors consider today their first duty to prolong as much as possible the most awful and desperate sufferings of agony'. They behave 'as if they believed that any, however terrible, suffering is better than those which await us in the great Unknown' (1993: 13–14).

Banished from thought, modern death invaded and colonized life, though in a way totally different from its predecessor, from that death which remained daily uppermost in the Christian mind. That other death demanded mortification of the body; it sent vanguard patrols to torment its future wards, collecting advance payment for the gifts it had in store for them; in the total account of penitence and redemption, pain and suffering were credited against sins and guilt. On the other hand, letting the body loose in pursuit of its desires, aiding and abetting its inborn levity, indulging its craving for pleasure, were both vain and sinful; they invited trouble, to come after the body loses its desires as well as the capacity to satisfy them, and to mar the eternity of the soul's existence. Lust, gluttony and sloth loomed large among the seven deadly sins, casting a long dark shadow on all carnal pleasures. All in all, the pre-modern death put no premium on the care for the body and no obligations upon its owner to keep his possession in good shape. The new, modern death did not usher in the era of leniency and indulgence for the body. But, like everything else in the modern world, the body was loudly proclaimed a private possession, and with private ownership came the duties and responsibilities of the owner. At the top of the long list of obligations was now placed the care for *health*; caring for health meant first and foremost fighting *disease*. Modernity, that epoch of reason and realism, could not and did not declare war on death. But having deconstructed the big and invincible prospect of death into a multitude of bigger or smaller, but in principle conquerable, threats to life, it transformed the totality of living into a battlefield, on which big and small skirmishes against the regular or guerrilla detachments of the army of death were engaged in battle and fought daily. Repulsing the enemy became now the daily task of the owner of the body permanently threatened with invasion. It called for constant vigilance and meticulous observance of the rules of self-defence and engagement. The enemy to be fought was the disease; the ramparts to be defended were those of health.

The opposition between health and disease was an instance of the modern obsession with the idea of *norm* and *abnormality*; in the ongoing struggle to impose a legible order upon the confused and dissipated human world, the clear notion of a 'norm' for every area and aspect of life (a notion that defined everything else as a *departure* from the norm, and thus something abnormal, pathological and in need of radical cure or excision) was a necessity. One can view the opposition between the *norm* of 'health' and the *abnormality* of a disease as a pattern-setting specimen of the large class of notions which combined into the modern image of the world and of the human vocation in the world; one can say then that modernity in general embodied the 'medical stance' towards reality – it 'medicalized' the world.

Modernity was the era of mass industrial labour and mass (conscript) army. Modern society engaged (integrated, 'functionalized', disciplined) the bulk of its members through industrial labour and soldiering, and the factory and the army were throughout modern times the principal socializing-disciplining-surveying institutions for all males[2] deemed incapable of self-regulation or not trustworthy enough to be allowed a self-rule. To go through several years of a gruelling, exacting army drill and to spend most of one's life under the close and obtrusive surveillance of factory bosses was the norm for the great majority of the male population. For individuals and states alike this was 'a must' – not only because industrial labour was needed for wealth, profit or 'the economic potency of the nation', while a mass army was needed to keep the neighbours quiet or under one's thumb; but also (and perhaps in the first place) because the huge drilling/supervising institutions of factory and army were the major modern mechanisms of order-building and maintenance. Hired labourers might have been economically exploited in the factories that hired them, and the conscripts might have been groomed for the role of cannon-fodder – but they were also, and most importantly, taught the art of submission and discipline and kept under close observation and so away from trouble.

The norm of health was made to the measure of these human destinations: the measure of health was the capacity for factory work and army service. To be healthy meant, ultimately, to be fit for the chores of industrial labour and soldiering. To be unfit for factory employment and army service meant to stay beyond the reach of the principal ordering/integrating social agencies, and that spelled trouble for the society at large. The nineteenth century and the beginning of the twentieth were punctuated by panics into which the enlightened elite of nations kept falling whenever alerted to a large number of industrial invalids or army rejects. The industrial/military might of the nation was at stake, for sure; but the alarm reached deeper, down to the very foundation of orderly society (the enormous popularity of the ancient adage, *mens sana in corpore sano* – resurrected, overhauled and given a new tinge in the nineteenth century – could have been due to adumbrating this deeper implication).

The healthy body was thus a strong, enduring body, capable of prolonged exertion; but also a body with no excessive demands, easy to satisfy and to keep in a 'workable' condition, remaining 'in a steady state' – a body controllable and controlled. Of such a body the medical opinion, and in its wake public opinion at large, thought in terms of the 'normal state' which was seen as simultaneously minimal and maximal, setting the lowest and highest limits of the desirable condition. The dangers of excess equalled, if not excelled, the horrors of deprivation. Through the nineteenth century and still well into the twentieth, charitable and reform-bent minds were busy working out the 'minimum basket' of nourishing substances which needed to be consumed by a human male to keep his body in a healthy state; but the same minds were keen to decry everything above the minimum as a sign of harmful self-indulgence and a symptom or seed of moral depravity. Asceticism was no longer to be hailed as the attribute of saintliness; but neither was intemperance as the sign of decent life.

From all this thinking about the regime of health, the thought of death is absent. It has no role to play in a life already given sense and fully structured by realities of – as Scheler would say – work and acquisition. Death was indeed a distant event, which was only tenuously, if at all, related to the events of life lived 'from one day to another': just the last event in the eventful life, the last day of many. For Spinoza, the free man who thinks little about death was a dream, a postulate, an exhortation; for the modern man, not thinking about death is the fate administered by his life conditions. The impotence of the 'deconstructed' death in shaping and running daily life has been increasingly acknowledged and reinforced through the cultural ban imposed ever more rigorously on speaking of death and watching death, as well as on public displays of mourning and bereavement. The practice of public execution, for centuries the most popular communal spectacle of death, ground to a halt. The agony of bereavement was gradually medicalized and made itself into a kind of disease, an abnormality calling for medical and psychiatric treatment.

The more vociferous and militant the stance taken against the 'agent of death', the disease as 'abnormality', the more complete was the numbness in the face of the real thing, the death itself. Life subjected to instrumental norms and to the requirements of functionality spawned no language suitable for a conversation with a dying person: when there is nothing to be done, nothing is left to be said. To speak of death and to address the dying, a special professional language needs to be developed, incomprehensible to ordinary mortals, and referring to the clinical, not lay and daily, experience. The devising of such language went hand in hand with the segregation of the dying, banishing them from the context of lay life and entrusting them to the wardenship of the specialists. The experience of dying was now part of hospital routine.

The taboo on speaking of death and watching the dying, however, has been gradually relaxed. Like all other human emotions (once suppressed, declared shameful and utterly private and as such frowned upon and censured if displayed in public, but now freely vented and commanding widespread and legitimate public interest) feelings triggered by death and bereavement are now continually and keenly encouraged to be openly manifested, talked about, shared with others. Innumerable talk-shows demonstrate how to do this, setting the pattern for public display and offering the expressive symbols to be used on the occasion. Death is arguably the most common sight on ubiquitous mass media screens, a daily and hourly occurrence inside that virtual reality which, by common consent of culture analysts, becomes today 'more real', and certainly more picturesque, spectacular, impressive and attention-catching, than 'ordinary' reality.

Does this mean that the 'thought of death', banished to a great extent from the quotidianity of modern men and women, has returned to haunt the mentality of their postmodern descendants? And, above all, does this mean that, having returned from exile, that thought is likely to invade, conquer and colonize daily life the way the pre-modern fearful fascination with the afterlife did?

Confronted with the growing evidence of the rehabilitation of public display of nudity, eroticism, violence and other strong emotions, Norbert Elias (the author of a highly influential, though controversial, historical interpretation of the 'civilizing process') suggested that what we are witnessing here is not so much going back on the lasting changes engraved on human cohabitation by the advancing modern civilization, as gathering the fruits of its unqualified success: the civilized pattern of intercourse and self-control have been so deeply and solidly entrenched that we can now afford to vent in public aspects of human existence which previously, before the civilizing process took off, were too explosive and too likely to trigger violence to be given free rein. The apparent return to long suppressed forms of public behaviour means, in Norbert Elias's view, that we have acquired by now the skills and the habits needed to defuse their potentially explosive power and thus render them harmless. It seems that a similar opinion may be expressed about the return of death to the realm of keen public attention.

Death, we may say, is returning today in a thoroughly sanitized profane form; deflated to the size of one among those many 'problems' which fill modern life to the brim, which we face every day and know how to grapple with or know how to learn to grapple with. In the course of modernization death lost, irretrievably, its character as a gateway ushering the person into a new existence, an existence more long-lasting and thus more important than its earthly overture; it has lost, therefore, the power to dictate its rules to life and to pass judgement on the value and sense of mundane activities. In other words, death may be allowed back into life because it is harmless – impotent to interfere with the 'normal' run of life affairs. And it is harmless because we have been successfully trained to judge life activities by their own intrinsic merits and have acquired by now the skills needed to defend these activities against alien invasion and colonization. In other words, there is no question of going back on the accomplishments of modernity; the return of death to daily life testifies to the victory, not defeat, of the 'modernization process'.

But what are these intrinsic merits, by which we tend now to decide the value or worthlessness of our life activities? In this respect, much has changed since the years of 'classic' modernity. The framework in which our new skills and habits were moulded has been by now discarded. Contemporary affluent and high-tech societies need neither gigantic industrial plants nor massive conscript armies; going through the drill of factory work and/or military service is not a realistic prospect for the great majority of the population. On the other hand, if the bulk of the population used to be integrated into the 'classic' modern society through ideological indoctrination, coercion and normative regulation, it is now held in place with the help of seduction, needs' arousal and advertising. In other words, the late-modern or postmodern society does not need its members in the role of producers and soldiers – certainly not the great majority of its members. But it does need them in the role of *consumers* (to 'clear the supply', to 'lead the recovery', and altogether to keep the wheels of the market economy well lubricated). It is through the role of consumers that the twin tasks of reproducing life conditions ('keeping the economy going') and the patterning of routine behaviour is now performed.

The body of a producer/soldier and the body of a consumer are, sociologically speaking, two different bodies. The first is evaluated by its capacity to work and fight; the other, by its capacity to consume – and this means the ability to be aroused, a finely tuned sensitivity to pleasurable stimuli, readiness to absorb new sensations and openness to new, untested and therefore exciting, experience. To put it differently, the first is a normatively regulated body, and the norm by which it is regulated is the state of health; the other is a norm-defying and norm-transcending body, as a body defined as a receptor of sensations (in opposition to a body defined as a purveyor of work) must be, since the subjectively, 'internally' lived-through, sensations have no ascertainable minima and particularly no maxima, no objective measures and no ways to compare them intersubjectively.

The postmodern body is first and foremost a receiver of *sensations*; it imbibes and digests *experiences*; capacity of being stimulated renders it an instrument of *pleasure*. That capacity (to distinguish it from the ideal of 'health') is called fitness; obversely, the 'state of unfitness' stands for languor, apathy, listlessness, dejection, lack of stamina or *élan vital*, lackadaisical response to stimuli; for a shrinking or just 'below average' capacity for, and interest in, new sensations and experiences. To keep this body fit means to keep it *ready to ingest, absorb and to be stimulated*. It is not so much the performance of the body that counts, as the sensations the body receives in the course of the performance; those sensations must be deep and deeply gratifying – 'thrilling', 'ravishing', 'enrapturing', 'ecstatic'.

It has been mentioned already that the depth of sensation is much less amenable to exact measurement and target-setting than performance, assessed in terms of its tangible products and objective results. A side effect of the shifting emphasis is therefore the devaluation of the once central notion of 'normality' (and, by the same token, of 'abnormality'). Modern medicine struggled to draw a clear and visible line between health and illness, and thus made the distinction between the normal and the abnormal into its major concern; the distinction was to be, ideally, defined in empirically testable and quantifiable terms and then measured precisely – much as the normal temperature of the body is measured with a medical thermometer. This is hardly a viable prospect in the case of sensation, always a subjectively lived-through event, impossible to articulate in intersubjectively communicable terms and so to convey, put alongside somebody else's sensation and objectively compare. Because all comparison is, under such circumstances, as subjective as the sensation itself, the owners of a fit or struggling to be fit body are condemned to live forever in doubt as to whether their own sensations match the standard, and – more poignantly still – whether they reach the peaks that other people are capable of climbing. However deeply experienced, one can never say whether the sensations could not be deeper – and so one can be never sure that they are deep *enough*. Whatever happens can be bettered – in every ointment of achievement there is a fly of suspicion that the actually felt experience was but a pale shadow of what the 'real' experience could be (and if it *could*, it *should*). The idea of 'normality' does not make sense under this condition. There is a sliding, ascending and infinite scale of rapture which, when applied to the actually experienced, casts on every experience a deep shadow of 'malfunction'. The sliding scale of pleasure turns into a sliding scale of dysfunction, and spawns endless disaffection, condemning the victim to perpetual restlessness.

Given the notorious side effects of each pleasurable activity of the body – any, however spectacular and satisfying, exercise of fitness is also poisoned by a bitter taste of foreshadowed unfitness; and unfitness portends losing out on the chances of foretold pleasure. All in all, the search for the 'truly fit' body is plagued by anxieties which are unlikely ever to be quelled or dispelled. The body's capacity for vivid sensation and ecstasy is doomed to be forever short of the elusive ideal – hence no amount of care or drilling of the body is likely ever to put paid to the gnawing suspicion of malfunctioning.

No remedy is likely to emerge victorious from the test; remedies keep their authority as long as they are dreamed of and feverishly sought, but are disqualified almost at the moment of their application. One follows the recipe of 'sensual enhancement' diligently and arduously, yet each really achieved improvement is bound to stop short of that promised and expected. Remedies are rapidly discarded, new and improved ones must replace them at an ever increasing pace; fitness of the body is not an end which can be reached, and there is no moment in sight when one would be able to say with unclouded conviction: 'I got it.' Impatience climbs the ceaselessly rising pile of successive disappointments.

The whole of organic life, not just the relatively rare, by definition unusual and exceptional state of illness, becomes thus the potential object of medical and psychiatric intervention. There is no upper limit to which fitness could be raised, and so there is no point in sight in which the demand for medical or psychiatric assistance and intervention could grind to a halt. Demand for expert help is boundless – and rising in the course of its satisfaction. This casts the 'body care' profession into a totally new situation, sharply different from those times when medicine was, purely and simply, about 'fighting disease' and pushing back the moment of death. The cultural expectations regarding the medical services are now such that the prospect of medicine ever reaching the point when 'everything that could be done, has been', when its further progress, as it used to be hoped a century or so ago, may be stopped or at least slowed down because 'all known diseases have been conquered' and the state of health of the population has been secured, is unlikely ever to materialize.

This is not to say that the functions which modern medicine developed to serve have been declared null and void. Curing the sick and prescribing the way to ward off the disease, and above all discovering the heretofore unidentified 'causes of death', spotting and carving out ever new 'disease units' and designing the means to fight them – is now, as it used to be, what one expects the medical profession to do. The splitting and slicing of death into ever more minute, named causes has reached an unprecedented level thanks to the accelerated division of labour and expertise, aided and abetted by the development of ever more specialized technology of diagnosis and treatment. One may guess that the moment when the idea of the death's natural causes will be finally discarded is nigh; already now the inability to name 'the cause of death' is perceived, shamefacedly, as the sign of medicine falling behind its task. But alongside its traditional functions, the medical profession of our times is increasingly burdened with the new task: to make and keep the sensation-gatherer *fit to gather more sensations.* Unlike in the case of the original functions of medicine, even in wildest fantasy one cannot visualize that latter task ever being finished. As a disease-fighting and health-guarding institution, the medical profession could think of itself (counterfactually to be sure, but still . . .) in terms of a progressive movement – coming slowly perhaps, but relentlessly, closer to the target. Such thinking, though, makes little sense once the traditional functions are overlaid with the demand to make the patient 'feel good' – since any state of good feeling wears off fast and is easily dwarfed and blackened by the option to feel better still. As Sigmund Freud warned, long ago:

> what we call happiness in the strictest sense comes from the (preferably sudden) satisfaction of needs which have been dammed up to a high degree, and it is from its nature only possible as an episodic phenomenon. . . . We are so made that we can derive intense enjoyment only from a contrast and very little from the state of things.
>
> (Freud 1973: 13)

No wonder the doctors have such a difficulty in locating the roots of the most conspicuously postmodern ailment, the true existential affliction of the sensation-gatherer: 'feeling ill', 'feeling weak', 'being not myself', 'being unable to cope', 'wishing to get away from it all' – the many symptoms (or, rather, articulations) of the one, diffuse yet acutely felt, unspecific yet painful, perpetually gnawing suspicion of inadequacy. The difficulty is not the doctors' fault. The affliction is, indeed, non-specific and as such admits no specific cure (it may be responded to only with chemical products as unspecific as itself – stimulants, tranquillizers, Prozac, narcotic drugs – all, for this reason, assured of their constant popularity and unfailing market demand). This affliction spills all over the patient's condition, desperately seeking an object on which to condense, but sets off again the moment it tries, in vain, to focus and finds out that the symptoms continue and so the point of focusing must have been wrongly chosen. Collectively and individually, the fitness-bent gatherers of sensations need ever new recipes for pinning down their troubles, as the prescriptions of yesterday are bound to be discredited (and so forfeit their healing force) if not today, then certainly tomorrow. In this respect the plight of the fitness-seekers is not dissimilar to that of the beauty-and-charm seekers, stumbling from one promising product to another and discarding them one after another as the promises one by one fail to come true.

In a certain sense the situation described is another version of the paradox of the disease-fighting modern medicine, which, having defeated one named and described cause of death after another, had to discover and confront ever new causes in order never to face up to the fact that death will arrive anyway – cause or no cause, and whatever the cause. The distance between the finite and the infinite is still infinite, and no amount of pinpointed and defeated causes of dying will make death less inevitable than it was at the start. There is an essential incommensurability between the ways and means of disease-fighting and the stern reality of human mortality, and the two do not become 'more commensurate' as the ways and means get more refined and effective; but the amount of continuous attention and effort which the disease-fighting-and-preventing requires helps enormously to obscure, or at least temporarily push aside, the chilling thought that death tolerates no cheating and allows no escape. Like the escape from death, so the attainment of 'peak experiences', full and untarnished happiness, being able to imbibe and enjoy everything the world has to offer, entering a state of permanent ecstasy, living through a kind of sensation that devalues and dwarfs all other sensations, one's own and those of the other people – are inachievable targets and unfulfillable goals.[3] But chasing after them may be a full-time, perhaps even lifelong, occupation. And living that occupation as a vocation (given the amount of attention and hard work such living demands) may help us to forget, or at least to cast temporarily aside, that chilling thought that the spectre of inadequacy will be never exorcized and that 'perfect fitness' will stay forever round the next corner. Or perhaps the one after the next.

NOTES

1 It is tempting to surmise that paving the way for the 'spirit of capitalism' (or modernity rather), accomplished according to Max Weber by the Protestant ethic, was in decisive degree linked to the Calvinist decision to break the causal connection between earthly deeds and the verdicts of Divine Providence. If the matters of salvation and condemnation have been decided beforehand, if they depend entirely on inscrutable Divine Grace and there is nothing humans can do to influence God's decisions – self-inflicted punishment in life loses its instrumental value, as far as the posthumous bliss or sufferings are concerned; there is no obvious penalty for attending to the needs of the flesh. In view of the absence – blindness and deafness – of the Calvinist God, the thought of death could turn yet more tormenting and anxiety-generating than in its Roman Catholic version, but it did not militate against the conduct of daily life and did not clash with assiduous concern with life and its demands.

2 The family was the 'capillary extensions' of basic discipline-training institu-

tions. The male 'head of the family' was assigned, in the relation to women and children, the same disciplining role which was exercised towards him by the factory foreman or army corporal.

3 Recent research has shown, not unexpectedly, that rising income (and so rising consuming potency) correlates with increased happiness and increase of 'feeling good' factor at the bottom end of the wealth scale, but the correlation gets smaller as one moves up the hierarchy, and vanishes altogether in its upper regions. It is tempting to explain these findings by a supposition, that the closer one comes to the full attainability of the currently available happiness-offering goods and services, the less is left to put one's trust in and so the hope of ever finding what one is after, easily entertained at the bottom, loses its credibility and fades.

REFERENCES

Anderson, Ray S. (1986) *Theology, Death and Dying*, Oxford: Blackwell.

Bauman, Zygmunt (1988) *Freedom*, Milton Keynes: Open University Press.

Delumeau, Jean (1990) *Sin and Fear: The Emergence of a Western Guilt Culture, 13th–18th Centuries*, trans. Eric Nicholson, New York: St Martin's Press

Freud, Sigmund (1973) *Civilization and its Discontents*, trans. Joan Riviere, London: Hogarth Press.

Huizinga, Johan (ed.) (1961) *Jesień Średniowiecza*, trans. Tadeusz Brzostowski, Warsaw: PIW. (Orig. 1918 *Hersttij der Middeleeuwen*.)

Maeterlinck, Maurice (1993) *Śmierć*, trans. Franciszek Mirandola, Warsaw: Tulipan. (Orig. 1913 *La Mort*.)

Scheler, Max (ed.) *Cierpienie, Śmeirć, Dalsze Życie*, trans. Adam Węgrzecki, Warsaw: PWN. (Orig. 1916 *Von Sinn des Leides*.)

Index